Also by Anthony Slide

The Griffith Actresses (1973)
The Idols of Silence (1976)
The Big V: A History of the Vitagraph Company (1976; revised 1987)
Early Women Directors (1977; revised 1984)
Aspects of American Film History Prior to 1920 (1978)
Films on Film History (1979)
The Kindergarten of the Movies: A History of the Fine Arts Company (1980)
The Vaudevillians (1981)
Great Radio Personalities in Historic Photographs (1982; revised 1988)
A Collector's Guide to Movie Memorabilia (1983)
Fifty Classic British Films: 1932-1982 (1985)
A Collector's Guide to TV Memorabilia (1985)
The American Film Industry: A Historical Dictionary (1986)
Great Pretenders (1986)
Fifty Classic French Films: 1912-1982 (1987)
The Cinema and Ireland (1988)
Sourcebook for the Performing Arts (1988)
The Television Industry: A Historical Dictionary (1991)
Nitrate Won't Wait (1992)
Before Video (1992)
The Slide Area (1992)

With Edward Wagenknecht:

The Films of D. W. Griffith (1975)
Fifty Great American Silent Films: 1912-1920 (1980)

Editor:

Selected Film Criticism: 1896-1911 (1982)
Selected Film Criticism: 1912-1920 (1982)
Selected Film Criticism: 1921-1930 (1982)
Selected Film Criticism: 1931-1940 (1982)
Selected Film Criticism: 1941-1950 (1983)

Selected Film Criticism: Foreign Films 1930-1950 (1984)
Selected Film Criticism: 1951-1960 (1985)
International Film, Radio, and Television Journals (1985)
The Best of Rob Wagner's Script (1985)
Selected Theatre Criticism: 1900-1919 (1985)
Selected Theatre Criticism: 1920-1930 (1985)
Selected Theatre Criticism: 1931-1950 (1986)
Filmfront (1986)
Selected Radio and Television Criticism (1987)
Selected Vaudeville Criticism (1988)
Picture Dancing on a Screen (1988)
Silent Portraits (1989)
They Also Wrote for the Fan Magazines (1992)

EARLY AMERICAN CINEMA

by

Anthony Slide

Revised Edition

The Scarecrow Press, Inc.
Metuchen, N.J., & London
1994

The original edition of this book was published in 1970
by Zwemmer/A. S. Barnes.

British Library Cataloguing-in-Publication data available

Library of Congress Cataloging-in-Publication Data

Slide, Anthony.
     Early American cinema / by Anthony Slide. — Rev. ed.
       p. cm.
     Includes bibliographical references and index.
     ISBN 0-8108-2711-5 (cloth). — ISBN 0-8108-2722-0 (paper)
     1. Motion pictures—United States—History. 2. Silent films—United
States—History and criticism. I. Title.
PN1993.5.U6S55 1994
791.43'0973—dc20   94-13282

In Memory of Blanche Sweet

Contents

Introduction

In 1970, I published my first book, *Early American Cinema*. At that time, it was the first volume giving serious consideration to the early years of the American film industry—prior to 1920—as a separate subject. I would like to believe that it led, in part, to an increase in interest in that period. Happily for me, it led to my being awarded a Louis B. Mayer Research Fellowship with the American Film Institute and the start of what has become a long-term exile from my native England.

With this new edition of the book, I have undertaken a complete rewrite of *Early American Cinema*. Quite obviously, in the intervening years, much new information has been uncovered by me and by other film historians. My attitudes and opinions have changed. New areas of research have opened up, new paper collections have become available, and films have been rediscovered or (just as significant) become accessible within archives.

The publication of a number of books and many articles on the subject at hand has in no way made the necessity of a book such as *Early American Cinema* less valid. Indeed, it has increased the demand for a single volume providing a concise history of the era. I hope that this new edition of *Early American Cinema* is just such a book. It should serve as both a "solid" introduction to the period as well as a textbook history. All relevant areas are covered, and I have taken care to provide birth and death dates for all important figures discussed in the text.

Research for the original edition of *Early American Cinema* was undertaken in England with my primary resources being the James Anderson Collection of scrapbooks and clippings in the National Film Archive of the British Film Institute. I was lucky that the Archive's curator, Ernest Lindgren, agreed to my cataloging the collection; thus, I gained special access to materials. The then-head of the British Film Institute's Information Services, Brenda Davies, was equally helpful in this regard. (In recent years, it has become fashionable to denigrate Ernest Lindgren, and certainly I was one of his leading critics when he was alive. Such criticism, which is often quite offensive, seems, in retrospect, unfair. Lindgren *did* create the National Film Archive and was one of the leaders in an initial film preservation movement.)

I was aided in the chore by two Englishmen, Harold Dunham and the late Bert Langdon, and one Irishman, Liam O'Leary, not only in the academic study of the period, but also, and perhaps more importantly, in my feeling a great deal of pleasure and satisfaction in the task. My love of silent films was awakened and nurtured through Bert Langdon's screenings of original 35mm nitrate prints in his North London council flat. Little did the Camden Town City Council realize what happiness—not to mention fire risk—existed every Saturday night in one of its apartment buildings.

There are other people in England who deserve recognition and thanks: Peter Cowie, who agreed to publish the first edition of *Early American Cinema* through his Tantivy Press, Kevin Brownlow, Leslie Flint, John Lanchbery, Bessie Love, Audrey Wadowska, Patricia Coward, John Cunningham, Paul O'Dell, and David Francis.

In the United States, I must first of all acknowledge Edward Wagenknecht, a scholar and a gentleman in the true sense of both words, whom I regard as my mentor. He has always been supportive of my work, and it has been my privilege to work with him on two volumes: *The Films of D. W. Griffith* and *Fifty Great American Silent Films: 1912-1920.* Others whose friendship and scholarship helped in my study of the era are Robert Gitt, Sam Gill, Eileen Bowser, Charles Silver, Herb Sterne, Arthur Lennig, George J. Mitchell, the late Charles G. Clarke, John Dewar, Alan Gevinson, Pat and Steve Hanson, John Belton, Marty Kearns, the late George Pratt, Richard Koszarski, John Kuiper, Paul Spehr, David Parker, Patrick Sheehan, and Q. David Bowers.

When I first came to the United States, I was made more than welcome at the Margaret Herrick Library of the Academy of Motion Picture Arts and Sciences by Mildred Simpson and Alice Mitchell. Other U. S. institutions with resources I have used include the Doheny Memorial Library of the University of Southern California, the Department of Special Collections and the Theater Arts Library of UCLA, the Library of Congress, the Museum of Modern

Art, the International Museum of Photography at George Eastman House, the Wisconsin Center for Film and Theater Research, and the Lincoln Center Library for the Performing Arts.

It has been an honor to know many of the pioneers of the era: Mignon Anderson, Beverly Bayne, Ruth Clifford, Miriam Cooper, Viola Dana, Carter De Haven, Dorothy Devore, Claire DuBrey, William P. S. Earle, Lillian Gish, Ethel Grandin, Victor Heerman, Madge Kennedy, Emily Lubin Lowry, James Morrison, Jane Novak, Olga Petrova, Arline Pretty, Billie Rhodes, Edward Sloman, Blanche Sweet, Phil Tannura, Marian Blackton Trimble, James Van Trees, and Margery Wilson.

To all, I give my thanks and to many, my love.

1

Pre-Cinema

J ust as no one country nor one individual can claim responsibility for the invention of the motion picture, neither can one event at one time in history be said to have led directly to that invention. It might well be argued that the concept of "moving pictures" has its origins in the drawings of cave dwellers in prehistoric times, or in Chinese and Javanese shadow plays, all of which are a precursory form of the motion picture. However, on a more practical and documentable level, "pre-cinema," or the immediate period prior to the invention of the motion picture, can be firmly dated from the seventeenth century.[1]

In 1646, Athanasius Kircher (1601-1680), a Jesuit priest, published the first treatise on the magic lantern, titled *Ars Magna Lucis et Umbrae*; a second edition was published in 1671. The magic lantern, the first practical means of projection (a crucial element in motion pictures) owed its existence to the discovery of concave glass, originally discussed in Giambattista della Porta's *Natural Magick* (1589). This discovery permitted the projection of objects and formed the basis for the camera obscura, about which Leonardo da Vinci wrote in the late 1400s.

Magic lantern demonstrations took place throughout Europe in the late seventeenth century. Thomas Walgerstein presented magic lantern performances in Paris, in Rome, and before the King of Sweden. In 1665, Samuel Pepys records a demonstration of the magic lantern in his diary, writing: "Comes by agreement Mr. [John] Reeves [an optician and maker of optical instruments], bringing me a lathorn [sic], with pictures in glass, to make strange things on a wall, very pretty."

Writing in 1740, Benjamin Martin commented that the magic lantern "has been since used to surprise and amuse ignorant people, and for the sake of lucre, than for any other purpose, and thence it has its common name." By the nineteenth century, the magic lantern was in use not only as entertainment, but also as an educational tool—the first audiovisual aid; as such, it was still used well into the twentieth century. From a simple device using a candle as a light source, the magic lantern developed into a reasonably complex piece of machinery, often using three separate lenses, which made it possible to dissolve one image into another from one slide to the next, and with the invention of the oxy-hydrogen limelight, it could also be used to project images from a considerable distance before audiences of several hundreds. At least one major early filmmaker, the English Cecil Hepworth (1874-1953), began his career as a magic lanternist and carried over many of the simple techniques of the magic lantern (particularly the gentle transition from one scene to the next) into his motion picture work.[2]

The concept of projection had its origins in the magic lantern. The theory of the persistence of vision, which enables the viewer to see a series of still photographs as a continuous moving image, was first suggested by Peter Mark Roget (1779-1869), who is better remembered for his *Thesaurus*, in 1824 at a lecture to the Royal Society. The same theory was also developed by Joseph Antoine Ferdinand Plateau (1801-1883). Both men discovered that sixteen images viewed consecutively in one second give the impression of motion. This simple fact is still a crucial element in motion pictures, with films during the early years of the silent era projected at an average speed of sixteen frames per second. Plateau demonstrated his theory with a toy called the phenakistiscope, which used a series of drawings on a revolving disc. Other toys that illustrated the persistence of vision included Dr. John Ayrton Paris's thaumatrope, William George Horner's zoetrope, and Emile Reynaud's praxinoscope. The last, created by Reynaud (1844-1918) in 1877, combined the theory of persistence of vision with projection, and Reynaud was able to present his exquisite moving drawings before a large audience of delighted Parisians.

One final element was necessary for the invention of the motion picture, and that was photography, which can be dated back as far as 1727, when a German named Johann Heinrich Schulze experimented with a mixture of silver nitrate and chalk and discovered that the substance could hold an image. As with the motion picture, the invention of photography cannot be attributed to any one individual, but among the names crucial to its creation are Nicéphone Niepce, Louis Jacques Mandé Daguerre, Hippolyte Bayard, William Henry Fox Talbot, and Niepce de Saint Joseph Victor.

Most historians agree that the Father of the Motion Picture is the English-born Eadweard Muybridge (1830-1904), who photographed a series of images in such a way as to give the impression of continuous movement. In the mid-1870s, the former Governor of California, Leland Stanford, commissioned Muybridge to prove, through a series of photographs, that a running horse had all four feet off the ground at the same time. Muybridge's photographs showed this to be the case, and as a result, Stanford supposedly won a $25,000 wager. Muybridge projected his photographs through a device that was, in part, a magic lantern and partly a zoetrope, and which he called a zoopraxiscope. He also photographed an eleven-volume series of animals in motion titled, appropriately, *Animal Locomotion*, first published by the University of Pennsylvania in 1887. This was followed by a series of photographs of men, women, and children (the majority of whom were nude) intended for scientific purposes, but, one suspects, with more than a passing prurient interest for both reader and photographer.

In 1881, Muybridge demonstrated his work in France, and it came to the attention of physiologist Etienne-Jules Marey (1830-1904), who continued Muybridge's experiments, utilizing a gun-like camera (invented in 1882) that photographed motion by using glass plates. At the Paris Exposition in 1889, by which time he had commenced using photographic paper rather than plates, Marey met Thomas Edison, and this meeting might well be considered a turning point in the history of the invention of the motion picture.[3]

However, before considering Edison's contribution, it is necessary to document the work of others in the field. Celluloid, without which there could be no motion pictures, was first discovered by the Englishman Alexander Parkes in 1885; in the United States, the Reverend Hannibal Goodwin perfected nitrocellulose film in 1887, and in 1888, George Eastman (1854-1932) introduced celluloid in roll film form for use in his new Kodak cameras.

Throughout Europe in the late 1800s, men were at work inventing what became the motion picture. Englishman Wordsworth Donisthorpe was one of the earliest, with his experiments dating to the mid-1870s. Also in England, French-born Louis Aimé Augustin Le Prince (1842-?) developed a camera in 1889 that might have superceded all later claims to the invention of the motion picture, but Le Prince disappeared mysteriously in September of 1890 after boarding a train at Dijon for Paris—he never arrived at his destination, and neither his luggage nor his body was ever found.[4]

Englishman William Friese-Greene has been the topic of much discussion in Britain and was even the subject of a 1951 feature film, *The Magic Box,* in which he was portrayed by Robert Donat. But Friese-Greene's experiments in the late 1880s have been discounted by most historians as having no practical value. Another Englishman—although American-born—experimenting with the principles of motion picture photography was Birt Acres (1845-1918), who worked closely with Robert W. Paul and *did* present a public demonstration of moving pictures in the English township of Barnet in August 1895.

In Germany, the Skladanowsky brothers—Max and Paul—demonstrated their motion picture equipment in the late 1890s. However, it was in France that many might argue that the motion picture was truly born through the work of two brothers, Louis (1864-1948) and Auguste (1862-1954) Lumière. Although they have always shared credit, it is Louis who is generally considered to have been the chief inventor of a combined projector/camera with which the two men gave a public performance in Paris on March 22, 1895. The first film screened was *La Sortie des Ouvriers de l' Usine Lumière / Workers Leaving the Lumière Factory.*

The Lumière Brothers should also receive credit for having produced the first fictional film and the first screen comedy, titled *L'Arroseur Arrosé / The Sprinkler Sprinkled,* in which a small boy pinches the gardener's hose and releases it when the gardener looks down the nozzle, resulting in the latter receiving a faceful of water.

In 1888, Thomas Alva Edison (1847-1931) initially conceived of a device that would combine his phonograph invention with Muybridge's projector. When such an invention proved impossible, Edison assigned William Kennedy Laurie Dickson (1860-1935) to work on a camera/projector device at his Orange, New Jersey, laboratory. Although it has been proven—notably by historian

Gordon Hendricks[5]—that much of the credit for the "invention" of the motion picture should go to Dickson rather than Edison, one should not overlook the fact that the original concept was Edison's, and it was Edison who supervised and employed Dickson. In a capitalist society such as in the United States, it was commonplace and acceptable that the employer, rather than the employee, receive ultimate praise and benefit from any discovery or invention created while in his employment.

The Edison invention was initially only a viewing apparatus called a "Kinetoscope," first demonstrated in 1891. The Kinetoscope machines proved popular enough that Edison found it necessary to produce a regular supply of films—an average of sixty seconds in duration—for them. He built his famous Black Maria studio, also located in Orange, New Jersey, and generally considered the world's first motion picture studio, in 1893.

With his perforated film and an intermittent film transport using two loops (which had been invented by Americans C. Francis Jenkins and Woodville Latham, and rights to which had been acquired by Edison), Edison was able to present the first public performance of moving pictures in the United States on his "Vitascope" projector at Koster and Bial's Music Hall at 34th Street and Broadway in New York City on April 23, 1896.

"The Vitascope is a big success," reported *The New York Dramatic Mirror* (May 2, 1896), "and Mr. Edison is to be congratulated for his splendid contribution to the people's pleasure." The Lumière films were first presented publicly in New York City in July of the same year, followed in October by the first presentation of the films of the American Mutoscope and Biograph Company.

Despite the valid claims of many rival inventors, it was Thomas Edison and that first public performance that paved the way for exploitation of the motion picture in the United States. Edison's claims were to create serious legal problems for other early film producers; they eventually led to the establishment of the film industry on the West Coast and the rise to power of the industry's first moguls, Carl Laemmle and William Fox. Although he, himself, seemed to take but scant interest in the new invention—he once called it "a silly little device for making pictures that would dance"—Thomas Edison was, albeit innocently, the spark that lead to the establishment of the motion picture as a major entertainment force and, ultimately, the first basically American art form.

Notes

1. Useful general books dealing with pre-cinema are: John Barnes, *Precursors of the Cinema: Shadowgraphy, Panoramas, Dioramas and Peepshows Considered in Their Relationship to the History of the Cinema* (St. Ives, UK: Barnes Museum of Cinematography, 1967); C. W. Ceram, *Archaeology of the Cinema* (New York: Harcourt, Brace, 1965); Olive Cook, *Movement in Two Dimensions: A Study of the Animated and Projected Pictures Which Preceded the Invention of Cinematography* (London: Hutchinson, 1963); Martin Quigley, *Magic Shadows: The Story of the Origin of Motion Pictures* (Washington, DC: Georgetown University Press, 1948); and David B. Thomas, *The Origins of the Motion Picture: An Introductory Booklet on the Pre-History of the Cinema* (London: Her Majesty's Stationery Office, 1964).

2. Cecil Hepworth's father, T. C. Hepworth, was the author of *The Book of the Lantern, Being a Practical Guide to the Working of the Optical (or Magic) Lantern* (London: Hazell, Watson and Viney, 1894). Hepworth authored what is probably the first popular handbook of cinematography, *Animated Photography, or the A. B. C. of the Cinematograph* (London: Hazell, Watson and Viney, 1897).

3. For more information, see Marta Braun, *Picturing Time: The Work of Etienne-Jules Marey (1830-1904)* (Chicago: University of Chicago Press, 1993) and François Dagognet, *Etienne-Jules Marey: A Passion for the Trace* (Cambridge, MA: Zone Books/The MIT Press, 1993).

4. For more information concerning this fascinating pioneer, see Walter H. Stainton, "A Neglected Pioneer," *Films in Review,* Vol. XIV, No. 3 (March 1963), pp. 160-166, and Christopher Rawlence, *The Missing Reel* (New York: Atheneum, 1990).

5. Gordon Hendricks, *The Edison Motion Picture Myth* (Berkeley, CA: University of California Press, 1961).

2

The Motion Picture Patents
Company and the Film Establishment

On January 7, 1894, W. K. L. Dickson submitted a series of photographs for copyrighting by the Library of Congress of Edison employee Fred Ott (1860-1936) sneezing. Although it was the second Edison film to be registered for copyright—the actual registration date is January 9, 1894—it is better known and indicative of Dickson and Edison's acknowledgment of the commercial potential of the new invention.[1] However, neither Dickson nor Edison were major participants in the development of the company later known as either Thomas A. Edison, Inc., or the Edison Manufacturing Company.

Edison appeared in a number of actuality films, one of the earliest of which is titled *Mr. Edison at Work in His Chemical Laboratory,* which was, in reality, filmed in the Black Maria studio and copyrighted on June 5, 1897. Aside from occasional film appearances such as this, Edison's chief interest in the motion picture was as an educational tool, a use that he constantly advocated in the early years of this century.

In 1916, Edison clarified his position somewhat:

Did it ever occur to you that people don't like to be educated by force? My suggestion of education by means of film was taken too literally. People had an idea that film education might be crammed down their throats. That was not my intention at all. The eventual picture—the popular film of the distant future—

will have what we might call an educational tone. It will not be labelled educational.[2]

The business aspects of the motion picture part of Edison's empire were overseen by William E. Gilmore, who was succeeded in 1908 by Frank L. Dyer. The creative success of the Edison films was due to one man, Edwin S. Porter (1869-1941), who initially worked as a projectionist before becoming a part-time cameraman for Edison in 1900 and, eventually, the individual responsible for all Edison production. Influenced by European filmmakers who were arguably superior, Porter was one of the first in the American film industry to devise story films and realize the potential of editing for dramatic effect. He was rightly described by *Motography* (November 15, 1913) as "The father of motion picture production and master of that spectacular art." He was cameraman, director, and editor—an auteur in the truest sense.

Two of Porter's films, *Life of an American Fireman* (copyrighted on January 21, 1903) and *The Great Train Robbery* (copyrighted on December 1, 1903), have taken on almost mythical proportions in the history of the American cinema and are often considered as important in their own time as was *The Birth of a Nation* some twelve years later. The films are certainly relevant to the development of the motion picture industry, but they did not suddenly spring from nowhere and should not be considered as prominent samples of Porter's entire work.

Life of an American Fireman, whose uncredited leading players are Arthur White and Vivian Vaughan, has an obvious antecedent in British producer James Williamson's 1901 film *Fire!* and Porter himself also acknowledged a debt to French pioneer Georges Méliès and his 1902 film *Le voyage dans la lune / A Trip to the Moon.* (Méliès was also an obvious influence on Porter when the latter made *Jack and the Beanstalk,* copyrighted on June 20, 1902; but its visual effects are poor in comparison to the Frenchman's work.) Even if from a modern viewpoint, the two films do not particularly stand out among other Porter productions, it is worth noting that *The Great Train Robbery* was popular enough in its day to warrant an unauthorized remake in the following year by the Lubin Company, and it is also interesting for the appearance (uncredited) by future Western star Broncho Billy Anderson.

Edwin S. Porter remained with Edison through 1909, but after 1906, his filmmaking techniques failed to expand with the medium. He formed his own company, Rex, and, in 1913, joined Adolph Zukor's Famous Players Company. He continued to direct until 1915, with his last production being *The Eternal City* starring Pauline Frederick. Based on the turgidity of his direction in the surviving Famous Players films, it was wise of Porter to quit production and concentrate on technical aspects of the industry, notably the manufacture of the Simplex projector, which he invented.[3]

When Porter joined the Edison Company, its studios were in New York City at 41 East 23rd Street. In 1906, the company moved to a new studio at 2826 Decatur Avenue in the Bedford Park area of the Bronx. Built appropriately of Edison Portland Cement, the studio was able to withstand a 1914 fire with little damage. Here in 1909, Horace G. Plimpton became what was termed "manager of negative productions," meaning supervising producer, taking over from Porter and turning out five reels of film a week (by 1912) at an average total cost of 50 cents a foot. He built up a stock company of players including Mary Fuller, Laura Sawyer, Mabel Trunelle, Marc MacDermott, Miriam Nesbitt, Viola Dana, Gertrude McCoy, Bessie Learn, Herbert Prior, and Charles Ogle. (Plimpton resigned in 1915 and was replaced by Leonard W. McChesney.)

Charles Ogle (1865-1940) and Marc MacDermott (1881-1929) are of particular interest. Ogle entered films in August 1909, and a year later was seen as the monster in Edison's (and the first screen) version of *Frankenstein*. An extremely underrated and versatile actor (as witness his three highly different characterizations in the 1920 William Fox production *While New York Sleeps*), Marc Mac-Dermott is the star of a notable 1912 Edison film, *The Passer-By,* released on June 21 and directed by Oscar Apfel,[4] in which the camera moves in from a long shot to a close-up of the leading man recalling the tragedy of his past for a group of guests at a bachelor party. Direction and photographic technique in this film are exceedingly sophisticated for the day and were noted by *The Moving Picture World* (July 6, 1912) in its review: "There is some clever camera work in the dinner scene when the machine is gradually pushed toward the speaker at the head of the table, and then withdrawn. The effect, of course, is that of the actor being drawn toward the spectators and then receding."[5]

Although it is seldom credited for such, the Edison Company produced a considerable number of films based on major literary works. Among the authors from whom it borrowed were Charles Dickens, Robert Browning, Mark Twain, George Eliot, O. Henry, Sir Gilbert Parker, Edgar Allan Poe, Robert Louis Stevenson, James Whitcomb Riley, Richard Harding Davis, Wilkie Collins, and Frederick Schiller. A 1913 adaptation of Schiller's play *Mary Stuart* is very poor; it is little more than a series of historical tableaux with linking titles and well indicates why Edison's reputation diminished in the teens. Aside from the aforementioned authors, Rex Beach contributed a number of stories to the Edison Company in 1911, and director-to-be Rex Ingram was also a scenario writer there.

The Edison Company did not limit its activities to the United States. In January 1909, it sent a cameraman to Jamaica, Haiti, and South America. It began producing films in Canada in the summer of 1910. Director J. Searle Dawley first took a company of players to Bermuda early in 1912, and the company also filmed there in 1913 and 1914. Later in 1912, Ashley Miller, Marc MacDermott, and Miriam Nesbitt sailed for England, where they produced a number of films and were later joined by actress Mary Fuller. In 1913, Nesbitt and MacDermott, along with director Charles Brabin and cinematographer Otto Brautigan, returned for a second visit to England; they were there almost six months. Director Richard Ridgeley also took a company to Cuba in 1915 to produce a series of five-reel features.

Edison's entry into feature film production led to the establishment in July 1915, of a new distribution set-up—the Kleine-Edison Feature Film Service.[6] The new company was to release features from both Edison (which planned to produce one a month) and George Kleine. The first film from the new distributor was *Vanity Fair,* starring Mrs. Minnie Maddern Fiske and directed by Eugene Nowland. The second Edison release through Kleine-Edison was to have been *The Poor Little Rich Girl,* starring Viola Dana (who had commenced her screen career with Edison) in an adaptation of her hit Broadway play, but the rights were acquired by Adolph Zukor for Mary Pickford. Instead, Dana starred in *Children of Eve,* written and directed by John H. Collins.

If the Edison Company still held a position of prominence from the mid-teens until its demise in 1918—its last production was *The Unbeliever,* directed by Alan Crosland—it is because of John

Hancock Collins. He was responsible for the design of all interior settings for Edison films from 1911 onwards.[7] Later, he became an assistant director and casting supervisor, and eventually, in 1914, was promoted to director with *Jim's Vindication*. Collins worked closely with Viola Dana, whom he married, and with whom he moved, as her director, to Metro in 1916. In their films together, the couple display a sensitivity and artistic sense lacking in many other dramas of the period. Because of his background in design, Collins was particularly adept at lighting effects.[8] *Motion Picture News* (August 28, 1915) noted the qualities that show clearly in his work: "Strikingly quiet and modest at and about his work, never raising his voice, never hurried, and having a faculty for working with his players more than arbitrary directing, he has every mark of the man who knows his business and knows it well." His death, as a result of the 1918 Spanish influenza epidemic, was a major loss to the industry.[9]

W. K. L. Dickson parted company with Thomas Edison on April 2, 1895. He joined forces with an engineer and photographer named Herman Casler, and was associated with him in the invention of a motion picture camera and the Mutoscope, a device by which a single individual could view a series of cards that were flipped rapidly enough to give the impression of movement. Also involved in these endeavors was Henry Marvin, who worked with Casler initially at a machine shop in Syracuse, New York, and later in Canastota, New York.

Casler, Marvin, and Dickson, along with a fourth man, E. B. Koopman, pooled their resources and patents, and in January 1896, formed the American Mutoscope Company. With offices at 841 Broadway, New York City, they made plans to begin filming on the roof of the building. G. W. "Billy" Bitzer (1870-1944) was already in the employ of Koopman, and he was appointed the company's cameraman. In his autobiography, Bitzer recalls:

> The first pictures we took were of loom-weaving materials which the traveling salesmen could use to show merchants what they were buying. We also photographed very large machines, whose working parts could be demonstrated by this method better than they could by chart. All the salesman needed was to carry a lightweight box with a cord to hook into an electric plug. Inside the box was a series of postcard-size flip pictures, which

could be stopped at any point for discussion or inspection, and were a great boon to sales.[10]

In September 1896, Bitzer and Dickson visited Canton, Ohio, and made the first motion pictures of an American president, William McKinley, reenacting his receipt of the Republican nomination for president.

The first "official" presentation of the company's films was at New York City's Olympia Theatre on October 12, 1896, with Bitzer operating the projector. The event was reported in *The New York Dramatic Mirror* (October 24, 1896):

> The Biograph, called on the programme "the *dernier cri* in the art of producing light and motion," was shown for the first time with great success. The pictures are very large and are remarkably clear and free from vibration. The views included *Stable on Fire, Upper Rapids of Niagara, Trilby and Little Billee, Joseph Jefferson in a Scene from Rip Van Winkle, A Hard Wash, The Empire State Express, Sixty Miles an Hour, McKinley and Hobart Parade at Canton, O,* and *Major McKinley at Home.* The last showed McKinley walking across his lawn, reading a telegram handed him by his secretary. On Monday evening, a large number of prominent Republicans were present, including Garret Hobart, candidate for vice-president, Matt Quay and his son Dick, J. H. Manley, Mack Osborn, C. N. Bliss, Powell Clayton, and General Horace Porter. The house was crowded and the pictures of McKinley set the audience wild. Seldom is such a demonstration seen in a theatre. The entire audience rose to their feet, shouting and waving American flags, and it was several minutes before they settled down quietly to enjoy the rest of the performance.

At this time, the American Mutoscope Company was not using film of 35mm width, which was to become the industry standard by arrangement with Edison and George Eastman, but film that was 2-3/4 inches wide. Perhaps this width explains why the film appeared clearer on screen than the Edison presentation.

It is interesting to note that as early as 1896, the word "Biograph" was in use to describe the American Mutoscope's presentation. It was not until 1899 that the company officially became known as the American Mutoscope and Biograph Company, and not until 1909 that it was more generally called the Biograph Company.

Aside from Bitzer, the company used a former stage director, Wallace McCutcheon, Sr., to direct, write, and hire players, along with a former newspaperman named Lee Dougherty. Dickson and his sister, Antonia, left the United States for good in May 1897, and settled in London. Dickson helped expand the company's operations in Europe—in Britain, it was known as the British Mutoscope and Biograph Co., Ltd.—and he photographed many subjects, notably the Boer War in 1899 and 1900. (Dickson recorded his experiences in the latter conflict in *The Biograph in Battle: Its Story in the South African War* [London: T. Fisher Unwin, 1901].)

In 1903, the company moved to a new studio in what had been a New York brownstone residence at 11 East 14th Street. Stanner E. V. Taylor became director for a while, replacing an ailing McCutcheon. Financial setbacks resulted in the company coming under the direct control of the Empire Trust Company, which had helped finance its organization; R. H. Hammer was named president, a position that he held until 1913. In 1906, its first office in Los Angeles was opened, although it was not until 1910 that the company began producing films on a regular basis in California.

D. W. Griffith's joining the company in 1908 marked the beginning of the "golden era," which was to continue until the director's resignation in October 1913. Between October and December, Bitzer and most of the players whom Griffith had nurtured at Biograph also left. It was the beginning of the end.

In 1912, Biograph built a new studio at 807 East 175th Street in the Bronx. The studio was to be used, in part, to film screen adaptations of plays owned by the theatrical company of Marc Klaw and Abraham Erlanger. New directors, including T. Hayes Hunter, Lawrence Marston, and Travers Vale, joined the company, but their films lacked style, and the Klaw and Erlanger adaptations looked like nothing more than they were—filmed stage plays. The company limped along, producing new films at both the Bronx and the West Coast studios, as well as reissuing the early D. W. Griffith films through 1916. In 1917, it reissued *Judith of Bethulia* in a longer version, thanks to the addition of more subtitles, as *Her Condoned Sin*. The company officially ceased to exist in 1919, and the Bronx studios were used as rental facilities.

Although it did not have a director of the calibre of D. W. Griffith in its company, Vitagraph must take pride as the most important of early producers. This status can be accorded, in part, because of the company's longevity. Unlike its contemporaries, which slowly faded out of existence in the teens, Vitagraph was able to expand and grow with the years. It entered the decade of the twenties with studio facilities on both coasts, a major distribution setup with offices in London and Paris, and a small, but important, roster of stars, including Corinne Griffith, Alice Joyce, Antonio Moreno, Larry Semon, and Earle Williams. All of these assets made it a desirable purchase for Warner Bros., which took over the company in April 1925.

Aside from its longevity, Vitagraph can lay claim to building up the first major roster of stars, beginning with Maurice Costello and Florence Turner, and to introducing John Bunny, the American cinema's first major comedian, to the screen. Its early films were sophisticated, if sometimes stagebound, and were always at the forefront of popularity with contemporary audiences. Above all, Vitagraph had as its co-head a remarkably talented Englishman named J. Stuart Blackton (1875-1941), whose interest in painting led to his becoming not only Vitagraph's first animator but also America's. His best-known work was *Humorous Phases of Funny Faces,* copyrighted in 1906 but possibly made in 1904. With films such as *The Haunted Hotel* (1907) and *Princess Nicotine* (1909), Blackton perfected the technique of trick photography in American films with his work closely rivalling that of the Frenchman Georges Méliès (1861-1938). As early as 1898, Blackton realized the propaganda potential of the motion picture, with the production of two films (*Tearing Down the Spanish Flag* and *The Battle of Manila Bay*) intended to stir up anti-Spanish feeling following the sinking of the U. S. battleship *Maine.* Crude as these two films were, they are important antecedents of similar productions to come, notably Vitagraph's propreparedness feature of 1915, *The Battle Cry of Peace.*

The Vitagraph Company of America had its origins in an entertainment group called variously "The Royal Entertainers," "The International Novelty Company," and "The Celebrated Reader, Smith and Blackton Combination," formed by Blackton with Ronald A. Reader and Albert E. Smith (1875-1958). The group presented magic tricks, magic lantern slides, and "lightning sketches" (executed by Blackton), and it was relatively unsuccessful. In 1897, the men became involved with film, as yet another novelty to add to their act, following the purchase of one of Edison's Projecting Kinetoscopes, and in May of the same year, Smith and Blackton (Reader had temporarily left the company) produced their first film, *The Burglar on the Roof,* filmed on the roof of the company's offices in New York City's Morse Building.

In 1899, a third partner, William T. "Pop" Rock, joined Smith and Blackton. He brought business sense to the company and was to work behind the scenes securing good distribution for Vitagraph's productions and ensuring that the company had a solid financial base from which to operate. The company produced a few films between 1897 and 1900, but it was in the latter year that Blackton was seen in the title role of "The Happy Hooligan" in a series of short films that, with other productions from 1900, number more than Vitagraph had made in total up to that time. In 1905, Vitagraph began building its studio at East 15th Street and Locust Avenue in the Flatbush area of Brooklyn, and two of the first films shot there were of the stage actor J. Barney Sherry in *The Adventures of Raffles, the Amateur Cracksman* and *The Great Sword Combat on the Stairs* (a scene from Sherry's 1901 theatrical success, *A Gentleman of France*). With the studio fully operational in 1906, Vitagraph began building up a stock company of players that included Paul Panzer, James Morrison, Clara Kimball Young, Charles Kent, Mary Maurice, Van Dyke Brooke, Edith Storey, Lillian Walker, Norma Talmadge, Anita Stewart, Maurice Costello, and Dorothy Kelly. Florence Turner (1887-1946) joined Vitagraph in 1907 and was initially billed as "The Vitagraph Girl." She was an actress of considerable talent on screen and offscreen in the early years she also doubled as bookkeeper and cook at the studio. John Bunny (1863-1915) joined Vitagraph in 1910 and quickly became America's best-loved and admired comedian. Although he was capable of considerable pantomimic style, it is difficult for modern audiences to understand why this repulsive fat man should be considered funny. Apparently, he was a temperamental and difficult star, actively disliked by most who worked with him, including his long-time leading lady, the thin and spinsterish Flora Finch (1869-1940).

A monthly newsreel, *Current Events,* which later became *Hearst-Vitagraph Weekly News Feature,* began distribution in August 1911. The following year, Vitagraph sent a company of players and technicians, including Maurice Costello and his daughters Helene and Dolores, and Clara Kimball Young and her husband, James Young, on a filmmaking trip around the world. By 1914, the company had become so prominent that it was able to take over the Criterion Theatre on Broadway, rename it the Vitagraph, and begin presenting its films there prior to their release nationally. The first Vitagraph program at the renamed Criterion opened on February 7, 1914, and consisted of *A Million Bid,* directed by Ralph Ince and starring Anita Stewart; the delightful movie melodrama satire *Goodness Gracious!,* directed by James Young and starring Sidney Drew and Clara Kimball Young; and a live playlet, *The Honeymooners,* written by J. Stuart Blackton and performed in mime by James Morrison and Mary Charleson.

As it expanded, Vitagraph did encounter some difficulties. "Pop" Rock's death in the summer of 1916 was a major blow to the company. His death led to Vitagraph becoming embroiled in a complicated scheme hatched by Benjamin B. Hampton (who was later, in 1931, to author *A History of the Movies*) for Vitagraph's merger into a "moving picture consolidation," which was to include not only Vitagraph, but also Paramount, Lubin, Essanay, Selig, the Oliver Morosco Company, and Pallas. The scheme backfired badly and resulted in Blackton's quitting Vitagraph in June 1917—he did not return until 1923—and the company's experiencing financial problems that were not fully resolved until 1919. Hampton's project does, however, very clearly indicate the importance of the Vitagraph Company and place it on par with such prominent producers of the later teens as Paramount, Fox, and Metro.[11]

Undoubtedly the most engaging, colorful, and down-to-earth personality among the pioneers of the film industry was Siegmund "Pop" Lubin, a German immigrant who came to the United States in 1876 and labored as an itinerant peddler of household wares before settling in Philadelphia in 1882 and opening a small optical shop. There he produced song slides, the most popular of which was for the 1896 song, "In the Baggage Coach Ahead," whose unidentified leading man (the bereaved husband) was Theodore Dreiser's brother, Ed. He began experimenting with motion pictures soon after they were first seen in Philadelphia in 1895, and began the manufacture of projectors and cameras on the third floor of his establishment at 21 South 8th Street.

There is nothing remarkable about Lubin's films. Indeed, they seem singularly lacking in artistic significance. They are cheaply made, and it shows. His directors—Joseph Kaufman, Barry O'Neill, Romaine Fielding, Arthur D. Hotaling, Edgar Lewis, and others—were competent, but certainly not major directors. Yet, here was a pioneer who grasped at any opportunity that the motion picture might offer. Following Edison's success with *The Great Train Robbery,* Lubin released his *Great Train Robbery,* a shot-by-shot reenactment, in August 1904. Lubin was able to persuade *The Philadelphia Inquirer* to praise it lavishly in its issue of June 26, 1904. The story is also told of Gaston Méliès visiting Lubin's offices and of the entrepreneur trying to sell him copies of his or his brother Georges' films, all of which Lubin had duped and pirated. Cinematographer Fred Balshofer insisted, "He made more money out of duping than the companies themselves" made from legitimate sales of their films.[12]

It is little wonder that Lubin was involved in a longstanding legal battle with Edison. Lubin recalled for *The Moving Picture World* (March 1, 1913), "When Mr. Edison started in to fight me I told my lawyer I wanted nothing to do with that man. My lawyer said to me: 'Well Mr. Lubin, you may want to have nothing to do with that man, but he wants to have something to do with you.' "

Lubin was the first pioneer to realize the necessity of owning theatres where his company's films could be screened. In 1899, he opened a theatre on the midway of the National Export Exposition in West Philadelphia, and by 1908, he was in control of 100 East Coast establishments, presenting both films and vaudeville entertainment. In that same year, he opened Lubin's Palace at 926 Market Street, Philadelphia, which *The Moving Picture World* (September 12, 1908) described as:

> . . . unquestionably the largest and most elaborate moving picture theater in the world. . . . The theatre is an ornate, thoroughly fireproof building, erected at a cost of $132,000, upon ground which commands a price, it is said, of $665,000. The architects arranged it so that it comfortably seats 800 persons, and the present plan of the management is to give a dozen performances a day.

Interestingly, when New York's Madison Square Garden became a film theatre on May 22, 1915, it was Lubin's production of
The Sporting Duchess, directed by Barry O'Neill and starring Rose
Coghlan and Ethel Clayton, that was selected for the opening (but
replaced at the last moment by *Silver Threads Among the Gold,* a
minor and unimportant production).

The company's players, who included Mae Hotely, Harry
Myers, director-to-be Henry King, Louise Huff, Ethel Clayton, and
Ormi Hawley, are of relatively little interest. Lubin's most important stars were Arthur Johnson (1877-1916) and Lottie Briscoe
(1881-1950), who were teamed in a series of romantic short subjects. The filmmaker seems to have held little regard for the acting
profession, telling *The Moving Picture World* (March 1, 1913), "I
have many innovations in my studio for the benefit of my employees, all except the actors; I have no sympathy for the actors." Lubin
did, however, recognize the value of star names. In January, 1913,
Helen Marten, known as "The Gibson Girl," joined the company.
Lubin tried, without success, to sign Alla Nazimova to a contract
in 1915, but it was to be another year before the actress made her
film debut in an adaptation of her stage success, *War Brides,* for
Herbert Brenon Productions. He was able to lure theatrical star
Nance O'Neil away from William Fox in October 1915.

Perhaps the most important stage performer to work for Lubin
was Marie Dressler (1869-1934), who came to the company in April
1915, following the success of *Tillie's Punctured Romance,* in
which Chaplin and Mabel Normand had supported her the previous
year at Mack Sennett's Keystone Film Company. Dressler was
starred by Lubin in what may be considered a sequel, *Tillie's
Tomato Surprise,* directed by Howard Hansell and released in
September 1915.

Dressler told a contemporary fan magazine:

> Both Acton Davis, the author of my new play, and myself
> pride ourselves on the fact that in spite of *Tillie's Tomato Surprise*
> being a five-reel comedy you will not find in it either a police-
> man, a syphon, a telephone, or a revolver, and any one who has
> ever seen a comic moving-picture will realize that in avoiding
> these features we have attained at least some feat and are going
> to give the public something new in the line of vegetables, if not
> of photo-plays.

Marie Dressler made one further "Tillie" film, *Tillie Wakes Up,* for William Brady's World Film Corporation; it was released in January 1917.

Lubin made his earliest films in the late 1890s in the backyard of his house at 1608 North 15th Street, Philadelphia. He specialized in re-creations of famous boxing contests and produced more than 150 of them between 1897 and 1905. The use of the family backyard created problems, as Lubin's daughter, Emily Lowry, recalled, "The neighbors would think, 'Oh those Lubins, they've got naked men.'"[13] In response, Lubin moved his filmmaking activities to the roof of a building at 912 Arch Street and later to space above the Palace Theatre, approached through a curtained door at the side of the ticket office. The company prospered, and its trademark of the Liberty Bell and its claim for the photographic quality of the prints (although somewhat inaccurate), "As Clear as a Bell," became familiar to nickelodeon audiences. As a result, Lubin was able to move to a new and expanded studio complex at 20th Street and Indiana Avenue in Philadelphia.

The new studio, which officially became operative in May 1910, was christened "Lubinville" and included both a five-story and a two-story building, as well as a studio space, measuring 158 feet by 60 feet, enclosed in glass on three sides. According to *The Moving Picture World* (March 30, 1912), it was "the largest in the country." Presiding over the new studio was Emily Lubin's husband, Ira M. Lowry, who held the title of Secretary and General Manager.

Aside from the studios in Philadelphia, Lubin operated a studio in Jacksonville, Florida, where a company of players and technicians, including Oliver Hardy, spent the winter months. He also sent companies out to film in Cape Elizabeth, Maine (summer of 1912); Atlantic City, New Jersey; Atlanta; and the West Indies (spring of 1910). Romaine Fielding (1879-1927), who served as director, writer, and star, was, arguably, the most ambitious leader of the travelling Lubin companies, working in Arizona, New Mexico, Colorado, and Texas between 1912 and 1915.

From a studio in Los Angeles (with one stage measuring 100 by 150 feet) at 4560 Pasadena Avenue, the Lubin Company moved to a new West Coast studio in Coronado, just outside of San Diego, which opened on September 24, 1915, under the direction of Wilbert Melville (who had joined Lubin in the summer of 1911).

Lubin traveled to San Diego for the opening of his new studio and September 25, 1915, was officially declared Lubin Day at the San Diego Exposition.

Edward Sloman (1885-1972), who enjoyed a prominent career with American Flying A and Universal, began his directorial career at the Coronado studios in 1915. As he recalled,

> Melville turned to me and said, "How would you direct that?" So I said so-and-so-and-so-and-so. In those days the actors didn't have a script; there was a little black book that the director had. Right then, the book-keeper came and told the Captain [Melville] he was wanted on the phone. He said, "Go ahead, and direct that scene the way you told me it should be." So I did, and later on, around lunchtime, he came on the stage, and said, "What are you sitting around here for?" I said, "What do you mean? It's lunchtime!" He said, "Have you directed the scene?" I said, "No." He said, "Go ahead with the rest of them." That's how I became a director.[14]

Sloman's first film for Lubin, in which he both starred and directed, was *Vengeance of the Oppressed,* released on January 6, 1916.

Lubin's most ambitious undertaking was the acquisition of the 500-acre Betzwood Estate, the former home of a Philadelphia brewer, on the banks of the Schuykill River. The estate was centered around an English-style manor house that served as the summer home of the Lubin family. When it officially opened in the summer of 1914, the complex included a full-scale laboratory, along with a three-story administrative building. Scenery available included mountains, prairies, a quarry, a factory, farmyard, riverbank, and railroad, all of which led W. Stephen Bush in *The Moving Picture World* (July 11, 1914) to describe Betzwood as "the largest and best equipped motion picture factory in the world."

Among the features filmed here were the Civil War drama *The Battle of Shiloh* (1913), directed by Joseph Smiley and featuring John Ince; *Threads of Destiny* (1914), also directed by Joseph Smiley and starring Evelyn Nesbitt in her screen debut; and *Michael Strogoff* (1914), directed by Lloyd B. Carleton and starring Jacob P. Adler. The last was the first feature film from Popular Plays and Players and was produced in association with Lubin.[15]

In February 1913, Lubin made arrangements to acquire screen rights to an important group of plays by Charles Klein, including *The Lion and the Mouse* and *The Third Degree*. A year later, in January 1914, Lubin negotiated with producer Henry W. Savage for a number of his popular stage successes, including *The College Widow, The County Chairman,* and *The Prince of Pilsen*.

It must have seemed to Lubin that nothing could go wrong with his filmmaking world. Sadly, he failed to take into account the new producers coming along with bigger and better features and the loss of revenue from the European market as a result of the First World War. A third blow came on June 13, 1914, when Lubin's film storage vaults at 20th Street and Indiana Avenue in Philadelphia were destroyed by an explosion. Damage was estimated at between $500,000 and $1,000,000.

Within three years, it was all over for "Pop" Lubin. From September 10 through 14, 1917, the real estate, machinery, and equipment of the Lubin Manufacturing Company were disposed of · in a liquidation sale. The Betzwood Studios were taken over by the Betzwood Film Company early in 1918 and continued in operation for a short while longer.

Lubin returned to his optical business. He died at his summer home in Ventnor City near Philadelphia on September 11, 1923, at the reported age of 72 years. (Lubin's exact date of birth is unknown.)

Lubin symbolizes the hard-working immigrant who seized the opportunity that the motion picture offered. At the same time, he never forgot his roots. He told *The Moving Picture World* (July 11, 1914), which reported on his looking out of his office window at the crowds below, "I am the friend of all of these people. I have myself risen from the depths of poverty. I can feel just as they feel and I know the bond of loyalty between us will last while I live."[16]

George K. Spoor (1872-1953) first became involved with motion pictures in 1894, when he provided initial capital to E. H. Amet for the development of a film projector. Spoor was operating the local opera house in Waukegan, Illinois, and Amet had a workshop there. With their projector, christened the Magniscope, Spoor and Amet began presenting film shows throughout Illinois until 1900 when Amet sold the equipment (to Spoor's annoyance) to a major Philadelphia company, Williams, Brown and Earle.[17] It seems probable that the claim in *The Moving Picture World* (January 23,

1909) that Spoor was the first man to present a moving picture exhibition west of New York City is correct.

A few years later, Spoor joined forces with a new partner, Gilbert M. "Andy" Anderson (1884-1971), a vaudeville performer whose real name was Max Aronson and who had appeared in *The Great Train Robbery* and also worked for both Vitagraph and Selig. Taking the first letters of their names, Spoor and Anderson incorporated the Essanay Film Manufacturing Company on February 5, 1907. Spoor's chief reason for creating the new company was that he needed to produce films for his two distribution outlets, the Kinodrome Circuit and the National Film Renting Company. Essanay's first film, *An Awful Skate, or The Hobo on Rollers,* was produced at the company's original headquarters at 501 Wells Street, Chicago.

In the summer of 1909, Essanay moved to a new studio complex at 1055 Argyle Street, Chicago, and converted its former plant to office accommodations. Henry McCrea Webster became head of production.

Anderson was keen to produce films further west than Chicago, and he first took a company of players in that direction in 1908. In September of the following year, Anderson led a group of eight actors, cameramen, and assistants on a longer filmmaking trip, traveling by train to stops in Denver, Portland, San Francisco, Los Angeles, El Paso, and Mexico. Anderson returned East in the summer of 1910, but announced that the Essanay Western Stock Company, as it was now known, would remain in Colorado. ("Colorado is the finest place in the country for Wild West stuff," Anderson told *The Denver Post.*) In reality, the company moved to Santa Barbara and then, in late 1910, to San Jose. From San Jose, they journeyed to Redlands, California, where they were to remain for three months. Essanay brought out a number of cowboys from Los Angeles, but they went on strike in March 1911, claiming that they were endangering their lives and were entitled to higher pay. Essanay's response was to try to hire new men to replace them.

The Essanay Guide (March 15, 1910) expounded on the quality of the photography by the Western Company's Jesse Robbins:

> Every one familiar with the Essanay Company's splendid
> Western films has noted the clear almost stereoscopic photogra-
> phy, which makes the figures apparently stand out from the

screen in such a splendid perspective that it is hard to realize that one is not actually looking upon the scene of the picture itself. This is due chiefly to the absolute purity of the atmosphere, which seems to carry not a particle of dust, smoke or hazy fog. Clearly outlined to very minute detail objects several miles distant can be photographed with all the clearness and correctness as when seen with the naked eye.

By the summer of 1911, the Western Company was shooting in Santa Monica Canyon and from there, it moved to San Rafael and Los Gatos, outside of San Francisco. Early in 1912, the company moved to Lakeside, and from there to Niles. Located a reasonable distance from San Francisco, Niles was to become the Essanay Company's permanent Western location. A railroad car that served as a laboratory was placed on a siding there, and a temporary studio established in a barn. Eventually, on June 16, 1913, Essanay opened a specially built (at $50,000) studio at Niles with one indoor stage, ten dressing rooms, a carpenter's shop, property room, wardrobe room, and one outdoor stage. Ten cottages at the end of the property served as homes for the principal players. The studio was operated on a permanent basis by Essanay through April 1916, and then again, briefly, in 1917.

It was on these Western trips that Anderson was able to create and develop his cowboy character of "Broncho Billy." The character of "Broncho Billy" had been used earlier in at least one Vitagraph film, circa 1905 or 1906, with Paul Panzer in the role. Anderson acknowledged that he had stolen the name from a story by Western writer Peter Kyne. Anderson starred as "Broncho Billy" in a series of hundreds of Westerns produced over a seven-year period, and although the films are simplistic and lacking the drama of the William S. Hart vehicles or the humor of the Tom Mix features, they are important as the first Western series produced by the screen's first cowboy star.

Aside from Anderson, Essanay's most important early star was J. Warren Kerrigan (1879-1947), who made his debut early in 1910. He was a popular, if somewhat effete, leading man, and when an independent production company, the American Film Manufacturing Company, was established in Chicago in the fall of 1910, it quickly lured Kerrigan and other employees away from Essanay.

In 1913, Essanay joined forces with Buffalo Bill Cody, then aging and heavily in debt, to form the William F. Cody Historical Picture Company. Cody wanted to film a re-creation of the Battle of Wounded Knee, the last major conflict between white and Native Americans. He was able to persuade Lieutenant General Nelson Appleton Miles, army commander during the battle, to participate, along with Sioux Indians from the Pine Ridge Reservation in South Dakota, some of whom had actually fought in the battle. The Indians objected that the site of the battle was now a sacred burial ground and nothing should be filmed there. They also threatened that in the new battle, they would be the winners. Nevertheless, shooting took place without incident, and *The Indian Wars* received very limited release in the summer of 1914. Following Cody's death, the film was reissued in January 1917, under the title *The Adventures of Buffalo Bill*.[18]

It is often suggested that by the mid-teens, the work of the early, pioneering film producers, compared to the work of newer companies, can be dismissed. As is apparent from Essanay alone, such is far from the truth. The company produced a number of interesting features, including an adaptation of Edgar Allan Poe's *The Raven*, released in October 1915, with Henry B. Walthall starring as Poe under the direction of Charles J. Brabin. In the spring of 1916, Essanay produced a seven-reel version of *Sherlock Holmes*, starring William Gillette in the most famous of his stage characterizations.

Sherlock Holmes was released by V-L-S-E, a company created by Vitagraph, Lubin, Selig, and Essanay. On September 22, 1917, *Essanay News*, the company's house organ, announced the creation of a new organization, Perfection Pictures, whose films were to be produced by Essanay, Edison, and George Kleine, and distributed by Kleine. Among the first Perfection Pictures from Essanay, all produced in the fall of 1917, were *Fools for Luck* and *The Small Town Guy* (both featuring Taylor Holmes) and *The Fibbers* (with Bryant Washburn and Virginia Valli).

One of the most attractive juveniles in the teens and early twenties, Bryant Washburn (1889-1963) was featured in a series of films based on the character of "Skinner" created by Henry Irving Dodge for stories in *The Saturday Evening Post*. The first of the group was *Skinner's Dress Suit*, released in January 1917, which was followed by *Skinner's Bubble* and *Skinner's Baby* (also released in 1917). Harry Beaumont directed all three features. Earlier,

Washburn had been featured in adaptations of George Barr Mc-
Cutcheon's *Graustark* (1915) and *The Prince of Graustark* (1916).
Both were directed by Fred E. Wright, and the former starred
Francis X. Bushman and Beverly Bayne.

Francis X. Bushman (1883-1966) and Beverly Bayne (1895-
1982) had joined the company in, respectively, 1911 and 1912.
Bushman quickly became the most popular of all early leading men
and was paired with Miss Bayne in a series of romantic dramas.
While at Essanay, the two were secretly married, and in 1916, both
moved over to Metro, where they co-starred that same year in
Romeo and Juliet.

As early as June 5, 1909, *The Moving Picture World* dubbed
Essanay the "House of Comedy Hits," in part because of its having
cross-eyed Ben Turpin under contract. Essanay's ties to comedy
were considerably strengthened in 1914 when the company,
through the efforts of Anderson, was able to sign Charlie Chaplin
to a contract. The comedian was dissatisfied with Keystone, where
he had been since 1913, and impressed by Essanay's offer of a
salary of $1,250 a week plus a $10,000 bonus (which never mate-
rialized).

Chaplin made his first Essanay film, appropriately titled *His
New Job,* at the Chicago plant, but decided to make his other
Essanay films at Niles, which was a considerably warmer location
than Chicago. Interestingly, two "bit" players at Essanay were in
His New Job, and both became major Hollywood stars: Gloria
Swanson and Agnes Ayres. Chaplin made twelve other films at
Essanay, all but the last released in 1915: *A Night Out, The Cham-
pion, In the Park, A Jitney Elopement, The Tramp, By the Sea, Work,
A Woman, The Bank, Shanghaied, A Night in the Show,* and *Charlie
Chaplin's Burlesque on Carmen.* The last was released in 1916,
after Chaplin left Essanay, and expanded, without the comedian's
approval, from two to four reels.

When the comedian's contract came up for renewal early in
1916, Spoor was unwilling to meet Chaplin's demands, which
included a bonus of $150,000. Chaplin signed a new contract with
the Mutual Film Corporation. The one lasting element from the
Essanay contract was Chaplin's new leading lady, Edna Purviance,
who was first seen in his second Essanay production, *A Night Out.*

With Chaplin's departure, Spoor looked around for another
comedian and found him in the prominent French star Max Linder

(1883-1925), to whom Chaplin had acknowledged a considerable debt. Spoor signed Linder to a contract in August 1916, at a reported (but probably inflated) salary of $260,000 a year. Linder made only a handful of films for Essanay, beginning with *Max Comes Across* (1917), but ill health, not to mention limited commercial success, hastened the comedian's return to France.

Two very disparate literary figures were active at Essanay in the mid-teens. One was gossip-columnist-to-be Louella Parsons, heading the scenario department. The other was Katherine Anne Porter, who had worked as a cub reporter for the *Chicago Tribune* and gone to Essanay to write a story on the company.

"I was just coming out into the world and trying to find myself," she recalled, and in the finding, became an extra at Essanay. "I stayed there about six months. The company raised me little by little, and by the time I was ready to go I was making $12 a day."[19]

Other writers at Essanay included William Anthony McGuire, who was to write some of Eddie Cantor's biggest stage successes, such as *Kid Boots* and *Whoopee;* Ring Lardner; and Anthony Paul Kelly, who became a prominent screenwriter in the twenties.

G. M. Anderson resigned from the Essanay Company—he had held the title of Secretary—in February 1916, and his stock was acquired by George K. Spoor. Anderson returned to the screen in 1918 with a feature titled *Shootin' Mad.* In *Motion Picture Classic* (January 1919), Frederick James Smith thought it "quite hopeless," adding, "Mr. Anderson doesn't seem to believe that the photoplay has advanced since he left it." Essanay ceased production in 1918— one of its last features was the first screen version of *Ruggles of Red Gap,* starring Taylor Holmes in the title role—but Spoor continued working in the film industry through the twenties, experimenting with three-dimensional production and with widescreen, 70mm film.[20]

Despite its longevity, there is little to recommend Chicago's other producer, the Selig Polyscope Company, for a prominent place in film history. Its greatest claim to fame was that it was the first company to establish a studio in Los Angeles. Also, it was the company that introduced not only Tom Mix, but also the distinguished and talented actor Hobart Bosworth to the screen. Selig made the first film versions of *The Spoilers* and *The Garden of Allah*, and it was noted for the wild animals readily available for any of its productions from the Selig Zoo, set up in Los Angeles in December 1911.

The company was formed by Colonel William N. Selig (1864-1948). The "Colonel" was a self-awarded title. Selig had served an apprenticeship in the decorating and upholstering trade before entering on a career as a minor magician. He billed himself as "the celebrated and wonderfully gifted medium, Prof. Selig." He first came to California in 1890, and there formed a minstrel troupe, "Selig and Johnson's Colored Minstrels," a company of twelve who traveled the state by horse-drawn wagon. At the same time, Selig was working on the development of a motion picture projector and camera. He returned to Chicago and, in a loft at 43 Peck Court, established his first company, The Multiscope and Film Company, in 1896. The Selig Polyscope Company was incorporated in 1900 with capital of $50,000. Four hundred shares in the company were owned by Selig, with the remaining 100 shares held by two lawyers, Ephraim and Thomas Banning. (Selig later acquired the Banning shares.)

As its logo, the company selected the letter "S" in a diamond. The choice was not without controversy when, in 1910, materials from Selig were seized at the Russian border on the misunderstanding that the logo was a socialist emblem. After the matter was resolved, *The Moving Picture World* (October 1, 1910) primly noted: "If Mr. Selig is guilty of anything, it is in trying to educate and elevate the nations by means of decent, clean and moral pictures."

In April and May 1901, Selig produced a series of films for Armour and Company, documenting the operation of its slaughterhouses and meat packing plant. In return for the later use of these films in an effort to answer Upton Sinclair's attack on the company in *The Jungle,* Armour provided free legal counsel for Selig when his operation became involved in a patent suit with Edison. Selig claimed that his first fictional film, *Humpty Dumpty,* was made in 1904.

Selig moved to a new studio at Irving Park Road and Western Avenue in September 1907. Thomas S. Nash became general superintendent, a position that he held at the West Coast studio from 1912 onwards. Otis Turner was Selig's first major director at the new studio, and he remained with Selig almost until his death in 1918. Here, on April 8, 1910, Selig filmed the great operatic tenor

Enrico Caruso. Never intended for release, the film was probably the first of Caruso, who later starred in a 1918 Famous Players-Lasky feature, *My Cousin.* Another important film from the Chicago studios of Selig was *The Coming of Columbus,* a three-reel production on incidents in the life of the explorer, starring Charles Clary as Columbus, and released on May 6, 1912.

As early as 1907, Selig sent director Francis Boggs on a Western filmmaking expedition, but the director's time in the Los Angeles area was limited to the filming of a scene for *The Count of Monte Cristo* on the Santa Monica beachfront. (Selig also produced a three-reel version of *The Count of Monte Cristo* in 1912.)

On January 8, 1909, Boggs left Chicago for Los Angeles with the intention of establishing a studio there. The initial location was the site of a Chinese laundry in downtown Los Angeles at 7th Street and Olive, and here Boggs directed Selig's first Los Angeles production, *The Heart of a Race Tout,* released on July 29, 1909.[21] The original company that came to Los Angeles with Boggs consisted of Tom Santschi and Jean Ward (leading men), Harry Todd, (comedian), Charles Dean (character man), Silence Tower (character woman), James L. McGee ("heavy"), and James Crosby (cameraman).

Another early production from the West Coast studio was *In the Sultan's Power,* released on June 17, 1909, prior to *The Heart of a Race Tout.* It featured a stage actor named Hobart Bosworth (1867-1943), who had temporarily retired from the theatre because of ill health and who became a major figure in motion pictures for the next two decades, noted for the commanding stature of his performances and soon dubbed the "Dean of the Film Industry." Bosworth recalled his first visit to the Selig studio in Los Angeles:

> The plant was a vacant lot with an old building on it that served as a dressing room. I will never forget my first visit to it. My heart sank into my boots when I viewed the frightful disorder of the place. The stage was covered with carpets and debris and, viewing my ill-concealed repugnance, Boggs said: "Never mind the floor, we will only cut to your knees; the rest won't show."[22]

Bosworth soon changed his attitude towards the motion picture and the Selig Polyscope Company. Within weeks, he was also writing and directing for Selig and, when he left the company, he was proud to claim that he had written 112 scenarios there and had directed 84 of the 140 films in which he appeared.

Aside from Bosworth, the only interesting director to have worked for Selig was Colin Campbell (circa 1866-1928). He was described by *The Moving Picture World* (March 27, 1915) as "among the foremost directors in the making of photoplays in America," and by *Photoplay* (May 1916) as "a pace-maker in the picture-telling of great dramatic picture stories." Campbell joined Selig in 1911 and was chiefly active at the West Coast studios. He first came to attention early in 1912 when he took a company of players, led by Bessie Eyton, to Catalina Island to film a series of one-reel productions.

Specializing in dramatic features, Campbell was known for the coldness of his direction and for the clarity of his sharp, intellectual mind. He directed *The Spoilers* for Selig in 1914, and his other Selig features include *The Rosary* (1915), *The Ne'er Do Well* (1915), *The Crisis* (1916), and *Little Orphant Annie* (1919).

The Chinese laundry site proved to be only a brief stop for the Selig Western Company. In November 1909, it acquired a parcel of land at the corner of Clifford and Allessandro Streets (the latter is now Glendale Boulevard) in the Edendale section of Los Angeles and here built a studio in the style of a California mission. Cinematographer Fred Balshofer describes the studio in his autobiographical *One Reel a Week*.

His studio in Edendale covered a city block on Allessandro Street and was half a block wide, surrounded by a high, vine-clad wall. Huge wrought-iron gates of Spanish design formed the entrance to the studio, and just beyond the gates was a lush tropical garden.[23]

It was at this studio on October 27, 1911, that Francis Boggs was shot and killed by a Japanese gardener named Frank Minnimatsu. The 29-year-old Japanese also shot and wounded William Selig and attempted to shoot actress Bessie Eyton before being overpowered by Tom Santschi and Hobart Bosworth. The gun came from Selig's property room, and no reason was ever uncovered for Minnimatsu's behavior.

Tom Mix (1880-1940) began his screen career with Selig in 1910, when he was seen in a one-reel short titled *The Range Rider,*

released on June 6 and filmed in Flemington, Missouri. Selig was
impressed by Mix and arranged for him to join his company's
Florida unit in the winter of 1910. A year later, while in Dewey,
Oklahoma, Mix was filmed in *Ranch Life in the Great Southwest*.
He worked steadily for Selig. Initially a supporting actor to William
Duncan, by 1914, Mix was considered a prominent member of the
company. His films were cheaply made and produced by a self-con-
tained unit that included Hoot Gibson, Leo Maloney, Wally Wales,
Joe Ryan, Dick Hunter, Boss and Goober Glenn, George Pankey,
Pat Chrisman, Dick Crawford, and Victoria Forde, who became
Mix's leading lady in 1915 and, later, his fourth wife. In Selig's
adaptation of Winston Churchill's novel *The Crisis* (1916), Mix
performs a spectacular stunt in which he and his horse go over a
hill, rolling over and over to the bottom. Mix left the Selig Polyscope Company in 1917 and signed a long-term contract with the
William Fox Company where he enjoyed his greatest success in the
twenties. As evidence of his later popularity, *Weekly Review* (October 8, 1927) hailed him as "The king of cowboys, the prince of
western heroes."[24]

In April, 1915, Selig joined Vitagraph, Lubin, and Essanay to
form V-L-S-E to distribute features from all four companies. In
September 1916, a new organization, K-E-S-E, was formed, with
George Kleine and Edison replacing Vitagraph and Lubin as feature
film distributors. Selig's features for the new distributor were
labelled Selig Red Seal Plays.

Despite Selig's ambitious distribution plans, the company was
approaching the end of its life. On June 7, 1919, *Exhibitor's Trade
Review* announced that the world rights to all of the Selig films had
been acquired by Exclusive Features, Inc., which planned to reissue and reedit the productions. In May 1919, producer Harry
Garson acquired Selig's Edendale studio. Finally, in July 1920,
Selig sold his Chicago studios to a newly organized automobile
concern. "The sale sounds the knell of Chicago as a picture producing center, which it once promised to become," commented *Variety*
(July 16, 1920). William N. Selig continued as an independent
producer through the mid-twenties, chiefly concentrating on the
production of such serials as *The Lost City* (1920), *Miracles of the
Jungle* (1921), and *The Jungle Goddess* (1922), all of which made
use of the animals in the Selig Zoo.[25]

The last of the major pioneering producers was Kalem, organized in 1907. The subject of only scant attention since its demise, Kalem is one of the more interesting production companies because of its continuing use of natural locations for its films. While other producers were filming against studio backdrops and clinging to a theatrical tradition of artificiality, Kalem was shooting on location, not only in the United States, but also in Europe and the Middle East. Kalem's productions are some of the most visually attractive of early films, and generally have a crisp and vibrant quality that carries the viewer into the storyline. The naturalness of the settings of the Kalem films is matched by the natural quality of much of the acting from a small group of stalwart players, most of whom never amounted to much once they left the company.

There can be little doubt that credit for the sparkle of the Kalem productions lies with the company's first and most active director, Sidney Olcott (1872-1949), whose later career included directing major starring vehicles for Mary Pickford, Marion Davies, and Rudolph Valentino. Based on his work at Kalem, it is easy to understand writer Martha M. Stanley's comparing him to the greatest of the early 20th century theatrical producers, David Belasco, by dubbing Olcott "the Belasco of the Open Air."

The Kalem Company, Inc., derived its name from the first letters of the last names of its founders: George Kleine, Samuel Long, and Frank Marion. The company's president was George Kleine, who owned the Kleine Optical Company of Chicago, while both Long and Marion had been with the Biograph Company.

According to Kalem's first leading lady, Gene Gauntier (1891-1966), who was known as the "Kalem Girl" (a title she later relinquished to Ruth Roland):

> They secured a floor in a loft building at 131 W. 24th Street [New York], partitioned off a small room dividing it into two offices, installed the simplest of laboratories in the rear and were ready for business. It was all very primitive and looked as if a slight shove might push apart the walls. No provision had been made for a studio.
>
> The general procedure for taking a picture was the same. There was never a scenario on hand, and Sid [Olcott], after finishing up the previous week's work, would hang about the lean-to office waiting for something to turn up. About Wednes-

day Mr. Marion would come down from his home in Connecticut, a black scowl on his face and an unfriendly attitude towards
everyone. And Sid would whisper, "Either his liver is bad or he
has a story to get off his chest," and would "beat it" until after
lunch, returning to face a smiling, buoyant Marion looking
expectantly over his desk.

"That you Sid? The report is for good weather tomorrow.
You'd better get your people together and run out to Shadyside
and take this picture. It's about a horse thief and there's a dandy
climax. The last scene shows him, after the vigilance committee
has lynched him, hanging over the Palisades by his neck. Here's
the dope. You'd better get busy on the phone right away."

And he would hand Sid a business envelope (used) on the
back of which, in his minute handwriting was sketched the
outline of six scenes, supposed to run one hundred and fifty feet
to the scene—as much as our little Moy camera could hold. A
half dozen words described each scene; I believe that, to this day,
Mr. Marion holds the championship for the shortest working
scenario.

Olcott practiced the strictest economy. . . . If we found we
were running behind, or clouds began to gather, rehearsals were
cut. Sometimes, even, the action would only be told us and we
would "take a chance" on getting it without a rehearsal. But not
often, for one of Sid's pet economies was not to waste film.
Negative cost three cents a foot. The length of each of the six or
seven scenes had been carefully reckoned beforehand and the
director held a stopwatch on the last rehearsal. If, during the
actual filming, he heard the cameraman saying quietly, "Speed
up, Sid; film's running out," he would dance up and down
shouting, "Hurry up, folks; film's going. Grab her, Jim; kiss her
not too long. Quick! Don't wait to put her coat on—out of the
scene—Hurry! Out! "[26]

Olcott directed Kalem's first film, *A Runaway Sleighbelle*
(1907). He also directed two films that resulted in legal actions that
had a major influence on filmmakers. In January 1908, Kalem
released *The Merry Widow,* which it claimed was "done by the
original Viennese cast," and included an adaptation of Franz
Lehar's score for live synchronization with the film. New York
producer Henry W. Savage, who owned the rights to the operetta,

quickly sued in the U. S. Circuit Court, claiming that film producers should pay royalties to copyright owners. Savage also pointed out that the film did not include performances by the original cast, but was filmed in New York City with New York actors and actresses. The Court directed Kalem to hand over all the negatives and films in its possession to the complainant.

The second lawsuit is better known and concerns Kalem's 1907 production of a one-reel version of *Ben-Hur*. Kalem promoted the film as follows:

> Scenery and Supers by Pain's Fireworks Company. Costumes from Metropolitan Opera House. Chariot Race by 3rd Battery, Brooklyn. Positively the Most Superb Moving Picture Spectacle Ever Produced in America. In Sixteen Magnificent Scenes.

Again in the U. S. Circuit Court, a suit to recover damages for infringement of property rights in the dramatization of *Ben-Hur* was commenced by publisher Harper and Row, by Klaw and Erlanger, the theatrical producers owning dramatic rights, and by Henry L. Wallace, son of the late General Lew Wallace (author of the original work) and administrator of the estate of his mother, Susan E. Wallace. It was not until the spring of 1909 that the Circuit Court issued a major ruling that a moving picture exhibition was held to be a stage representation, and unless the producer had acquired the necessary copyright, the film violated the author's rights. Kalem maintained that a film was no more than a pantomime and not a dramatization, but the Court felt that "the essence of the matter in the case . . . is not the mechanism employed but that we see the event or story lived."

So important was this issue considered by film producers at the time, who were far from happy with the notion that they should have to pay for screen adaptations of any works, that all members of the Motion Picture Patents Company agreed on March 17, 1910, to finance counsel in an (unsuccessful) argument before the Supreme Court.

The photographic quality of the Kalem films was readily acknowledged by trade paper writers. The company's first two cinematographers, Max Schneider and Knute Rahmn, had both been still photographers who were hired on the strength of their work.

Kalem's third cameraman, George K. Hollister, joined the company in April 1910, and based on the films of his that survive, it is apparent that he was a superb craftsman. (His wife, Alice, was also with Kalem as an actress.)[27]

An early observer of the industry wrote under the name of Lux Graphicus for *The Moving Picture World*, and his comments always offer valuable contemporary insights, as in the following from the February 27, 1909, issue:

> Photographically the Kalem Company's films are some of the grandest I have seen, and my experience of moving picture work dates back a few years. These pictures are very refined, delicate pieces of photography, and I have been surprised not to see them in some of the New York moving picture theaters. However, on Saturday last, I came across *The High Diver* at Harlem and on Fourteenth Street, and I am sure the public appreciated this very ingenious film. The Kalem work is technically so very beautiful in its photography that for that reason alone it is bound to be popular wherever it is shown. And it is surprising how little good photography there is in modern fillums—beg pardon, films.

Aside from the New York facility, Kalem initially used a studio close to Frank Marion's home in Stamford, Connecticut. It also used other Connecticut locations, such as the estate of Ernest Thompson Seton for a 1908 production of *As You Like It*. Later, in April 1909, Kalem moved its offices to the Eastman Kodak Building at 235-239 West 23rd Street and operated a studio on New York's 19th Street, as well as two studios in New Jersey at Cliffside Park and Rockaway.

Kalem first sent a company to film in Jacksonville, Florida, in December 1908, and Sidney Olcott and Frank Marion selected as their headquarters the Roseland, a large, old hotel with three acres of grounds on the banks of the St. John River in the Jacksonville suburb of Fairfield. *The Moving Picture World* (December 5, 1908) characterized the trip to Florida as part of Kalem's policy of using "real scenic effects instead of studio paintings." The company remained in Florida until April 1909. In the late fall of that year, Kalem sent a company to Canada. A Southern company was reorganized to return to Jacksonville that same year, and wintering in Florida became the norm for the Kalem Company until March 1917.

At the same time, Kalem also had a company at work in Southern California, and in 1911, it established a permanent studio on Verdugo Road in the Los Angeles suburb of Glendale. A second studio, in Santa Monica, California, opened in 1911 and remained active until the spring of 1914. Kalem also filmed in New Orleans in the winter of 1911-1912. In the summer of 1912, director George Melford, who had joined Kalem in Florida in November 1909, took a company of players to New Mexico, and among its members was Mae Marsh, usually associated with the films of D. W. Griffith. In the winter of 1912-1913, director J. P. McGowan, who had joined Kalem in New York in 1909, had a company of players at work in Birmingham, Alabama.

Although, as already noted, a number of early producers made filmmaking trips abroad, none did so on the scale or importance of those by the Kalem Company. Kalem appeared to have a genuine desire for realism—so much so that it even made a joke of the subject with *Too Much Realism,* released on December 8, 1911, in which one of the cowgirls working with a film company gets tired of the same old Western films and decides to make a real Western.

In the spring of 1910, Frank Marion suggested to Sidney Olcott that he make a filmmaking trip to Ireland. Irish-American Olcott (who, according to Gene Gauntier, "possessed all the sparkle and sentiment of that emotional race") was delighted to agree. In August 1910, he, Gene Gauntier, actor Robert Vignola, and cameraman George K. Hollister landed at Cobh, Ireland. They found an ideal site for their filmmaking activities in the village of Beaufort, just outside of Killarney, and here the group filmed *The Lad from Old Ireland.* They also filmed a number of Irish beauty spots and edited the footage together under the title of *The Irish Honeymoon.* Enroute back to the United States, the quartet stopped in Germany to film scenes for *The Little Spreewald Maiden.* (Additional scenes for both this film and *The Lad from Old Ireland* were shot in New York.)

In the summer of 1911, a larger contingent of Kalem personnel returned to Ireland and to Beaufort, beginning their filming activities with *Rory O'More,* the story of an eighteenth-century Irish revolutionary hero. Other films produced at this time included *The O'Neill, You Remember Ellen,* and most importantly, *The Colleen*

Bawn and *Arrah-na-Pogue,* three-reel adaptations of Dion
Boucicault plays.

The company returned to New York City on October 6, 1911,
and journeyed briefly to Florida before departing from the United
States yet again—this time for Egypt and Palestine. There, they
filmed a number of interest shorts, including *Making Photoplays in
Egypt,* released on June 10, 1912, as well as several fictional films
such as *The Fighting Dervishes of the Desert,* released on May 27,
1912; *Captured by Bedouins,* released on June 26, 1912; *A Prisoner
of the Harem,* released on July 19, 1912; and *Winning a Widow,*
released on July 5, 1912.

It was initially Frank Marion's intention that the company
produce a film in Egypt on the life of Moses. Instead, it was decided
to film a feature-length version of the life of Christ, released as *From
the Manger to the Cross.* (As early as 1908, Kalem had made a
one-reel short titled *Jerusalem in the Time of Christ.*)

Gene Gauntier wrote the script and also played the Virgin Mary.
Christ was played as an adult by a British actor named R. Henderson
Bland. Other roles were played by members of the company and
whoever happened to be available. For the Feast of Cana, the
bridegroom was played by a Cairo tailor, and his bride, by
Gauntier's Armenian maid.

The film proved a huge success for the Kalem Company, but
Marion was unwilling to allow Olcott and Gauntier to share in the
success with increased salaries. As a result, after one more summer
trip to Beaufort in 1912 (which included the production of three-reel
versions of *The Kerry Gow* and *The Shaughraun),* Olcott, Gauntier,
and Jack Clark (Gauntier's husband) left Kalem and formed their
own company, the Gene Gauntier Feature Players. This group
returned to Ireland in 1913. In 1914, Olcott again came to Ireland,
but with a new leading lady, his future wife, Valentine Grant, this
time making films for his own company, Sid Films.[28]

From her temporary home in Stockholm, Sweden, Gene Gauntier wrote, on December 16, 1928:

> So our family of pathfinders disbanded, as pioneers will do
> when the long trail is ended, and each one departed into new
> environments, to build for himself. As settlers in a new land,
> some were submerged while others went blithely on to the top
> crest of popularity. Life never stands still, nor would we wish it

to. Suffice for us the memories of that epoch in our lives, with
its joys and its sorrows, its thrills and adventures, its affections
and achievements. We would not live through them again, nor,
yet, would we desire to part with the memories of those days
when we were blazing the trail.

The O'Kalems, as the group was called while working in
Ireland, and the El Kalems, as they were known in Egypt, left
Kalem, but the company continued, albeit without the excitement
of its early years.

Its "Ham and Bud" series of comedies featured Lloyd Hamilton
(1891-1935) and Bud Duncan (1883-1960) and began with *Ham at
the Garbage Gentleman's Ball,* released in March 1915. These
comedies were a staple of the Kalem program through 1917. There
was also Marin Sais, featured in such series as *The Social Pirates*
(1916), *The Girl from Frisco* (1916), and *The American Girl* (1917),
as well as the popular *Hazards of Helen* episodes starring Helen
Holmes and, later, Helen Gibson.

"Speaking of Kalem," wrote *Picture Play* (October 9, 1915)
facetiously, "Alice Joyce has left, Tom Moore has left, Guy Coombs
has left. Who's left?"

The company was slowly dying. In April 1915, it began reissuing one-reelers featuring Alice Joyce and Carlyle Blackwell from
three or four years earlier. In the spring of 1916, it began releasing
old episodes of *The Hazards of Helen* as if they were new productions, simply because there were no new productions. Certainly, the
company was still in business. In May 1916, it signed British actress
Ivy Close to star in one-reel comedies, and later that same year, it
announced the signing of a long-term contract with actor George
Larkin.

On July 18, 1915, Kalem president Samuel Long died. Marion
was elected to replace him, and William Wright was elected secretary and treasurer. Wright had been with Kalem almost since its
inception, initially serving as general sales and advertising manager. He was not in touch with current trends and staunchly advocated a policy that Kalem should limit its production to one- , two-,
and three-reel films. By January 1917, Wright had announced that
Kalem would produce no film over two reels in length. *The Moving
Picture World* (January 13, 1917) reported:

Its determination to stick to the short-length pictures that are
the logical kind for the smaller theatres to exhibit, is based upon
carefully tabulated statistics which prove, to Kalem's satisfaction, that one and two reel features are as necessary to the
industry as films of greater length.

With such shortsightedness, there is little wonder that Kalem's
days were numbered. In 1919, the Vitagraph Company acquired
Kalem, including the services of William Wright. That same year,
the company's Cliffside Park, New Jersey, studios were purchased
by the newly formed Creation Films, Inc.[29]

While Edison, the American Mutoscope and Biograph Company, the Vitagraph Company, Lubin, Selig, Essanay, and Kalem
were establishing the film industry, others were taking it to the
hinterland of America. From his homebase in Wilkes-Barre, Pennsylvania, Lyman H. Howe (1856-1923) pioneered the concept of
travelling film shows. Rejecting William N. Selig's Polyscope as
too delicate a mechanism, he designed and built his own heavy-duty
projector. Between 1912 and 1919, Howe had six travelling road
companies operating in the United States and parts of Canada. He
was also active as a producer from 1905 onwards. Director-to-be
Fred Niblo (1874-1948) had a similar, smaller operation, but
Howe's only major competitor was Burton Holmes (1870-1958),
who screened films of his travels around the world to enthusiastic
audiences. He began his career presenting stereopticon slides in
1891, then started taking motion pictures, and formed his own
corporation in partnership with Oscar DePue in 1897. Holmes was
the first person to use the word "travelogue" in 1904.

These three showmen were so prominent that they were invited,
in October 1909, to become participants in the Motion Picture
Patents Company. They were "permitted" to import films for their
shows, providing they paid a royalty of one-half cent a foot and $5
per week. So powerful was the Motion Picture Patents Company
that Howe, Niblo, and Holmes were happy to pay its "tribute."

Incorporated in New Jersey on September 9, 1908, the Motion
Picture Patents Company was intended to create a monopoly in the
film industry by the simple expediency of controlling all patents
relating to motion picture projectors and cameras. It was, in essence, a patents pool, in which were immersed the patents of
Edison, the American Mutoscope and Biograph Company, Thomas

Armat, Francis Jenkins, and the Latham family (Woodville and his sons, Otway and Grey), inventors of the "Latham Loop," which was crucial to the operation of the motion picture projector.

In theory, the Motion Picture Patents Company was now in total control of the production and presentation of motion pictures, a control further enhanced by an exclusive contract with the Eastman-Kodak Company for the manufacture of raw stock. This was not the first time that a group of producers tried to gain control of the industry. The United Film Service Protective Association, formed on November 16, 1907, and the Film Service Association, formed on February 8, 1908, had been created with a similar end in mind, but did not succeed because of the refusal of the American Muto-scope and Biograph Company to join.

The founding members of the Motion Picture Patents Company were Edison, American Mutoscope and Biograph, Essanay, Kalem, Lubin, Vitagraph, Selig, Gaumont (for its sound films only), importer George Kleine, Gaston Méliès, and Pathé Frères (which had been active in the United States since 1904). Aside from the moving picture machines built by the founding members, the Motion Picture Patents Company also licensed the following machine makers: American Moving Picture Machine Co., Armat Moving Picture Machine Co., Edengraph Manufacturing Co., Enterprise Optical Company, Nicholas Power Company, and Eberhard Schneider.

Initially, the Company licensed individual exchanges, controlling two-thirds of all film exchanges in the country. However, in April 1910, the Motion Picture Patents Company created a separate organization (to which it claimed no legal ties), the General Film Company, for the express purpose of distributing films, equipment, and advertising matter.

Jacques A. Berst was general manager of Pathé from 1904-1907 and its executive head from June 26, 1908. In November 1915, he became president of the General Film Company, so perhaps his explanation of why the latter came into being is the most acceptable:

> The idea was to establish an ideal exchange which would give an ideal service so all the exhibitors who were dissatisfied could go to a place of business where they would receive fair treatment. . . . Most of them [the exchanges] were conducted by people who were not reliable, people which [sic] would not keep their agreement or their arrangement with the exhibitors. . . . The

films were not inspected properly by the exchanges. . . . The manufacturers in order to do a good business have to give a certain [amount] of credit, at least once a week, and it was very unsafe to do it. We never knew if we would get our money or not.[30]

The Motion Picture Patents Company served as a trade organization, in much the same way as does the current Motion Picture Association of America. When a major copyright issue affecting the film industry came up with regard to the Kalem Company's screen adaptation of *Ben-Hur,* all the producer members of the Company agreed on March 17, 1910, to finance counsel to argue on Kalem's behalf before the Supreme Court. In December 1910, it impressed upon its members the importance of using nonflammable film, but there was no support for the proposal.

The Motion Picture Patents Company had a strongly negative attitude towards the use of films for advertising purposes. In May 1910, it took up the issue of theaters screening advertising films for which exhibitors, of course, did not have to pay, upon discovery that Anheuser Busch was producing such films. Later in 1910, it rejected a proposal from Proctor & Gamble whereby the latter would exchange soap wrappers for theater tickets. On October 11, 1910, it resolved that none of its members could accept compensation for promoting a product in any film without permission of the majority of members and that if such permission was granted, the compensation received was to be shared by all.

In 1910, the Company authorized J. Stuart Blackton to incorporate a publishing company with a capital of $100,000 for the publication of what was to be the cinema's first "fan" magazine, *The Motion Picture Story Magazine.* The journal was to be strictly for the promotion of the films of member companies, with the frontispiece each month to be a picture or scene from a film of the Licensed Manufacturers and Importers, as follows:

Lubin—March
Vitagraph—April
George Kleine—May
Selig—June
Gaston Méliès—July
Essanay—August

Pathé Frères—September
Edison—November
Biograph—December

The company also published its own trade journal, *The Film Index,* and its refusal to sell this publication to the trade paper *The Moving Picture World* in September 1910, led to the latter's adopting a negative attitude towards the Motion Picture Patents Company. Earlier, *The Moving Picture World* had published a four-page retrospect and appreciation, announcing "the continued existence of the Patents Company and the conservation of its policy are things to be desired."[31] The change of attitude by *The Moving Picture World* towards the Motion Picture Patents Company certainly helped those within the industry who were opposed to its policies and, in the long run, was to be instrumental in the downfall of the Company. Without the advertising that trade papers such as *The Moving Picture World* provided to those against the Motion Picture Patents Company, there would have been less consolidated opposition to the organization. Such opposition was gradually building, but in 1910, it must have seemed to the members of the Company that they were preeminent and likely to remain so. They had created an organization dedicated to making unprecedented amounts of money. They had created an organization that made it very clear that they were the establishment and they were here to stay.

Notes

1. For more information, see Paul C. Spehr, "Edison Films in the Library of Congress," *The Quarterly Journal of the Library of Congress* (January 1975), pp. 34-50.
2. "Edison Talks of the Future," *Motion Picture News,* Vol. XIV, No. 26 (December 1916), p. 4177.
3. Charles Musser has researched Porter's career extensively; he coordinated a 1978 Museum of Modern Art tribute to Porter and is also the author of "The Early Cinema of Edwin Porter," *Cinema Journal,* Vol. XIX, No. 1 (Fall 1979), pp. 1-38 and *Before the Nickelodeon: Edwin S. Porter and the Edison Manufacturing Company* (Berkeley, CA: University of California Press, 1991).
4. It is remarkable how film history has ignored Oscar Apfel (1879-1938). He codirected Cecil B. DeMille's first film, *The Squaw Man.*

5. The film is preserved in the British National Film Archive.

6. Earlier Edison features were distributed by the General Film Company or Paramount.

7. Some of Collins's more memorable designs and effects are documented in "John Hancock Collins," *The Moving Picture World* (December 13, 1913), p. 1263.

8. The few of Collins', Edison and Metro productions that survive are preserved at the International Museum of Photography at George Eastman House.

9. The following are major contemporary articles and other items dealing with the Edison Company: Alan Crosland, "How Edison's 'Black Maria' Grew," *Motography*, Vol. XV, No. 17 (April 22, 1916), pp. 911-914; Antonia and W. K. L. Dickson, *The Edison Vitascope*, Privately printed, 1894; *Edison's Invention of the Kineto-Phonograph* (Los Angeles: Pueblo Press, 1939); *History of the Kinetograph, Kinetoscope and Kineto-Phonograph* (New York: Arno Press, 1970); Louis Reeves Harrison, "Studio Saunterings," *The Moving Picture World* (April 13, 1913), pp. 127-131; "Edison Progress," *The Moving Picture World* (December 11, 1909), pp. 833-835; James S. McQuade, "Kleine-Edison Merger Formed," *The Moving Picture World* (July 24, 1915), pp. 626-627; George J. Svedja, *The Black Maria Site Study* (Washington, DC: Office of Archeology and Historical Preservation, 1969); and T. B., "Edisonia," *Exhibitor's Times*, Vol. I, No. 15 (August 30, 1913), pp. 1, 4.

10. *Billy Bitzer: His Story* (New York: Farrar, Straus and Giroux, 1973), p. 9.

11. The complete history of the Vitagraph Company is adequately documented in two books: Anthony Slide with Alan Gevinson, *The Big V: A History of the Vitagraph Company* (Metuchen, NJ: Scarecrow Press, 1987); and Paolo Cherchi Usai, ed., *Vitagraph Co. of America, Il Cinema Prima di Hollywood* (Pordenone, Italy: Edizioni Studio Tesi, 1987).

12. Interview on file with the American Society of Cinematographers.

13. Interview with Anthony Slide, October 7, 1971.

14. Interview with Anthony Slide, January 7, 1972.

15. The following contemporary articles provide good documentation on Betzwood: "Betzwood Film Co. Buys Lubin's Betzwood Plant," *The Moving Picture World* (February 16, 1918), p. 952; "Betzwood on the Perkiomen," *Motography* (August 23, 1913), pp. 121-122; W. Stephen Bush, "Betzwood, the Great," *The Moving Picture World* (July 11, 1914), pp. 274-275; "Get Off at Lubin," *The Moving Picture World* (September 13, 1913), pp. 1159-1160; and "Lubin's New Home," *Exhibitor's Times* (September 27, 1913), pp. 12-14.

16. A good introductory text on the Lubin Company is Joseph P. Eckhardt and Linda Kowall, *Peddler of Dreams* (Philadelphia: National Museum of American Jewish History, 1984). Other texts on Lubin include W. Stephen Bush, "A Day with Siegmund Lubin," *The Moving Picture*

World (July 11, 1914), pp. 209-210; Louis Reeves Harrison, "Studio Saunterings," *The Moving Picture World* (March 30, 1912), pp. 1142-1144; and Linda Kowall, "Siegmund Lubin: The Forgotten Filmmaker," *Pennsylvania Heritage,* Vol. XII, No. 1 (Winter 1986), pp. 18-27.

17. Speech by George K. Spoor, Waukegan Chamber of Commerce, May 10, 1944.

18. This is one of the most sought-after "lost" films. Prints were given to the War Department and the Department of the Interior after the film's completion, but such prints were not among the records of these departments handed over to the National Archives on its establishment in 1934. A letter in the files of the Bureau of Indian Affairs indicates that a print held by them was in bad condition as early as the twenties.

19. Interview with Anthony Slide, September 29, 1975.

20. Among texts on Essanay are the following: "The 'Acting' Member of Essanay," *The Moving Picture World* (January 6, 1912), pp. 27-28; "The Essanay Company Out West," *The Moving Picture World* (December 4, 1909), pp. 801-802; Ivan Gaddis, "The Origin of 'Broncho Billy,'" *Motion Picture Story Magazine* (March 1916), pp. 99-101; "In the Far West," *The Bioscope* (February 9, 1911), pp. 11-13; Charles J. McGuirk, "I Knew Them When," *Photoplay,* Vol. XXVII, No. 4 (March 1925), pp. 30-32, 113-116; Thomas Millstead, "The Movie the Indians Almost Won," *Westways* (December 1970), pp. 24-26, 55; Donald Parkhurst, "Broncho Billy and Niles, California," *The Pacific Historian,* Vol. XXVI, No. 4 (Winter 1982), pp. 1-22; and George K. Spoor, "Remarkable Growth of Motion Picture Industry," *The Moving Picture World* (July 9, 1913), p. 5.

21. Film pioneer T. K. Peters claims the first Selig studio was not at 7th Street and Olive, but on the roof of a loft building at Broadway and 8th Street.

22. Hobart Bosworth, "The Picture Forty-Niners," *Photoplay* (December 1915), p. 76.

23. Fred J. Balshofer and Arthur C. Miller, *One Reel A Week* (Berkeley, CA: University of California Press, 1967), p. 57.

24. For more information on Mix's Selig career, see Robert S. Birchard, "Earliest Days of the Tom Mix Legend," *American Cinematographer* (June 1987), pp. 36-41.

25. The only book-length study of the Selig Polyscope Company—Kalton C. Lahue, *Motion Picture Pioneer: The Selig Polyscope Company* (South Brunswick, NJ: A. S. Barnes, 1973)—is disappointing. The following are major contemporary articles on the company: Harry Hammond Beall, "The Packing House of Canned Drama," *The Rounder* (October 29, 1910), pp. 82-83; Leo Edwards, "An Afternoon at the Selig Studio," *Feature Movie Magazine* (April 15, 1915), pp. 34-39, 57; and "Selig's—The Great Moving Picture Plant of the West," *The Moving Picture World* (August 21, 1909), pp. 247-248. The papers of William N. Selig are

housed in the Margaret Herrick Library of the Academy of Motion Picture Arts and Sciences.

26. These and other quotes by Gene Gauntier are taken from her unpublished manuscript *Blazing the Trail*, which is in the files of the Museum of Modern Art.

27. The work of George K. Hollister is discussed in Roberta Courtlandt, "Troubles of the Camera Man," *Motion Picture Classic* (August 1916).

28. For more information, see Anthony Slide, "The O'Kalems," *Aspects of American Film History prior to 1920* (Metuchen, NJ: Scarecrow Press, 1978), pp. 87-97.

29. The following articles provide more information on the Kalem Company: Robert S. Birchard, "Kalem Company: Manufacturers of Moving Picture Films," *American Cinematographer* (August/September 1984), pp. 34-38; George Blaisdell, "Sid Olcott in Traveltalk," *The Moving Picture World* (January 17, 1914), pp. 272-273; W. Stephen Bush, "Samuel Long," *The Moving Picture World* (August 14, 1915), p. 1132; Lynde Denig, "The Kalem Viewpoint," *The Moving Picture World* (August 7, 1915), p. 1002; Louis Reeves Harrison, "Studio Saunterings," *The Moving Picture World* (July 6, 1912), pp. 23-26; "Kalem Sends Company to the Orient," *The Moving Picture World* (December 16, 1911), p. 880; "Kalem's Achievements as Pioneer," *The Moving Picture World* (March 10, 1917), pp. 1504-1505; and "Some Egyptian Pictures," *The Bioscope* (June 27, 1912), p. 937.

30. Testimony of Jacques A. Berst, July 10, 1913, *The Greater New York Film Rental Company vs. The Biograph Company and The General Film Company.*

31. "The Motion Picture Patents Company and Its Work: A Retrospect and Appreciation," *The Moving Picture World* (July 17, 1909), p. 84.

3

The Independents and a New Establishment

After the initial flush of interest in the motion picture in 1896, it fell into disfavor with the public. There was a limit to how many times an audience wished to see a train entering a station or a naive comedy in which a mother tries to bathe a recalcitrant infant.

"As we tired of the bicycle just as it was attaining perfection, so we tired of the biograph just as it was entering upon its career of supreme glory," wrote Rollin Lynde Hartt in 1909. "We early recognized how dreary, apart from the motion, were the pictures themselves. 'Man Eating,' 'Horse Walking,' 'Waves Waving,'—in these we beheld an art-for-art's sake futility not surpassed by our most infantile impressionists."[1]

Parents kept their children away because of the potential dangers that the motion picture represented. The new entertainment was the subject of much negative publicity as a result of a motion picture-inspired fire at the Charity Bazaar in Paris on May 4, 1897, which resulted in considerable loss of life. The poor quality of the picture image at many of the screenings led to rumors that the motion picture was injurious to the eyes.

By the turn of the century, film presentations had been relegated to the position of "chasers" on vaudeville bills. The motion picture appeared as the last item on the program—so uninteresting or disappointing that it would chase out the audience and thus clear the house for the next performance.

The motion picture as a novelty item was advanced in 1904, when two Kansas City entrepreneurs, George C. Hale and Fred W. Gifford, devised an entertainment consisting of a railroad Pullman car, at one end of which films were projected upon a screen, giving "passengers" in the car the experience of riding through different scenery. Known as Hale's Tours, the attraction was a major success at the 1904 World's Fair in St. Louis and was later seen as a permanent entertainment in many cities in the United States and abroad.

The rise of the motion picture to prominence began in 1905, when the first nickelodeon opened. Although now used as a generic term to describe most early film theaters, the name "The Nickelodeon" was first applied to a theater at 433-435 Smithfield Street, Pittsburgh, opened by John P. Harris on June 15, 1905. Pittsburgh's Nickelodeon was not, however, the first theater to be specifically opened for the screening of films; that honor goes to Thomas L. Tally's Electric Theatre, which opened at 262 South Main Street, Los Angeles, in April 1902.

Between 1905 and 1907, the number of five-cent theaters in America grew from 1 to between 4,000 and 5,000. By 1909, in New York City alone, there were 800 motion picture theaters, the majority custom-built for the presentation of films. Nationwide, the number rose to 10,000. It was estimated that between 500,000 and 1,000,000 people went to the movies daily in New York City. The movies were cheap—an entire family could enjoy an evening's entertainment for the price of one legitimate theater ticket. In 1907, children made up 33 percent of the audience. Americans of Spanish or South American descent were more consistent filmgoers than Irish or Jewish Americans.[2] Theaters catered to shop assistants, clerks, and office boys during their lunch breaks and to shoppers needing a place to rest their legs.[3]

"Of all the novelties in the field of popular amusement in recent years, none has made such headway or so completely taken hold of public favor as the moving picture," commented *The American Review of Reviews*.[4] The moving picture theater had become the people's theater. From a "chaser" on the vaudeville bill, the motion picture became the earlier amusement's partner, and in 1912, a number of theaters began alternating films with vaudeville acts. Despite the continuing relationship between the two media well into the forties, it was generally conceded in 1912 that film exhibition could only grow in stature if it became totally separate from the vaudeville stage.

The average weekly cost of operating a nickelodeon in 1907 was $190,[5] as follows:

Wage of manager	$ 25
Wage of operator	$ 20
Wage of doorman	$ 15
Wage of porter or musician	$ 12
Rental of films (changed twice per week)	$ 50
Rental of projector	$ 10
Rental of building	$ 40
Music, printing, "Campaign Contributions"(!), etc.	$ 18
Total:	$190

Nickelodeons boasted profits of between $300 and $500 a week, and offered opportunities to many immigrant groups with little or limited capital. The potential was there for quick profits with superficial regard for the well-being of patrons.

"Too many exhibitors had little conscience in their work and were interested only in raking in the nickels," wrote Bennet Musson and Robert Grau in 1912. "The converted theaters were generally dirty, unventilated, and dangerous in case of fire. Especially obnoxious was the fact that they were totally dark, and thus objectionable from a standpoint of good morals. Men of the lowest type of city politician found the motion picture a useful field for exploitation." Worst of all, pointed out the writers, "East Side Russian Jews, who are the greatest shoestring speculators in the world, reaped an enormous harvest."

A 1911 report on Conditions of Moving Picture Shows in New York City found much that was of concern:

> Third Avenue, Manhattan: This is a vile smelling place, and an attendant went round with a big pump atomizer spraying perfumery to allay the odor.

Pitkin Avenue, Brooklyn: Seats full and about two hundred
and fifty standing in the rear and in the aisles. A critical inspection of this place was impossible. The crowd was surging back
and forth, pushing and shoving for vantage points of view.
Quarrels were frequent. The air was fetid and stifling. Children
under sixteen years were admitted unaccompanied. This place is
without one single redeeming feature.[6]

The popularity of the nickelodeon is evidenced by the number
of standees this report found at each theater inspected:

Flatbush Avenue, Brooklyn	87 people
Graham Avenue, Brooklyn	86 people
Third Avenue, Manhattan	17 people
West 125th Street, Manhattan	46 people

Seven departments—Health, Police, Fire, Bureau of Buildings,
Water Supply, Gas and Electricity, Mayor's Bureau of Licensing,
and Tenement House—were charged with duties concerning film
exhibition in New York.

Criticism of nickelodeons led to exhibitors accepting a proposal
from a New York City civic organization, the People's Institute, for
the establishment of the National Board of Censorship of Motion
Pictures. Founded in October 1909, the Board arranged to censor
films from Biograph, Edison, Essanay, Kalem, Lubin, Selig, Vitagraph, Gaumont, Pathé, Méliès, and the British Urban Company
prior to their being sent to exchanges for distribution. In reality,
there was little to censor, because such companies had already
eliminated anything that might be considered objectionable. Images
to which the Board expressed opposition were those of crimes or
violence for their own sakes, indecency, and immoral suggestive-
ness. Additionally, the Board urged the use of the motion picture
for educational purposes. In 1916, its name was changed to the
National Board of Review of Motion Pictures, which continues to
the present, with its principal current activity being publication of
the magazine *Films in Review.*[7]

"This is the boom time in the moving-picture business. Every-
body is making money—manufacturers, renters, jobbers, exhibitors," said one press agent enthusiastically quoted in *Variety* in
1907. "Now this line is Klondike."[8]

A less commercial view was expressed two years later in *Scribner's Magazine:* "What all of us should realize is that this new department of the modern drama is—relatively—a virgin soil. Who knows what crops it may yet raise? And why assume that depravity —gross vulgarity even—is necessarily bound up in it?"[9] In other words, the film industry was ripe for takeover by producers outside of the Motion Picture Patents Company, producers who were to shape the future and become the industry's new establishment.

The newcomers to the industry had two characteristics in common: they were all immigrants from Eastern Europe, and they were all Jewish. With the exception of Siegmund Lubin—the token Jew in their midst—all of the men of the Motion Picture Patents Company were Christian, and many were anti-Semitic. J. Stuart Blackton s daughter, Marian, states categorically: "My father was anti-Semitic, a weakness in him that I could never understand. But he never spoke of it except in occasional close-family conversations, and I am certain he did not voice it in the studios."[10] When Warner Bros. took over Vitagraph, Blackton's partner, Albert E. Smith, spoke disparagingly of the Hebraic brethren.

Even more outspoken was George Kleine's daughter, Helen, who was quick to point out that her father's name was pronounced Klein-ee, Klein being Jewish. "I know they tried to keep the Jewish people out, because they thought they would ruin the business," she claimed. "They were sort of snooty—the pioneers—and they didn't want this new class of people coming in, the Jewish element." She shuddered with horror at the suggestion of inviting Siegmund Lubin to dine at her father's Chicago home.[11]

What Lubin thought of his Gentile colleagues is not recorded. Certainly, he was one of the first Jews in the industry to openly acknowledge his faith with the 1915 presentation of a meeting hall to the Congregation Keneseth Israel in Philadelphia. (The first program there was a lecture by Lubin director Joseph Smiley on "The Making of Moving Pictures.")

Lubin was also the only pioneer to openly assist the independent producers. When Jesse L. Lasky, Cecil B. DeMille, and Samuel Goldwyn (then Goldfish) discovered a problem with their negative on *The Squaw Man,* they took it to Lubin, who diagnosed faulty perforations of the film stock and was able to reperforate the film.

Samuel Goldwyn (1879-1974) came into his own in December, 1916, with the formation of Goldwyn Pictures Corporation, co-founded with Edgar and Archibald Selwyn. In 1918, Goldfish, as he was then known, took the company name as his surname.[12]

Goldwyn's ambitions were nothing compared to those of William Fox (1879-1952), who had started as an exhibitor in New York in 1904, forming the Greater New York Film Rental Company. In January 1914, he created Box Office Attractions Company, initially as a distributor and, later, as a producer. Winfield Sheehan, long associated with Fox, was the company's general manager. Box Office Attractions used the Eclair Studios (which Fox later purchased) in Fort Lee, New Jersey, and studios at Scott's Farm on Staten Island and in Jersey City. In 1915, Box Office Attractions Company became the Fox Film Corporation; a year later, Fox opened his studios on Western Avenue in Los Angeles. Fox, himself, operated out of the New York office, sending lengthy, often derogatory letters to his Los Angeles studio head, Sol Wurtzel, questioning every cent spent on production and the value of each and every one of his directors and stars. That so many of the extant Fox films of the teens and twenties are so good would seem to be in spite of, and not because of, William Fox.[13]

The person most influential in the downfall of the Motion Picture Patents group of companies was Carl Laemmle (1867-1939). Like so many of his contemporaries in the film industry, Laemmle was an immigrant—from Bavaria—and, again like so many other Jewish film pioneers, he had commenced his working life in the United States in the clothing industry, by managing a store in Oshkosh, Wisconsin.[14] Laemmle's first involvement with motion pictures came on February 24, 1906, when he opened the White Front Theater on Chicago's Milwaukee Avenue. That same year, he opened the Laemmle Film Service to purchase and rent films. By 1909, he claimed to be operating one of the largest film exchanges in the world.

Laemmle was totally opposed to the concept of the Motion Picture Patents Company and its insistence on licensing operations such as his. He refused to pay tribute, as he stubbornly called it, to the Motion Picture Patents Company and suddenly found himself cut off from the supply of films of its members. As early as October 16, 1908, he wrote to the Selig Polyscope Company:

> Conditions in the renting end of the moving picture business
> just at the moment are extremely bad. While I don't profess to

speak for any other renter than myself, still I know that none of us can make any profits the way things stand now.

There are three reasons for this:—First, the recent raise in price of films, approximating about 20 percent or more. Second, the fact that the films are all longer than they used to be, forcing us to buy a greater volume of film which, in turn, does not bring in any increased volume of rental money to the renters. Third, it is impossible for the renters to secure anything like fair rental prices from the exhibitors, owing to the unusually keen competition.[15]

(Laemmle's concern with increased lengths of films causing lower profits has been a continuing complaint of exhibitors to the present day. The longer the film, the fewer screenings a day, and this means a subsequent loss in admissions.)

Appealing to the licensed producers did Laemmle no good, and so, eventually, he took his fight openly to his fellow renters and exhibitors and ultimately, the public. He placed advertisements attacking the Motion Picture Patents Company in the pages of *The Moving Picture World* and other trade papers. The Motion Picture Patents Company acted foolishly in not inviting Laemmle to join them. Had they done so, the course of film history might have changed considerably. Initially, the Motion Picture Patents Company had an ally in Carl Laemmle. It is seldom noted that Carl Laemmle considered himself too important a member of the film industry to be labelled an "independent," and he tried to curry favor with the Motion Picture Patents Company through the dispatch of form letters such as the following, mailed to exhibitors on February 5, 1909:

Here are some COLD FACTS I want you to consider for ALL YOU ARE WORTH: —

First:—YOU are the Mainstay of the Moving Picture Business. Without you the Manufacturer and the Renter wouldn't last as long as a snowball in Hell. (Moral:—Therefore when anyone tells you that the Manufacturers or the Renters are trying to put you out of business, he must have an Ax to grind. Don't let him use you as a grind stone.)

Second:—Certain people, styling themselves "Independents" are urging you to fight Thomas Edison, the man who invented the very apparatus that gives you and me a chance to make a living. The REASON why they want YOU to put up the fight is that they cannot do it themselves. Furthermore, they cannot get a license from Thomas Edison. (Moral:—If Thomas Edison refuses them a license, there must be a damned good reason back of his refusal. If Thomas Edison thinks those people are a detriment to the Moving Picture Business, can YOU afford to do business with them? There s a Nigger in the Woodpile. Be sure you know what it is, before you accept any jackass advice.)

Third:—If you have any confidence in Me,—if you believe I am on the square—WHY do you suppose I decided not to join the so-called "Independents?" LISTEN to the answer:—It's because THEY HAVEN'T GOT A SINGLE LEG TO STAND ON. Their ONLY hope is that they can get their fight into the Courts and do business for perhaps half a year or so before they are thrown out by law altogether. They are banking entirely on the law's delays—one of the biggest fool schemes that was ever devised. They expect you to help put up a losing fight, and in the meantime submit to all sorts of annoyance and nuisance. (Moral:—DON'T pull another man's Chestnuts out of the Fire, because it is going to be about the hottest little fire that ever happened.)

Fourth:—You KNOW from experience that Europe has already taken a back seat in the production of good money-making Films. America is in the lead, after a long battle, and it is a cinch that she will not let go of her advantage. If you do business with the so-called "Independents," you'll have to use European stuff exclusively and you'll have to take whatever you can get. You won't have one tenth as big an assortment of subjects to choose from as you will if you deal with me—and I can prove it. (Moral: —Don't let a Dog in the Manger keep you from getting what you want.)[16]

Laemmle's next logical step was to become a producer. On June 5, 1909, he took out an advertisement in *The Moving Picture World* announcing:

EXTRA. Carl Laemmle Becomes a Film Manufacturer. Organizes a New Company To Be Totally Separate from the

Laemmle Film Service. Will Make a Tremendous Specialty of
American Subjects.

To emphasize the last, the new company was named Yankee,
but the name was quickly changed to the Independent Moving
Picture Company of America, more simply known as IMP. On
October 25, 1909, IMP released its first film, a one-reel adaptation
of Longfellow's *Hiawatha,* directed by William V. Ranous (usually
associated with the Vitagraph Company) and shot in Coytesville,
New Jersey, which is now a section of Englewood Cliffs.

The Moving Picture World (October 23, 1909) was lavish in its
praise of the production:

> It is stamped all over with the signs of success. The photog-
> raphy is good, the acting of the story is well sustained all through,
> and, barring a few minor blemishes of a technical nature, insep-
> arable from the haste of a first production, this film of *Hiawatha*
> is quite entitled right away to take rank as a first-class specimen
> of American-made film of an American subject by American
> labor.

In fact, compared with other one-reel subjects of the same year,
Hiawatha is well-made and a highly creditable first film.[17]

The IMP Company expanded with the addition to its ranks of
two former American Biograph Company players, Florence Lawrence and Mary Pickford. In 1910, Laemmle persuaded a group of
independent producers to get together and form the Motion Picture
Distributing Sales Company in answer to the Motion Picture Patents Company and the General Film Company. In 1911, IMP
opened its first studio in Los Angeles, at Sunset Boulevard and
Gower Street in the heart of Hollywood, deserting its former East
Coast studios at Coytesville and Bayonne, New Jersey. Also in
1911, IMP hired Herbert Brenon (1880-1958) as a scenario editor.
He became a director for the company the following year, respon-
sible for its first three-reel production, *Leah the Forsaken,* starring
Vivan Prescott in the title role and released on November 7, 1912.
In May, 1913, Brenon brought leading man King Baggot with him
to England to film an adaptation of Sir Walter Scott's *Ivanhoe* at
Chepstow Castle, Monmouth. Leah Baird played Rebecca of York,
and Brenon cast himself as Isaac of York. In Paris that same year,

the group filmed *Absinthe* and then journeyed on to Germany to make three further productions. Brenon's last major film for IMP was *Neptune's Daughter*, filmed over a three-month period in 1914 in Bermuda and starring Annette Kellermann.

On June 8, 1912, the Universal Film Manufacturing Company was formed, consisting not only of Laemmle's IMP Company, but also Pat Powers' Motion Picture Company, Mark Dintenfass' Champion Film Company, David Horsley's Nestor Company, and Charles Baumann and Adam Kessel's New York Motion Picture Company. In part, the formation of Universal was an answer to the founding of the Film Supply Company of America by Thanhouser, American, Majestic, Reliance, Solax, Comet, Gaumont, Great Northern, Eclair, and Lux, all of which had earlier been associated with the Motion Picture Distributing Sales Company and had now aligned themselves with the Mutual Film Corporation, which was to handle distribution of films by those producers under the leadership of Harry E. Aitken and John R. Freuler.

Major internal fighting broke out at both the Film Supply Company of America and Universal. The Mutual Film Corporation remained intact and continued in existence through 1918, but a new organization, Exclusive Film Corporation, was formed to handle releases from Great Northern, (Herbert) Blaché, and Solax. Following a bitter dispute at Universal, Kessel and Baumann departed and Carl Laemmle was elevated from the company's secretary to its president—gaining effective control of the organization.[18]

On June 22, 1912, Universal began publication of its house organ, *The Universal Weekly*. In its first issue, the company editorialized:

> Here in the United States, numerically at least, the Universal has the largest number of employees of any film manufacturing company. . . . The Universal represents the best possible scheme and organization for the manufacture and distribution of motion pictures on the largest possible scale.

In 1912, to emphasize its strength, the company opened branch offices in London, Berlin, Moscow, and other European cities, making the forays of the members of the Motion Picture Patents Group into the European market unimportant in comparison.

A number of "brand" names were used to identify Universal films, with a different day of the week designated for each brand:

Sunday—Rex films, directed by Lois Weber and Phillips Smalley, and starring Ella Hall and Rupert Julian (who later became a director and was noted for his portrayals of the German Kaiser, to whom he bore a striking resemblance).

Monday—Powers comedies, directed by Donald Macdonald and starring Laura Oakley, Marie Walcamp, and Howard Hickman; and Victor dramas, directed by Joseph MacDonald and starring J. Warren Kerrigan.

Tuesday—Gold Seal Films, one each from company No. 1 and company No. 2. Allan Dwan was the director of the first company, whose stars were his then-wife Pauline Bush, Murdoch Mac-Quarrie, and Lon Chaney, while Francis Ford directed and starred in the films for company No. 2, whose leading lady was Grace Cunard.

Wednesday—Joker comedies, directed by Allan Curtis and starring Max Asher; and Nestor dramas, directed by and starring Wallace Reid with leading lady Dorothy Davenport.

Thursday—Rex films, directed by Otis Turner and starring Robert Z. Leonard (later to become a director) and Edna Maison.

Friday—Nestor comedies, directed by Al Christie, and starring Eddie Lyons and Lee Moran; and Powers dramas, directed by and starring Edwin August.

Saturday—Joker half-reel comedies, directed by Allan Curtis; and Bison dramas, directed by Henry MacRae and starring William Clifford.

Additional films were produced by a second Bison company, directed by David Hartford, with leading lady Cleo Madison; and special "big" productions were directed by Otis Turner and Joseph MacDonald.[19]

In March 1914, with $3,500 down, Universal purchased the Taylor estate in the Lankershim Township on the north side of the Hollywood Hills in the San Fernando Valley. The total purchase price was $165,000. William Horsley was in charge of building Universal's new studio here under the supervision of general manager Isadore Bernstein, and ground-breaking took place on June 18, 1914. Universal City, as the studio was named, was officially opened by Carl Laemmle on March 15, 1915, with *Damon and Pythias*, starring Herbert Rawlinson, being the first film shot there (before the city had been opened); Rawlinson was named Universal City's first mayor.

Using only two 300-foot-long outdoor stages, 250 films were produced at Universal City in its first year of operation. By 1916, the studio had five open-air and two enclosed stages. When it first opened, tourists were encouraged to watch filming from bleacher seats built above the dressing rooms and boxed lunches were provided for them. Actress Ruth Clifford recalls that the audience would applaud at the end of each take. This open and friendly attitude towards visitors was a precursor of the Universal Studios Tours, which officially opened in 1964.

With the opening of Universal City, Carl Laemmle left little doubt about his prominence in the film industry. Irving Thalberg went to work for Laemmle in 1918 and was made director-general and head of production in the early twenties, a position that he held until 1923. One of Thalberg's first acts was to fire Erich von Stroheim, whom Laemmle had hired in 1918 to direct his first film, *Blind Husbands*.

Affectionately known as "Uncle Carl," in part because he had so many relatives working at the studio, Laemmle appears to have been a warm and caring employer, well-liked by both performers and technicians of his company.[20] The same cannot be said of Laemmle's fellow mogul, Adolph Zukor.

"Ruthless Zukor" would be an appropriate title for a biography of the man whose early career was marked by a relentless desire to destroy anyone who stood in the way of his plan to dominate the film industry. Adolph Zukor (1873-1976) had a lasting impact on the development of the film industry and his name will always be closely linked with Paramount Pictures, a company that he did not found and where he served merely as a figurehead after 1935, when the company was reorganized and taken over by others. In later years, he was characterized as a kindly old pioneer, venerated by his colleagues, to whom suitable tribute was paid by various Paramount contract stars who could easily be cajoled into making appearances at each of Zukor's more important birthdays. The reality was far removed from that later public persona.

From the late teens onwards, Zukor's plan was for Paramount to be the dominate force in production, distribution, *and* exhibition.

Through extensive and carefully considered advertising, the name "Paramount" became synonymous with the best in motion pictures (a not entirely dishonorable claim). Through various means, Paramount was able to have its films screened in 11,000 of the 16,000 motion picture theaters in the United States by 1921. In terms of theatrical screenings, Paramount was the leader, followed by Goldwyn, Metro, Universal, Fox, First National, and Pathé. Paramount's control of exhibition in 1921 was such that it became the subject of an investigation by the Federal Trade Commission and active opposition by the Motion Picture Theater Owners of America.

It was not until the forties that the government was able to force Paramount and other major studios to divest themselves of their theater chains. However, in the eighties, under the Reagan and later presidential administrations, Paramount and other studios have successfully acquired new theater chains without opposition from the Justice Department.

Paramount's financial demands from its exhibitors were anything but subtle. If an exhibitor refused to book Paramount features because of an increase in rental charges, the company would take out advertising in the local newspapers asking why the community was being denied access to Paramount features and suggesting that readers question their local theater management. A series of seven such advertisements was prepared for use in any American city, with blank spaces for the insertion of local data.

The owner of a theater in Mattoon, Illinois, was so angered by Paramount's activity that he placed his own advertisement in the local newspaper, stating:

There Must Be a Reason Why Paramount Pictures Are Not Being Shown in Mattoon.
Is it because the greatest of directors and the biggest stars have quit Paramount?
Because D. W. Griffith has quit Paramount?
Because Thomas Ince has quit Paramount?
Because Marguerite Clark has quit Paramount?
Because Mary Pickford has quit Paramount?
Because Douglas Fairbanks has quit Paramount?
Because all of these people are making wonderful pictures for other companies and we are running them?

Because inferior foreign-made pictures are being imported
by Paramount and foisted on the public under the Paramount
banner?[21]

The last is a reference to a policy adopted by Zukor after the
First World War, whereby he purchased European features cheaply
and released them on the Paramount program while cutting back
on production at home, including the 1921 closure of Paramount's
East Coast studio. Around the same time, Zukor instituted further
cost cutting by promoting his writers and directors as "stars," and
demanding salary cutbacks from his actor "stars" because their
names were no longer prominent in the promotion of their films.
This concept of promoting authors as celebrities—because writers
come considerably cheaper than players—was adopted by Samuel
Goldwyn in 1919 with his "Eminent Authors" series of features.

Adolph Zukor was particularly venal in his behavior towards
the Vitagraph Company. Albert E. Smith documents Zukor's activities in his autobiography, *Two Reels and a Crank*, but he was
apparently too intimidated by Zukor to mention the name of his
adversary. Smith discusses Paramount's production of feature films
similar to those of Vitagraph, and the former's release of these films
simultaneously with the Vitagraph release. He also recalls that on
the night of the premiere of Vitagraph's most important release of
the twenties, *Captain Blood,* Zukor hosted a dinner party for New
York's leading critics. Each was given an expensive wristwatch, and
one critic told Smith, "He [Zukor] said his feelings wouldn t be hurt
if we decided that *Captain Blood* was a lousy picture." [22]

Because Vitagraph claimed a loss of almost a million dollars in
revenue thanks to various restrictive trade practices of Paramount,
the company filed suit against Paramount in 1922, asking six
million dollars in punitive damages. Vitagraph was persuaded to
discontinue its suit by Will Hays, the head of the newly formed
Motion Picture Producers and Distributors of America, who promised that Paramount would similarly discontinue its activities
against Vitagraph. Vitagraph agreed, but Hays did not keep his
word. Because Paramount was the one studio closely linked to the
Hollywood scandals of the early twenties—all the participants were
Paramount contractees—and because the studio remained un-
scathed despite Will Hays' promise to clean up the industry, there
is more than a probability of close links between Hays and Zukor.

Nor should it be assumed that Adolph Zukor's ruthlessness was limited to the twenties. Even his control of Paramount in the mid-teens smacked of sordid business practice.

Hungarian-born Adolph Zukor came to the United States at the age of sixteen and gained employment with a fur manufacturer whose foreman was the brother of one of Zukor's school friends. On March 4, 1903, Zukor opened a penny arcade at Fourteenth Street and Union Square in New York City. He began a brief association with Marcus Loew and actor David Warfield, and opened three further penny arcades—each of which also included motion pictures—on New York's 125th Street, and in Newark and Boston. Loew parted company with Zukor and commenced opening a number of nickelodeons in partnership with Joseph and Nicholas Schenck, while Zukor also expanded his operation with combination vaudeville and film presentations and Hale's Tours. In 1909, Zukor merged his operation with Loew and Schenck, and a new corporation—Loew's Consolidated—was formed, with Zukor as its treasurer.

On June 1, 1912, Zukor incorporated the Famous Players Film Company, with its first acquisition being the French production *Les Amours de la Reine Elizabeth,* directed by Louis Mercanton and starring Sarah Bernhardt, which Zukor released in the United States as *Queen Elizabeth.* Zukor approached the General Film Company to handle distribution of the production. Although Pathé's Jacques Berst, along with Colonel Selig and Albert E. Smith, were in favor of the proposal, the majority of the board members of the General Film Company were not, and Zukor was rebuffed. There can be little doubt that Zukor remembered that slight in the years to come.

He distributed *Queen Elizabeth* on a states rights basis, as he did his following productions. Zukor announced plans to release six features per year starring famous theatrical personalities in the plays with which they were most closely associated. Additionally, another twelve features would star a well-known (but not famous) actor or actress in a well-known (but not necessarily famous) play, and another twelve films would feature members of the proposed Famous Players stock company. A states rights distributor would acquire two prints of each film for an appropriate license fee based on his territory. Thus, the states rights distributor for California, Arizona, New Mexico, and Nevada could acquire all thirty features for a grand total of $52,800.

Zukor purchased the U. S. rights to *Queen Elizabeth* for $40,000 and quickly netted a profit of $20,000.

Aside from a strictly profit motive, the creation of the Famous Players Film Company gave legitimacy to Zukor. He could talk pretentiously to the trade papers:

> Our aim is to have them [the films] within reach of the people who cannot afford to pay more than ten cents. I don't agree with the men who say we should charge 50 cents and a dollar for big productions. We believe that we are doing a sort of missionary work for the higher art—that we are aiding in the cultivation of a taste for better things. While of course we feel that our productions would command higher prices we want to encourage people to go to them. It may not be to our financial advantage at the beginning but in the end it will undoubtedly.[23]

Prominent in assisting Zukor in the creation of Famous Players was theatrical entrepreneur and producer Daniel Frohman, who served as the company's vice president and managing director. "Even then it was actually not hard to persuade [theatrical] stars to come to the films," he reminisced in 1920. "What they needed was proper assurance. Probably the stars had faith in me thru my previous association with many of them."[24]

Meanwhile, a distribution organization, Paramount Corporation, was founded on May 8, 1914, by William W. Hodkinson (1881-1971), who had commenced his career operating a film exchange and theater in Ogden, Utah, in 1909. Paramount was to distribute films from Famous Players, Master Productions, and the William L. Sherry Feature Film Company.[25] It was Hodkinson and not Zukor who founded Paramount, and as Hodkinson recalled:

> One summer evening in 1914, I met Zukor for a dinner appointment, following several months of hectic negotiations and the closing of contracts with the producers of the company I was forming; which I had originally planned to name Progressive Pictures Corporation—the name of the company which I had formed the year before, with operations on the Pacific Coast; I found upon telephoned advice from my attorney who had gone to Albany to push through the incorporation, that the name Progressive had been pre-empted in certain localities and that

something else must be chosen. Hoping to keep the name suffi-
ciently alliterative I picked up the New York telephone directory
on my desk and turned to names commencing with the letter "P."
One name on the page was "Paramount," the name of an apartment house. I decided that was it and hurriedly phoned my
attorney in Albany. While I was phoning I thought of Pike's Peak,
near where I had lived in Colorado and sketched, with pencil, on
a blotter a mountain, with the legend flying on two banners above
it, the prototype of the first Paramount trademark.

Adolph Zukor, the man to whom credit is falsely given for the
creation of Paramount, did not like the name. He urged Hodkinson
to call the company "Hygrade." "I explained," recalled Hodkinson,
"that there was merit in not being common; that our corporation
was an exceptional one, requiring something dignified." [26]
Shortly after Paramount's incorporation, the Jesse L. Lasky
Feature Play Company (incorporated in 1913), Bosworth Incorporated (founded by actor Hobart Bosworth in 1913)[27] and the Oliver
Morosco Photoplay Company (founded by the theatrical producer
in 1914) began releasing their films through Paramount. In the
summer of 1916, Lasky and Famous Players merged as the Famous
Players-Lasky Corporation. Zukor acquired a majority holding in
Paramount and Hodkinson was out, followed shortly thereafter by
both Bosworth and Morosco, neither of whom was adequately
compensated, although their companies remained with Zukor. In
November 1917, Hodkinson formed a new company, the W. W.
Hodkinson Corporation, which remained in existence through
1924. It never achieved the success it deserved, and Hodkinson
remained a bitter man, antagonistic towards Zukor until his death.
The relationship between Zukor and Lasky was a curious one
and remained so throughout the men's working relationship. Zukor
was the New York-based businessman, while Lasky headed the
West Coast studio, initially at Sunset Boulevard and Vine Street in
Hollywood and later, in 1926, at its present site at 5555 Melrose
Avenue. Lasky was never on first-name terms with Zukor. Every
letter to New York from Lasky's office begins "Dear Mr. Zukor."
Lasky might be the creative head of Paramount, but there was no
question as to who was the boss. In 1921, the two men made an
agreement whereby certain productions would be presented by
Zukor and others by Lasky (although all were supervised by the

latter). Adolph Zukor presented the films of William de Mille, Roscoe Arbuckle, Thomas Meighan, Betty Compson, Agnes Ayres, and Dorothy Dalton, while Lasky presented those of Cecil B. DeMille, George Melford, Gloria Swanson, Ethel Clayton, Wallace Reid, and Jack Holt.

Despite an apparent uneasiness between the two men and despite a May 1918, fire that caused $100,000 worth of damage at the West Coast studio, Paramount flourished. In July 1916, it created a new company, Artcraft, strictly for the release of Mary Pickford features, but later used for any major Paramount release.[28] It was a subtle move on Zukor's part, enabling his sales staff to persuade an exhibitor to sign a contract for a considerable number of Paramount features with the exhibitor presuming that Pickford's films would be among that number. Later the hapless exhibitor would discover that Pickford s films were not Paramount releases, but Artcraft releases. Similarly, in 1919, Realart Pictures Corporation was formed to handle lesser Paramount productions.

Despite the creation of Metro Pictures Corporation (the forerunner of Metro-Goldwyn-Mayer) in 1915, of First National in 1917, and of United Artists Corporation in January 1919, there was no question that by the late teens, Paramount was paramount in the American film industry, both from a business viewpoint *and* in terms of the quality of its features.[29]

Carl Laemmle and Adolph Zukor helped whittle away at the power of the Motion Picture Patents Company through the expansion of their companies from an industry viewpoint and that of the moviegoing public. On the legal front, the first major breakthrough for the independents came in 1912, when Laemmle successfully fought a suit against his Independent Moving Picture Company by the Motion Picture Patents Company. The most important case also came in 1912, when William Fox's The Greater New York Film Rental Company filed suit against the Biograph Company and the General Film Company, claiming an illegal monopoly and a restraint of trade. The General Film Company board tried unsuccessfully to buy off Fox and have him drop the suit. The matter came to the attention of the Department of Justice, which charged an antitrust violation against the Motion Picture Patents Company under the Sherman Act in August 1912. Hearings began in January 1913, and the case was decided in the government's favor in October 1915.

Following various reorganizations, both the Motion Picture Patents Company and the General Film Company were disbanded in 1918, long after they had ceased to be effective. The most succinct and accurate analysis of why the two organizations failed is provided by *Variety* in its issue of December 31, 1920:

> Put in a word, it was a matter of morals on the part of the principal men in the "trust." They were, for one thing, frenzied with money being deluged upon them; they would not take a long distance view of their interests, and they would not be subject to mutual counsel. Above all things, they were selfishly concerned with their own individual gains, jealous of each other, and imbued with the idea that their astounding success was the fruits of their own acumen rather than mostly an accident of circumstance.
>
> If the Patents Co., or more properly speaking, the General Film Co., in the days of its greatest height of power had had the foresight to accept into its circle the best of outside enterprise and business and artistic career, which all the time was striving for admittance, they probably would have established their huge amalgamation on a firm and permanent basis.[30]

When legal recourse failed, the Motion Picture Patents Company had, at times, turned to violence, hiring thugs to hound and destroy the photographic equipment of the independents. It also used the services of the remarkable Joseph Francis McCoy (1860-1938), who had first gained employment with Thomas Edison in 1880. McCoy was "the Edison Detective" who would mysteriously appear whenever an independent cameraman was at work. With beguiling charm, he would innocently ask the cameraman how his machine operated, and shortly thereafter, the independent would be served with an injunction containing a detailed description of his camera and showing its similarity to the Edison patent.

From a modern viewpoint, the Motion Picture Patents Company achieved little in its attempts to impede progress. In many respects, it helped, albeit accidentally, in the growth of the industry. Certainly, many companies of the Patents group went West to film. Within a few years of the birth of the motion picture, actuality footage had been taken of all the American states; as remote as Hawaii might have seemed at the time, films were first seen there on February 5, 1897, and Edison cameramen were shooting on the islands in May 1898. But the movement to California and other Western states took off as the independents tried to distance themselves from the harassment of the Motion Picture Patents Company. They set up studios throughout California, not only in Los Angeles, but also in San Diego and San Francisco. The American Film Manufacturing Company (founded in Chicago in 1910) opened studios in Santa Barbara in June, 1912, and employed such prominent directors as Allan Dwan, William Desmond Taylor, and Edward Sloman, together with the beautiful, but untalented, star Mary Miles Minter. In 1913, the Balboa Amusement Producing Company was formed in Long Beach, California. These are but two examples of the many independent companies that flourished in California.

There can be little doubt that the independents were crucial to the establishment of Los Angeles as the filmmaking capital of the United States and, eventually, the world. From a city that had once spurned filmmakers, Los Angeles became proud of its best-known industry. In February 1916, actress Louise Glaum even suggested that the slogan "Made in Los Angeles" be appended on all films produced in the city.[31] On January 4 of that same year, Jesse L. Lasky, D. W. Griffith, and David Horsley, representing the Motion Picture Producers Protective Association, met with Los Angeles Mayor Sebastian to discuss the ways in which the city benefitted from the film industry's presence.

By opening up the film industry, the independents also helped a number of European producers to establish studios in the United States. In 1907, Pathé Frères was the first, followed by Gaumont, which released its first American-made film in 1913. In 1911, Eclair opened a substantial Fort Lee, New Jersey, complex, which included two studio buildings, administrative offices, and a laboratory capable of processing 40,000 feet of film a day. Eclair's first American release was titled (appropriately enough) *Hands across the Sea in '76,* released on November 21, 1911, and, as the title suggests, the film documents the activities of the Marquis de Lafayette during the Revolutionary War.

The influx of foreign manufacturers such as Eclair was important because often their films were noted for artistic qualities seemingly lacking in productions of their American counterparts. Eclair's French films were notable for the participation of art director Ben Carré and director Maurice Tourneur. They were also highly praised for the photographic work. An anonymous critic in *The Moving Picture World* (January 14, 1911) commented:

> It seems that before they start the crank of the camera they study every detail of light, so as to bring out these wonderful effects. Their work is not the black and white outline drawing, it is as the full-toned oil painting in comparison. No matter where the Eclair folks place their camera, let it be in the studio, in the open air or in the woods, they know how to obtain figures in full relief, faces are well illuminated, showing every expression.

A March 1914, fire forced the closure of the Fort Lee plant, and the entire company was dispatched to Tucson, Arizona, where Webster Cullison was named managing director. (Before becoming a director to Eclair's Fort Lee studio, Cullison had organized two companies of players for the Lubin Company in Tucson.) The stock players with Eclair in Tucson included Robert Frazer, Carol Holloway, and Clara Horton, known as "The Eclair Kid" and featured in the films of the Eclair's Children's Comedy Company under the direction of Lucie K. Villa.[32]

"The enthusiasm of youth is the necessary thing in the making of future pictures," observed William Fox in a letter to Sol Wurtzel dated October 2, 1920. This comment may well explain why many of the Patents group of companies, those headed by the older pioneers, died, while one or two managed by younger, enthusiastic founders were able to survive. It may also explain why some independents, such as the Thanhouser Film Corporation, founded by Edwin Thanhouser, who had already enjoyed a long and successful career in the theater, remained active only from 1909-1918 and did not survive into the twenties.

The first batch of film pioneers was aging, and just as the screen's stars had to be much younger than they photographed, so those forming the new motion picture establishment could not afford to rest on their laurels—or even to grow old. The demise of William Fox, Carl Laemmle, and Adolph Zukor in the thirties had as much to do with the aging process—of the mind as well as the body—as with changes in the industry.

Notes

1. Rollin Lydne Hartt, *The People at Play* (Boston: Houghton Mifflin, 1909), pp. 125-126.

2. "The Nickelodeons," *Variety* (December 14, 1907), p. 33.

3. William Allen Johnston, "The Moving-Picture Show, the New Form of Drama for the Millions," *Munsay's Magazine* (August 1909), pp. 635-636.

4. "Moving Pictures Ad Nauseum," *The American Review of Reviews* (December 1908), pp. 744-745.

5. "The Nickelodeons," *Variety* (December 14, 1907), p. 33.

6. *A Report on Condition of Moving Picture Shows in New York, March 22, 1911* (New York: Office of Accounts), pp. 12-14.

7. Censorship remained a worrisome matter to the film industry. On August 28, 1917, *The Moving Picture World* stated, "Censorship is the Bogey Man of the Moving Picture Industry," and announced the availability, at cost, of a set of nine anticensorship slides. "As a means of self preservation," said *The World*, "exhibitors everywhere should constantly fight the proposed discriminatory control of their business. Picture theater patrons can aid materially in the fight and will if the subject is kept constantly before them." The slides featured such slogans as "Keep the pictures clean and keep them out of politics," "We do not believe the American people want censorship," and "We will not show objectionable films in this theater."

8. "The Nickelodeons," *Variety* (December 14, 1907), p. 33.

9. "The Point of View," *Scribner's Magazine,* Vol. XLVI, No. 1 (July 1909), pp. 121-122.

10. Letter to Anthony Slide, dated December 7, 1972.

11. Interview with Anthony Slide, August 17, 1984.

12. The best source of information on Samuel Goldwyn is Scott Berg, *Goldwyn: A Biography* (New York: Alfred A. Knopf, 1989).

13. A good summation of William Fox's early career is contained in "Penny Arcade to Theater Chain," *The Moving Picture World* (July 12, 1919), pp. 233-234.

14. Oshkosh is also famous as the birthplace of Orson Welles.

15. Letter in the Selig Collection at the Academy of Motion Picture Arts and Sciences.

16. Ibid.

17. *Hiawatha* is preserved at the Museum of Modern Art.

18. For a more detailed account of the in-fighting, see "Kinematography in the United States," *The Moving Picture World* (July 17, 1914), pp. 175-177.

19. See *The Universal Weekly* (November 22, 1913), p. 9.

20. The best general introduction to Universal is Richard Koszarski, *Universal Pictures: 65 Years* (New York: The Museum of Modern Art, 1977). The following is a listing of major contemporary articles on Laemmle and Universal: Mabel Condon, "The City Universal," *The New York Dramatic Mirror* (August 5, 1916), pp. 26-38, 44; Louis Reeves Harrison, "Studio Saunterings," *The Moving Picture World* (April 27, 1912), pp. 307-310; H. H. Hoffman, "The Newsboy Who Built a City," *Photo Play Topics* (September 20, 1915), pp. 8-9, 16-18; "An Interview with Carl Laemmle," *The Moving Picture World* (November 27, 1909), p. 764; "Universal's Chameleon City," *The Universal Weekly* (September 26, 1914), pp. 4-9, 37; and John Drinkwater, *The Life and Adventures of Carl Laemmle* (London: William Heinemann, 1931).

21. Information taken from *The Dearborn Independent* (November 19, 1921), p. 6.

22. Albert E. Smith, *Two Reels and a Crank* (Garden City, NY: Doubleday, 1952), pp. 266-271.

23. George Blaisdell, "Adolph Zukor Talks of Famous Players," *The Moving Picture World*, Vol. XV, No. 2 (January 11, 1913), p. 136.

24. Frederick James Smith, "Yesterday and Tomorrow in the Photoplay," *Shadowland*, Vol. II, No. 12 (August 1920), p. 55.

25. See "Big Combine Completed," *The Billboard* (May 30, 1914), p. 4.

26. Hodkinson's comments are taken from an unpublished manuscript, dated February 2, 1962, titled "Ruthless Zukor," a copy of which is in the author's collection.

27. For more information, see "Bosworth's Rapid Rise," *The New York Dramatic Mirror* (March 31, 1915), p. 32.

28. See *Motion Picture News* (November 4, 1916), p. 2815.

29. Will Irwin, *The House That Shadows Built* (New York: Doubleday, Doran, 1928) is strictly a studio-endorsed history of Paramount. Adolph Zukor's autobiography, with Dale Kramer, *The Public Is Never Wrong* (New York: Putnam, 1953) is both insipid and slight. The awe in which Zukor was held is evidenced by Julian Johnson, "The Man Who Put Fame in Famous," *Photoplay* (August 1917), pp. 73-74, 140.

30. For more information on the Motion Picture Patents Company, see the following: "The Motion Picture Patents Company and Its Work," *The Moving Picture World*, Vol. V, No. 3 (July 17, 1909), pp. 81-84; Janet Staiger, "Combination and Litigation: Structures of U. S. Film Distribution, 1896-1917," *Cinema Journal*, Vol. XXIII, No. 2 (Winter 1983), pp. 41-72; and Jeanne Thomas, "The Decay of the Motion Picture Patents Company," *Cinema Journal*, Vol. X, No. 2 (Spring 1971), pp. 34-40.

31. *Photoplay Art* (February 1916), p. 4.

32. See "Cullison Is New Managing Director of Eclair Productions," *The Universal Weekly* (August 22, 1914), pp. 8-9.

31. *Photoplay Art* (February 1916), p. 4.

32. See "Cullison Is New Managing Director of Eclair Productions," *The Universal Weekly* (August 22, 1914), pp. 8-9.

for no other reason than to prevent its use for the screening of films by a rival entrepreneur. Between 1908 and 1913, Marcus Loew (1870-1927) had risen from ownership of a penny arcade in Harlem to ownership of more than twenty important New York City theaters.

By 1915, there was no question as to the importance of the film industry in American life. In Milwaukee, the city's fifty theaters were filled to capacity eight to eleven times a week. In Cleveland, one in every six citizens attended a motion picture at least once every weekday, and one in three attended on weekends. Of the public who attended any form of theatrical entertainment, 73 percent went to the movies in Detroit, 65 percent in San Francisco, and 73 percent in Kansas City.[5]

Only vaudeville came close to the popularity of the motion picture, leading one writer to observe that:

> As vaudeville requires no thinking, so motion pictures require no listening. Their appeal is wholly to the eye. They tell their vivid pictorial story in a language all can understand, and bring from the ends of the earth the exact appearance of foreign scenes and peoples, thrilling adventures on land and sea, the story of great invention, all forms of work and play, and thus make the whole world kin in marvelous fashion.[6]

Or as drama critic Walter P. Eaton had it in 1913, "We as a nation are spending two millions of dollars daily to witness canned drama." [7]

Thanks to a social survey by the Rev. J. J. Phelan[8], it is possible to provide a detailed study of the rise of the motion picture in what may be considered a typical American city: Toledo, Ohio. Surprisingly, the number of theaters here decreased between 1914 and 1919, perhaps because the storefront nickelodeons were phased out as custom-built auditoria took their place:

66 theaters in 1914
60 theaters in 1915
50 theaters in 1916
48 theaters in 1917
58 theaters in 1918
49 theaters in 1919

Only four of these theaters had orchestras, with the remainder relying on a pianist or organist. Admission prices varied between seven and fifty-five cents. The average daily attendance was 45,000, with forty percent being male, thirty-five percent female, and twenty-five percent children. These same theaters rented films for between $200 and $2,000.

Each week in Toledo, 75,000 individuals under the age of twenty attended public film screenings, vaudeville, or burlesque shows. Forty thousand visited pool halls or bowling alleys. Twenty thousand attended public or private dances. Twenty thousand children under the age of eighteen supported themselves or their families, and less than five thousand attended any form of recreation provided by the city's churches. There is no documentation on how movie theaters faired in admissions compared to attendance at Toledo s 408 saloons.

The city's theaters provided little employment, with the total number of employees at most establishments being less than six. There were 344 male employees compared to 164 female employees, with five of the theaters owned by women, and the largest, the 6,000-seat Coliseum, managed by a woman.

Very few general publications in the teens gave serious consideration to the motion picture. Most articles in such periodicals dealt with the moral or health aspects of the motion picture: "Eye Strain from the Movie Habit" (*Literary Digest,* May 30, 1914), "Movies and Morals" (*Survey,* March 14, 1914), "Menace of the Movies" (*American Magazine,* September 1913), and " 'Filmitis,' the Modern Malady and Its Cure " (*McClure's,* January 1916). Aside from selected newspaper commentary, film reviews were limited to the trade papers and the "fan" magazines, where reviews were usually biased because studio publicists often critiqued their own product. If a film was considered important enough, it might be reviewed by the theater critic of one of the popular magazines, but many of these critics held strong, negative attitudes towards the motion picture. Typical was James Metcalfe, theater critic for the humor magazine *Life,* who was not only antifilms, but was also anti-Semitic. Therefore, he equated films with Jewish commercialism. Despite the rise of the feature film, the popularity of the motion picture, and its acceptance by a legitimate audience, the following commentary by Metcalfe from the February 21, 1918, issue of *Life* indicates that

An engraving after a painting by J. B. Schénau, showing a phantasmagoric
lanternist at work.

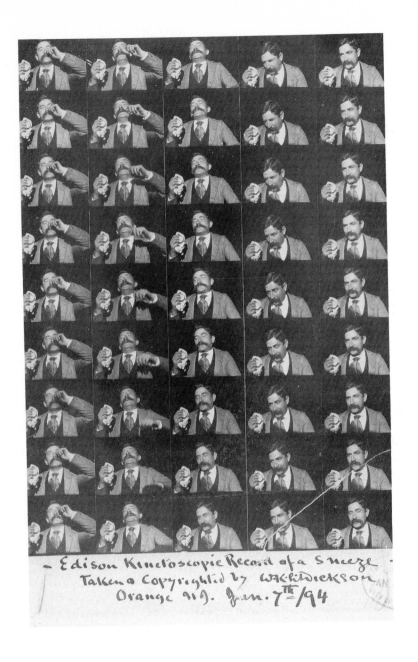

Fred Ott sneezes and the motion picture industry is born.

The Edison Studios at 2826 Decatur Avenue, the Bronx, New York, in 1908.

Marc MacDermott in *The Passer-By* (1912).

Edwin S. Porter.

A scene from a mutoscope reel, taken on the occasion of the formation of the Motion Picture Patents Company at the Biograph Studios on April 18, 1908, by Billy Bitzer. In the foreground, from left the right, are Albert E. Smith, Thomas Alva Edison, H. N. Marvin, J. Stuart Blackton, and Frank Marion.

G. M. "Broncho Billy" Anderson.

Siegmund Lubin.

George K. Spoor.

The birth of Christ in *From the Manger to the Cross* (1912). Gene Gauntier plays the Virgin Mary.

The Kalem Company in Ireland—Gene Gauntier and Sidney Olcott are standing on the far right.

Thomas Harper Ince.

Inceville, circa 1915.

The building of the new Ince studios in Culver City.

Victor Schertzinger, both a great director and a great composer.

D. W. Griffith.

the motion picture was still a long way from total recognition by the intelligentsia:

> The moving-picture business started as a sort of five-cent peep-show, and in its artistic standards has not advanced much beyond its original public. The nimble nickel is still the objective. The big-eyed, baby-girl heroine, the vamping adventuress and the slap-stick comedians are the great magnets for the coin of the multitude.
>
> The literature of the movie is confined to the badly written texts thrown on the screen, and dramatic construction is supplied by the shears of the person who cuts the celluloid films to secure startling effects.
>
> There have been a few exceptions where reckless expenditure, guided by some artistic impulse to produce stupendous effects, has appealed to the whole public. There has also been an occasional effort to transfer drama and acting to the screen, but invariably with unfortunate results to the backers, who did not know that the movie-picture public wants only the thing to which it has been accustomed, with such variations as the movie showman knows to introduce. More than this, the films can only be marketed through channels controlled by the cheapest kind of commercialism.
>
> Until the movie patrons tire of the sort of thing now supplied to them—and that may possibly happen—those of us who would like to see the screen drama developed with all its artistic possibilities must continue to grieve over lost opportunity.

Notes

1. For more information, see Robert S. Birchard, "Jack London and the Movies," *Film History*, Vol. I, No. 1 (1987), pp. 15-38.
2. *The Squaw Man* is preserved at the Library of Congress.
3. *The Spoilers* is preserved at the Library of Congress.
4. Letter dated December 21, 1914, in the Selig Collection at the Margaret Herrick Library of the Academy of Motion Picture Arts and Sciences.
5. Richard Henry Edwards, *Popular Amusements* (New York: Association Press, 1915), pp. 50-51.

6. Ibid., p. 53.

7. W. P. Eaton, "Menace of the Movies," *American Magazine* (September 1913), pp. 55-60.

8. Rev. J. J. Phelan, *Motion Pictures as a Phase of Commercialized Amusement in Toledo, Ohio,* Social Survey Series III (Toledo, OH: Little Book Press, 1919).

Thomas H. Ince

The name of Thomas Harper Ince looms large in the history of the American silent film industry. His position as a leading film producer of the era is partly secured not on the basis of the films that he made, but rather because of the gossip and innuendo surrounding his death, and because some left-wing critics/historians have sought to champion his cause over that of the politically unacceptable D. W. Griffith. Ince further helped his cause by heavily promoting himself as the sole creator of his films—an auteur, if you wish—and deliberately obscuring the identities of the true directors of his productions. (Whether Ince was knowingly involved in self-promotion for the cause of posterity cannot be discerned, but certainly there were others at the time who were accused of making films for posterity rather than the moment. Producer William Fox was continually writing letters critical of the Franklin brothers, Sidney and Chester, claiming that they were more interested in making a name for themselves and in how posterity would view their work than in making profits for him.)

An examination of the feature films made by Ince in the twenties indicates little justification for his prominent critical acclaim. Most are merely program pictures featuring the likes of Douglas MacLean, Doris May, Madge Bellamy, Florence Vidor, and Lloyd Hughes, and directed by reliable, if uninspired directors such as Lambert Hillyer and Roy William Neill. The exceptions are simply that—exceptions—the most notable of which is the first screen version of *Anna Christie*, directed by John Griffith Wray in

1923 and starring Blanche Sweet in the title role. The only other Ince features from the decade worthy of consideration are *Lorna Doone* (1922), a decidedly second-rate effort by director Maurice Tourneur, and *Human Wreckage* (1923), a "lost" feature directed by John Griffith Wray and featuring Mrs. Wallace Reid in a story influenced by her husband's death from drug addiction.

It is, therefore, on the basis of his work in the teens and earlier years that Ince's reputation stands or falls. The evidence from those years is cloudy, with Ince's success relying all too often upon the talents of others, although an ability to recognize and nurture such talent is, of course, on the plus side for any producer. Ince stamped his personality upon all of his productions, except for those of William S. Hart and Charles Ray, whose screen personalities transcended that of Ince. Ince's business sense was acute, assuring him precognition of a film's success long before production commenced. He had an uncanny knack for knowing just what the public wanted.

Some of these qualities are evidenced by *A Tour of the Thomas H. Ince Studios*.[1] Filmed studio tours were nothing new—Universal had produced one as early as 1914—but Ince used his three-reel short, released in the summer of 1920, not only to promote his players and his productions, but also to curry favor with the news media. In each city where the film was screened, the local newspaper was credited as the distributor, thus assuring an unprecedented amount of good publicity. Ince's acumen is apparent in his appointment of the man responsible for the direction of *A Tour of the Thomas H. Ince Studios*, Hunt Stromberg, who became Ince's publicity director in January 1920, and who was later to become a prominent Hollywood producer. The hiring of Stromberg typified Ince's ability for selecting talented people with whom to surround himself.[2]

On the whole, Ince was able to generate considerable loyalty from those in his employ. One of his contract stars from the twenties, Florence Vidor, recalled:

> One could not meet Thomas H. Ince in his studio without seeing that here was a great dynamic personality, having the brightest blue eyes, ready smile and charming manner; always interested in everything—perhaps the secret of his youthfulness.

On his desk was a small motto, "Nothing Is Impossible," and truly, to him, nothing was impossible.

It was a real privilege to be associated with him. His marvelous enthusiasm for each picture in preparation would make one feel that they wanted this to be the greatest picture they had ever made. Sensitive, emotional, always putting woman on a pedestal and always his pictures had a moral. If things went wrong he so gladly went on the set, would give the director just the help he needed or would often direct an entire sequence. I have never seen him in a temper or a bad mood. He could always handle the most difficult situations in a most diplomatic way. Many an actor had dashed up to his office in a rage about some mistreatment he had received, but once in his office, Mr. Ince, always charming, would soon quiet the emotional victim, pat him on the back and send him away smiling and happy, because he was associated with such a great organization, but never did Mr. Ince make concessions to his people.[3]

Some of the things that Ince did not do first are those for which many historians have given him credit. He did not introduce the detailed shooting script—the Edison Company was using these as early as 1911—although he did refine and modify such scripts to be the forerunners of the present-day shooting scripts. Ince did not introduce the star system, credit for which must go to the Kalem Company. And he was not the first to use natural and realistic locations, which can also be traced back to the Kalem Company.

In short, Ince was a mixture of both artistry and acumen, but a genius at neither.

Thomas Harper Ince was born on November 16, 1882, in Newport, Rhode Island, the second son of an English emigrant, John E. Ince, who had become a reasonably successful comedian, and Emma Brennan, an American actress. A third brother, Ralph (1887-1937), also entered the film industry, working as a director at Vitagraph in the teens—he joined the company as a prop boy in 1907—and ending his career making "quota quickies" in England from 1934-1937.

About 1890, Ince made his stage debut with Henry E. Dixey in a play titled *Seven Ages*. This debut was followed by a part in a touring vaudeville sketch, "Poets and Puppets," based on *Lady*

Windermere's Fan, with May Irwin, and two years touring with James Herne in *Shore Acres*.

Years later, Ince reminisced: "I'll always maintain that that was the greatest schooling I had—schooling, I mean, for what was in store for me. I was only a boy, very true, but I was at that impressionable age when a youngster absorbs everything that transpires about him."[4]

Ince's first important stage role—at the age of fourteen—was as Alec, a Negro Boy, in *A Southern Romance,* which opened at New York's Fifth Avenue Theatre on September 4, 1897, and in which his mother also appeared. He continued to appear regularly, if inauspiciously, on the stage for a number of years; in 1902, Ince had a small role in the William S. Hart's vehicle, *Hearts Courageous.* In 1902, he also appeared in *The Ninety and the Nine* (based on a once-popular hymn of the same name), which ran at New York's Academy of Music for 128 performances. In his review of the play in the *New York Herald* (October 8, 1902), noted critic Alan Dale wrote, "Thomas H. Ince showed sincerity and enthusiasm, and he will do something worthwhile one of these days."

That "something worthwhile" was a few more years in coming, and not on the stage. Ince continued his career, touring with the Beryl Hope Stock Company, appearing in revivals of the Civil War drama *Reverend Griffith Davenport, Home Folks,* and *When We Were Twenty-One,* and forming his own stock company, which played both vaudeville and the legitimate stage, and in which Ince was billed as "America's Favorite Comedian."

On October 19, 1907, Ince married Elinor Kershaw, an actress whose career had been as relatively undistinguished as his own. Ince worked with her in a vaudeville sketch that he had written, titled "Who Do You Love." In 1910, the couple joined the Chester Park Opera Company in Cincinnati, where Ince appeared in the title role of *The Sultan of Sulu,* as Mr. Pineapple in *A Chinese Honeymoon,* as Uncle Tom in *When Johnny Comes Marching Home,* and as Hans Nix, an inspector of telephones, in *The Telephone Girl.*

In search of work, Ince returned to New York City in the fall of 1910. Outside a Times Square hotel, he met fellow actor Joseph Smiley, who was working at Carl Laemmle's IMP Company and suggested that Ince also find employment there. That same day, Ince was hired to play a supporting role in a drama directed by Harry Salter. At the same time, Mrs. Ince was working as an actress at the

Biograph Company—she had appeared in two films there the previous year—and she was able to persuade director Frank Powell to use her husband in a one-reel comedy titled *His New Lid,* filmed in late October.

Ince did not remain at Biograph, nor did he take up an offer from Vitagraph, but returned to IMP, where he signed a contract to appear as an actor, with the understanding that when a directorial position became available, it would be offered to him. Legend has it that such a position became open almost immediately, and Ince directed his first film production, *Little Nell's Tobacco,* with Hayward Mack in the lead, late in 1910. Ince claims to have accompanied Carl Laemmle to a screening of the film at the Fourteenth Street Theatre and to have sweet-talked Laemmle into believing the film's reception was overwhelmingly positive. Such a story certainly sounds apocryphal, and it is hard to believe that as shrewd a businessman as Laemmle could be swayed by the boasts of a new, unknown director. Yet, when Mary Pickford was lured away from Biograph by Laemmle, it was Ince who was assigned to direct her, with their first film together being *Their First Misunderstanding,* released on January 9, 1911.

In order to escape unwanted harassment from the Motion Picture Patents Company, Laemmle decided to send Pickford to Cuba to star in films under Ince's direction. It was a far-from-happy excursion that the group made to an improvised studio in a hotel on the outskirts of Havana. On the voyage over, Pickford's mother, Charlotte, learned of her daughter's marriage to actor Owen Moore, who had been hired by Laemmle as Pickford's leading man. Ince and Moore took an extreme dislike to each other. Quite naturally, Pickford became antagonistic towards her director, who was certainly not in the same league as her former mentor, D. W. Griffith. Looking back on the experience, Pickford branded her films with Ince as poor and, based on the few that have survived, such an assessment would seem accurate, although the films were well-received at the time by trade paper reviewers. After twenty films with Ince, Pickford was assigned a new director at IMP, William Clifford.

Following the debacle with Pickford, Ince was lucky to be offered a directorial position with the New York Motion Picture Company, an independent producer formed in 1909 by Charles O. Baumann and Adam Kessel. The company first produced films in

Los Angeles in 1909 and now, in 1911, was looking for a new director to work at its studio in the Los Angeles suburb of Edendale (at a studio that was later associated with Keystone).

Ince's first meeting with Kessel and Baumann was probably the most important in his life, for his association with the two men marked the beginning of Ince's career as a major producing figure. In order to impress his potential employers, Ince borrowed a diamond ring from friend and IMP colleague C. A. "Doc" Willat, and he grew a mustache. In 1917, Ince recalled the meeting:

> Mr. Baumann surveyed me critically, and I could plainly see that he had taken cognizance of the fact that I was wearing a mustache and a diamond; also that he had apparently interpreted their presence as I had planned and hoped. "Well, Ince," he told me, "we'll give you a hundred dollars a week to go out there and make Western pictures for us." This, of course, startled me. But I kept cool and didn't betray my surprise. Instead, I tried to convey the impression that he would have to raise the ante a bit if he wanted me. Then, when he didn't say anything, I stood up and walked leisurely out of the office, promising to return a day or so later.
>
> In a few days I went back, and Baumann told me he would pay me a hundred and fifty a week; and, fearing that he might perchance change his mind—but not letting him observe my fear—I signed a contract for three months. Then I requested that he consent to my taking my leading woman, camera man, and property man with me. He readily consented—and that closed the deal.[5]

Within a week of his appointment, Ince was on a train bound for California. Accompanying him were his wife, actress Ethel Grandin, actor Charles Weston, and cameraman Ray Smallwood (whom Grandin later married). The films that Ince produced and directed were marketed under the brand name of "Bison," which was later abandoned in favor of "Broncho," to which were later added the brand names of "Domino" and "Kay Bee" (from the initials of the New York Motion Picture Company's owners). Ince's first film for the new company was *The New Cook,* which he claimed contained 53 scenes rather than the twenty or so scenes that comprised most one-reelers up to this time. It was almost antagonistic on Ince's part to go against the accepted industry standard so soon after his appointment. Perhaps it indicated his frustration with the smallness of the Edendale plant. It may well have been a precursor of Ince's determination to restructure the films that he was expected to make for it was during this time period that he uttered the famous criticism to his wife of the Westerns produced by the New York Motion Picture Company: "They ride uphill on Tuesday and downhill on Thursday."

Almost simultaneously with Ince's arrive in California, the New York Motion Picture Company acquired the services of the Miller Brothers 101 Ranch Wild West Show, which was spending the winter months in California. It is possible that Ince persuaded Baumann to rent the company while the latter was on a visit to Los Angeles. *The Moving Picture World* (December 9, 1911) reported the news:

> The surprise of the week is the announcement that the New York Motion Picture Company is abandoning the regular style of Indian and cowboy pictures it has been making for the past several years, and will hereafter produce nothing but sensational, spectacular Western subjects, with enormous casts, and that it has leased the Miller Brothers 101 Ranch Wild West Show, which is now installed at Bear Valley, Cal., having been consolidated with the regular reorganized Bison company of sixty people.

With the Miller Brothers 101 Ranch at his disposal, Ince was able to produce his first important film, *War on the Plains,* released early in 1912. It was the first two-reel film from the New York Motion Picture Company, and it proved to be so successful that the company announced that all of its future films would be two reels in length (a promise not entirely kept).

Ince had strong views on the subject of a film's length, arguing that the length should be determined by the subject matter:

> One of the first limitations to go will be that of a set length. Few photoplays do not suffer from having to be fitted into a given number of full reels. Again and again I have seen plays misfire in, say, four reels that would have succeeded in their original five or six, and we all know examples of weak four or five-reel dramas

that would have been excellent in two or, perhaps, two and a fraction.

Of course, one can in advance tell roughly what length a picture story is worth, but there must be a reasonable freedom to let the story make its own length for the best results—and only the best now stands a chance of life. A really honest artist does not write or paint to exact measure and if you try to make him do it, you get less than his best quality of work.

The true motion picture work of art may start as a two-reeler and end as a twelve, or it may be photographed to twelve reels and end logically with two and a quarter. Of course, we must try to meet within reason the natural and inevitable limitations of the business end of the industry, but these will gradually grow less so as to permit the capture of quality plays, whatever their length.[6]

War on the Plains was filmed in Santa Ynez Canyon, situated approximately where Sunset Boulevard today meets the Pacific Coast Highway, some four miles north of Santa Monica. Ince persuaded Kessel and Baumann to lease 18,000 acres of land here, at what became known as Inceville. When the producer first took over the property, he built tents and cabins for members of the Miller Brothers 101 Ranch, two dressing tents, and one stage for interior scenes, complete with a real stone fireplace (supposedly the first ever shown on the screen). "I always saw to it that that old fireplace remained undisturbed," wrote Ince many years later. "I regarded it as a sort of monument to pioneer realism." [7]

By 1916, as the following account indicates, Inceville had expanded to become certainly the largest and one of the most important studios in the United States.

It has been recognized by the United States government as a town, for it has its own post office. Everything required for the making of gigantic motion pictures is contained here. There are five stages, the main one being three hundred by one hundred feet, while the auxiliary ones are seventy-five by fifty feet each. Two hundred dressing rooms border the stages, and at either end are the scene docks, where more than five hundred distinct "sets" are kept in readiness for instant use. Then there are the administration buildings, where all of the business for the city is handled and where a working schedule is compiled every day; the commissary, where the hundreds of workers eat the noonday and often the evening meal; the arsenal, where thousands of firearms and boxes of ammunition and explosives are kept; the wardrobe buildings, containing hundreds of sets of various clothing from evening dress to ancient colonial costumes, and in which a modernly equipped tailor shop is to be found; the saddlery and stables for the horses, which number far into the three hundreds; a corral; a power house which furnishes electricity for the entire city; and a reservoir which does likewise with water. Besides these necessities, there are many "sets" that are kept standing all the time and used in pictures as required. Among these are a Dutch village with a genuine canal and windmill, a Japanese village, an Irish village, Canadian stockades, Southern log cabins, East Indian streets, Sioux Indian camps, and a real Scotch street that was used in Billie Burke's first play [*Peggy*].[8]

Ince spent his days directing, while Mrs. Ince researched scripts in the public library. As she recalled:

I never liked the acting part, but I did like the creative part—like writing scripts, doing research for his Indian Western films, helping him cut and edit the completed film—like attaching the film reel winder to the kitchen table, and while he would cut and examine every inch, I would paste back together and rewind. Then go and write out the works to be photographed the next day.[9]

As the company grew, Mrs. Ince devoted her time to raising the couple's three boys. However, as late as 1924, she was still selecting stories and advising on editing and production.

On June 1, 1913, Ince produced his biggest film to date, the five-reel *The Battle of Gettysburg,* a Civil War drama that *The New York Dramatic Mirror* (June 11, 1913) hailed as "a wonderful visualization of the greatest battle in American history." The film is notable for its use of eight cameras to film the battle scenes simultaneously. It was, perhaps, the first time that a producer used multiple cameras to shoot action that would be expensive to duplicate, indicating not only Ince's concern with avoiding retakes, but also his efficiency and cost effectiveness in ensuring that the additional filmed footage could be used in later features. It might have been another first in that the producer realized the value of what became known as "stock footage."

Even before *The Battle of Gettysburg* was filmed, Ince insisted on the preparation of detailed shooting scripts written by the producer in collaboration with either Richard V. Spencer or William H. Clifford. The scripts are notable for the phrase "See Mr. Ince," in reference to any problem that the assigned director might encounter.

As early as the summer of 1912, Ince had delegated half of the directorial chores to Francis Ford (1882-1953). The films that Ince and Ford directed have an unaffected energy to them, a quality helped by the naturalness of the acting, which both directors were able to obtain from Ethel Grandin, Ann Little, J. Barney Sherry, or which Ford himself (he often played the leading man) contributed. Those qualities instilled by Ford and Ince in these films may well have influenced Ford's younger brother John (1895-1973) when he became a director at Universal in 1917.[10]

With *The Battle of Gettysburg,* Ince ceased all directing and confined his activities to supervision. To help run his studio, he relied on E. H. Allen, who was appointed business manager in 1912. Allen is an important, if somewhat mysterious, figure in the Ince organization. Ethel Grandin remembers that he also worked the camera in the early years.[11] Actress Claire DuBrey paints a very vivid picture of Allen:

> Mr. Ince was absolutely charming. He never issued orders.
> He had a man to do that, as one should have. He had a stooge,
> and his name was E. H. Allen. He was an Irishman, and ignorant
> and foul-mouthed. He would come on the set and bawl the
> directors or the actors or anyone else out. Ince issued these
> orders, and we thought he was a dear. Allen was not so nice, but
> he got results.[12]

Francis Ford left Ince's employ in 1913, around which time Raymond B. West (who had been an assistant cameraman with Ince for a number of years) and Reginald Barker became the most important of Ince's directors. As with Ford, credit for their work went to Ince. Also on the Ince lot was a major Hollywood director-to-be, Frank Borzage (1893-1962), who would commence his directorial career in 1916, but had been working as an actor with Ince since 1912. Borzage is featured, along with Tsuru Aoki and her husband, Sessue Hayakawa, in a prominent feature-length Ince production of 1914, *The Wrath of the Gods,* directed by Reginald Barker with special effects by Raymond West. Aoki and a company of Japanese players had been signed by Ince in 1913 and they were featured in a number of films with ethnic themes, such as *The Wrath of the Gods,* which concerns a native girl's renunciation of her primitive religion in order to marry an American. The typhoon and volcanic explosion that mark the film's climax were highly praised by contemporary trade papers; *The New York Dramatic Mirror* (June 10, 1914) spoke of "triumphs of photography and directing resource."

As his company expanded, Ince, in obvious acknowledgment of his theatrical background, turned to the stage for his performers. He hired Rhea Mitchell, director-to-be William Desmond Taylor, Bessie Barriscale, Henry Woodruff, Enid Markey, H. B. Warner, Dustin Farnum, and others. George Beban, who specialized in Italian characterizations, was hired in the late summer of 1914 to play the lead in *The Italian,* a tragic story (directed by Reginald Barker) of the misery and corruption an Italian emigrant encounters in the United States.

"Long have I been a believer in the value of the stage star to the photodramatic production," announced Ince in 1916.[13] Never was this more evident than in Ince's hiring Billie Burke, one of the most prominent stage actresses of the day. For her 1916 feature film debut, *Peggy,* the producer spared no expense. He built a new stage for her at ground level, thus negating the actress's having to walk up and down steps to shoot a scene. He also returned to directing for one last time, aside from his appearing on stage to direct occasional scenes when confrontations between actor and director necessitated such action, as in one scene of Blanche Sweet's *Anna Christie.*

Billie Burke was paid $40,000 for her five weeks of work on *Peggy.* Prior to that, the largest salary Ince had paid an actor was that offered to Frank Keenan for playing the father in *The Coward.* Keenan's performance is melodramatic and bad, but the film served to make a star of Charles Ray, who plays the son in this Civil War drama. Prior to the release of *The Coward* in November 1915, Charles Ray (1891-1943) worked as an extra and bit player at the

Ince studios for two years. Following the success of *The Coward,* Ince put Ray under long-term contract, and the actor remained at the studio through 1920. He specialized in characterizations of small town and country youths who make good. His performances are best described as kittenish. Arguably, the best of his early features is *The Clodhopper,* directed by Victor Schertzinger in 1917. In it, Ray plays a banker's son who runs away from home after an argument with his father. He becomes a star in a revue, thanks to his hometown dance, "The Clodhopper Glide," which a title describes as "Perhaps not as finished as the works of Salome, but—," and which appears to have its origins in Russian Cossack dancing. It is unpretentious and fun. Unfortunately, Ray (largely at the insistence of his domineering wife) began to take himself too seriously and, as a result, his career floundered in the twenties.

The most important stage actor whom Ince brought to his studio was William S. Hart (1865-1946). He had been on stage since the 1890s and gained prominence with his portrayal of Messala in the original 1899 production of *Ben-Hur.* Hart had no direct connection to Western history, but as a child he had come to love its folklore. He wanted to capture the essence of its romance on films. With Tom Mix (1880-1940), Hart was to become the most famous cowboy star of the Silent Era. Mix's background was that of a real-life cowboy, yet his screen persona was entirely one of make-believe. No cowboy dressed like Tom Mix or had as much fun as he did in his films. Hart's features were infinitely more serious than those of Mix, which is, perhaps, why they do not appeal as much to modern audiences.

Hart joined Ince in 1914, with his first film being the two-reel *His Hour of Manhood.* Hart's third film, *The Bargain,* released in December 1914, and directed by Reginald Barker, is one of his best, in no small part thanks to the beautiful panoramic photography of the Grand Canyon. As with most of Hart's films, the actor portrays a "bad man" who is converted to the straight and narrow, thanks to the love of a good woman. Hart's actions and those of his leading ladies are spare, never melodramatic. Overacting and dramatic hysteria in Hart's films are always left to the vamp (often Louise Glaum) and the villain.

The French actor Charles Dullin, who bears a remarkable resemblance to Hart, summarized the William S. Hart screen characters well in a 1918 article:

He has the tenderness and simplicity of the hero who is always surprised at the evil intentions of men. He never doubts the word of others, since his own is sacred. He does not hate his enemy because of the harm he has done to him, but because of the contempt with which lies and treason inspire him. These generous traits are found in almost all of his roles. He never uses the artifice of theatrical "make up" to create his various roles, but searches within himself for the psychological traits which differentiate his characters.[14]

Hart's attitude towards women is one of decorum and quiet worship on screen. His heroines are virginal goddesses who are untouchable outside of the bonds of matrimony. In real life, his one marriage to leading lady Winifred Westover was a disaster, in no small part thanks to the interference of Hart's sister, Mary Ellen. At least three of his leading ladies—Ann Little, Margery Wilson, and Jane Novak—have told the author that Hart proposed to them.

There was certainly a cruel streak to his nature, as evidenced by the following story from Jane Novak:

They used to do all sorts of horrible things to me: Take my shoes and put them away, and say, "Now you have to get them." And I couldn't get up near the ceiling of the studio to get my shoes. One day, they tied my hands behind my back, then they put whiskey bottles all around me, and sat me on the floor with my knees tucked under my chin. Then they said, "Look over here," and I wouldn't look at the camera. I wasn't going to be photographed in this horrible position with all these bottles. So they took a piece of rope and tied it to the back of my hair and pulled my head until they got it into position.[15]

William S. Hart was far from happy under Ince's dictatorial influence, and although he remained under contract to the producer through 1919, he produced his films *his* way and with *his* hand-picked directors. The parting between the two men was far from amicable. As *Photoplay* (November 1920) reported:

Some years ago—we won't say how many—Bill Hart and Tom Ince were sharing pot-luck in a New York boarding house. Now when Tom passes Bill on the street he barely nods. Ince put

Hart into pictures; later Bill went his own way. Now J. Parker
Read, Jr., Ince's business associate, is suing Hart for $64,000
alleged to be due Read for services.

Hart continued to produce and star in features until 1925, when
he released what is probably the best known of his films, *Tumbleweeds*. One thing is evident in *Tumbleweeds* and in all of Hart's
films—the exhilaration the actor is getting from his performances.
As he wrote in his 1929 autobiography, *My Life East and West*, " I
love acting. I love the art of making motion pictures. It is the breath
of life to me." [16]
The prominence of the Ince organization in the film industry is
evidenced by its becoming part of the Triangle Film Corporation,
founded by Harry E. Aitken in July 1915. The new company was
an alliance between Ince, D. W. Griffith, and Mack Sennett, with
each man producing films independently of each other but releasing
them on the Triangle program. The program was booked at theatres
throughout the country, with the Knickerbocker in New York City
as the flagship. Ince's contribution to the first Triangle presentation
at the Knickerbocker on September 23, 1915, was *The Iron Strain,*
starring Enid Markey and Dustin Farnum and directed by Reginald
Barker.
Ince remained with Triangle until 1917, when he began releasing his films on the Paramount program. The new arrangement with
Triangle, in part, persuaded Ince to expand his studio operations
and to begin work on a new studio in Culver City, California. It was
announced that the new studios were initially intended to be used
for the production of society dramas, and they became officially
operational in February 1916. Four glass-enclosed stages housed
the companies of directors Reginald Barker, Raymond B. West,
Walter Edwards, and Charles Giblyn.
Ince's breakup with Triangle led to his losing the Culver City
Studios, which later became the home of Metro-Goldwyn-Mayer,
as well as the New York Motion Picture Company. As a result, Ince
opened new studios, also in Culver City, in 1919. Ince remained in
control here until his death, and the studios in later years were home
to David O. Selznick Productions, with the colonial-style administration building becoming a familiar sight to filmgoers as that
producer's trademark. Inceville was leased to the producing con-

cern of Robertson-Cole in 1920. Filmmaking ceased here entirely in 1922, and the last remaining sets were destroyed in a 1924 fire.

Although Thomas H. Ince remained an active producer for the rest of the decade, there is only one other feature from the teens that can be considered of major importance and that is *Civilization*. The most ambitious of all Ince's productions, *Civilization* was obviously the producer's answer to D. W. Griffith's *Intolerance*. A pacifist argument against America's entry into the First World War, the plot of *Civilization* concerns a submarine inventor's opposition to war following his religious conversion. His body is taken over by Christ, who shows the warring king the results of his belligerence. The film was dedicated to "That vast pitiful army whose tears have girdled the universe, the Mothers of the Dead." *Civilization* is not a great film in the manner that *Intolerance* is a great film. Its battle scenes are poorly directed and the allegorical moments are ludicrous. It is, however, an important historical document, and its direction by Raymond B. West and Reginald Barker is certainly on par with that of many other directors of the period.

Civilization is honored as an ideal rather than an achievement. It is a film that was influential in its day and may, as at least one newspaper claimed, have helped Woodrow Wilson, with his slogan of "He Kept Us Out of the War," win re-election.

Civilization was written by C. Gardner Sullivan (1884-1965), a former newspaperman who entered the film industry in 1913 and soon became head of Ince's scenario department. Among the many features that Sullivan wrote for Ince are *The Coward* (1915), *The Italian* (1915), *The Beggar of Cawnpore* (1916), *Peggy* (1916), and most of the William S. Hart features. (Sullivan may well have been crucial in the development of not only Hart's screen characterizations, but also those of Charles Ray.) He was active throughout the Silent Era—indeed, as late as the forties—and, apparently, adopted an unusual method of scriptwriting, in that he put all his subtitles down on paper first and then filled in the action linking them.

In October 1919, Ince ceased to produce for Paramount and began releasing his productions through Metro. At the same time, he created a new company, Associated Producers, Inc., in collaboration with Mack Sennett, Marshall Neilan, Allan Dwan, George Loane Tucker, Maurice Tourneur, and J. Parker Read. He continued to produce average, money-making films, but they lacked the vitality of his earlier works. The film industry was advancing, and Ince was simply marking time.

In November 1924, the producer boarded William Randolph Hearst's yacht to discuss filming certain stories from the publisher's *Cosmopolitan Magazine*. Rumors abound as to what happened on the boat, but the reality would appear to be that Ince suffered what would today be called a thrombosis. He died a few days later on November 19. As for the suggestion that Ince was shot by Hearst, both Mrs. Ince and the mortician who embalmed the producer's body have told this writer that there was no bullet hole.

One of the finest tributes to Thomas Harper Ince was by Frederick J. Ellis in the January 1925 issue of *Story World:*

> Thomas H. Ince to the audiences of the world, "T. H." to his studio employees, Tom to his friends, and Tommie to the more intimate of those friends, was one of the little group of pioneers that have blazed the trail for the generations of directors and producers that will follow. One of the sad aspects of the lives of movie makers is that their work is as pictures traced on the sand, to be effaced by the tides of time. The painter leaves his canvases, the author his books, the sculptor his statues, the architect his cathedrals, and the musician his operas or ballads. The producer and director leave negatives and prints, but these are destroyed or consigned to the oblivion of the storage vault. The Ince productions that are completed or in production will be exhibited for a few months. Some may be re-shown a few times in memory of their maker—and that will be the end. But Tom Ince will be a name held in glorious memory so long as their [sic] remains a living being who has witnessed one of his pictures.

Notes

1. It is indicative of Ince's ego that this short was also known as *A Trip Through the World s Greatest Motion Picture Studios.*

2. For more information, see "Ince Studios Launch Big Live Exploitation Drive," *Exhibitor's Trade Review* (August 7, 1920), p. 1059.

3. Unpublished interview with Florence Vidor in the files of the Museum of Modern Art.

4. Kenneth O'Hara, "The Life of Thomas H. Ince, Part II," *Picture Play* (February 1918), p. 221.

5. Kenneth O'Hara, "The Life of Thomas H. Ince, Part VI," *Picture Play* (June 1918), p. 252.

6. "Ince Predicts New Themes and Methods," *The Triangle* (November 1915), p. 1.

7. "Thomas H. Ince, The Early Days of Kay Bee," *Photoplay*, Vol. XV, No. 4 (March 1919), p. 44.

8. Robert C. Duncan, "The Ince Studios," *Picture Play* (March 1, 1916), pp. 25-26.

9. Letter to Anthony Slide, June 6, 1970.

10. The directorial relationship between Francis and John Ford is discussed in Tag Gallagher, *John Ford: The Man and His Films* (Berkeley, CA: University of California Press, 1986).

11. Interview with Anthony Slide, September 10, 1975.

12. Interview with Anthony Slide, November 22, 1971.

13. "Ince Says Stage Stars Help Films," *The Triangle* (January 15, 1916), p. 1.

14. "William S. Hart Judged by the Great French Actor Charles Dullin," *The New France* (December 1918), p. 314.

15. Interview with Anthony Slide, December 3, 1971.

16. For additional information on William S. Hart, see Diane Kaiser Koszarski, *The Complete Films of William S. Hart* (New York: Dover, 1980).

6

D. W. Griffith

To understand the importance of D. W. Griffith to the early
motion picture, it is necessary to comprehend the contempt in
which the medium was held by many critics. D. W. Griffith helped
the technological development of the cinema, but perhaps more
importantly, he helped develop the motion picture as an art form.

In 1921, the influential drama critic George Jean Nathan published an essay that, tinged as it is with anti-Semitism, still very
clearly indicates the attitude of many towards the film industry:

> Controlled in the overwhelming main by the most ignorant
> social outcasts, by the spawn of push-cart immigration, by hered-
> itary toothpick suckers, soup coloraturos and six-day sock
> wearers, controlled in the mass by men of a complete anaesthesia
> to everything fine and everything earnest and everything poten-
> tially dollarless, the moving pictures—the physic of the prole-
> tariat—have revealed themselves the most effective carriers of
> idiocy that the civilized world has known. Here in America, their
> fortress, they have cheapened a national taste, already cheap, to
> a point where cheapness can seem to go no farther. They have
> lurked near schoolhouses and seduced the impressionable minds
> of children. They have crawled up alleys and side-streets and for
> thirty pieces of copper have sold youth into aesthetic corruption.
> They have gagged the mouths of almost every newspaper in
> America with a rich advertising revenue; if there is a newspaper
> in the land that has the honor and the respectability to call the
> moving pictures by their right name, I haven't heard of it. They

have bought literature and converted it, by their own peculiar and esoteric magic, into rubbish. They have bought imaginative actors and converted them into face-makers and mechanical dolls. They have bought reputable authors and dramatists and have converted them into shamefaced hacks. They have elected for their editors and writers the most obscure and talentless failures of journalism and the tawdry periodicals. They have enlisted as their directors, with a few exceptions, an imposing array of ex-stage butlers and chauffeurs, assistant stage managers of turkey troupes, discharged pantaloons and the riff-raff of Broadway street corners. And presently they sweep their wet tongue across the American theatre.[1]

The American film industry needed a visionary who could represent the best that the motion picture could offer. It needed a man who could serve as a spokesman when the industry was attacked as being artless or when legislated censorship was urged. It needed a man of ego and a man of stature and, from the mid-teens onwards, it was very clear that D. W. Griffith was such a man.

D. W. Griffith did not invent editing or the close-up. He did not invent film grammar. What he did was take the work of his predecessors such as Edwin S. Porter and refine the techniques that those earlier pioneers had introduced. In many ways, he was the right man in the film industry at the right time. If Griffith had not been making films when he did, the industry would still have moved forward, and the techniques and advancements credited to Griffith would, eventually, have taken place. This is not intended in any way to diminish Griffiths importance, for, after all, he was there and he did do it. And not only did he do it as well as any man could, but he was also able to move with the times. Throughout the teens, Griffith was not a filmmaker who rested on his laurels.

Rather than a technical innovator, Griffith deserves credit for the emotional use to which he put the motion picture. Others might tell stories on screen, but Griffith presented *dramas* that were alive and that moved audiences. There is a vitality to the work of D. W. Griffith missing from the films of many of his contemporaries both in the United States and in Europe. His films have a poetic quality that transcends their sometimes dated storylines or occasional lapses into melodrama. He could take a rather pathetic old melo-drama—old even in 1920 when it was filmed—such as *Way Down*

East, and breathe such life and fire into its story that its excitement has not diminished with the passing of time.

Seduction, babies born out of wedlock, and last-minute rescues from ice floes are not the subjects of today's films. They are samplings from Victorian melodrama, which greatly appealed to D. W. Griffith, who had once tried to be a stage actor in the Victorian tradition of Henry Irving or Herbert Beerbohn Tree, and Griffith brought that melodrama to the screen as if it was the latest in contemporary fads. Griffith was a Victorian, but his story-telling techniques and his development and introduction of characters are similar to those of Charles Dickens—and just as the British novelist's works remain current, so do those of D. W. Griffith.

David Wark Griffith was born in the South—on a farm in Oldham County, Kentucky—on January 22, 1875, and Southern culture and history deeply affected his life and his films. In later years, he became the stereotype of a Southern gentleman, a little too fond of alcohol, attracted by and attractive to the ladies, but never lacking in public dignity. As a child, Griffith heard his father, "Roaring Jake" Griffith, recount his exploits during the Civil War, and Griffith was to document the Southern side of the conflict in a number of one-reel short subjects for the American Biograph Company and, of course, in *The Birth of a Nation.*

Griffith was also of the land. The family farmstead is still there, although the original building has disappeared and the city of Louisville encroaches upon it. Recent owners describe the land as "good."[2] Griffith's love of the countryside is apparent in Biograph shorts that compare the squalor of the city to the peaceful freedom offered in America's farmland, and in the feature-length rural dramas of *True Heart Susie, A Romance of Happy Valley,* and *Way Down East.* The Bartlett family in *Way Down East* had, perhaps, the same love for the land, the same basic belief in old-fashioned good and evil as did Griffith and his family.

From his early teens onward, Griffith had a fascination for the stage, and he quickly decided that his future was in playwriting. It was to be an impossible dream, but from 1895 through 1907, he devoted himself to the theatre. He achieved no major success as an actor, but he did write a vaudeville sketch, "In Washington's Time," first performed in 1901, and one play, *A Fool and a Girl.* The last was produced by James K. Hackett at the Columbia Theatre in Washington, D. C., and starred Fannie Ward, John W. Dean, and

Alison Skipworth. It ran from September 30 through October 12, 1907, and was not a success. *The New York Dramatic Mirror* (October 12, 1907) commented: "First class audiences will not accept it in its present form." [3]

Griffith's theatrical career was important for two reasons. First, because its failure led directly to his entering films, initially as an actor in *Rescued from an Eagle's Nest,* filmed by J. Searle Dawley for Edison early in 1908. It was ill-received by *The Moving Picture World* (February 1, 1908) which commented, "We looked for better things." Secondly, when Griffith turned to directing at the American Biograph Company after a brief tenure there as an actor with *The Adventures of Dollie* (released on July 14, 1908), he brought many theatrical devices to the screen, devices that he was able to adapt and modify for the new medium.

On August 17, 1908, Griffith signed a formal directing contract with the American Mutoscope and Biograph Company.

> To superintend and direct the "make-up" of all performers participating in indoor and open air performances, to thoroughly rehearse all performances, and to enforce such discipline as will prevent waste of time or performers while they are employed by the party of the second part. . . . The party of the first part further agrees to faithfully and energetically endeavor to increase the business and profits of the party of the second part by thoroughly and economically executing all the business of the party of the second part that is entrusted to him. . . . The party of the first part further agrees not to furnish information to other parties or to grant interviews to representatives of newspapers or other publications, relating to the business of the party of the second part.[4]

It heralded what must be acknowledged as the legitimate start of a directorial career that included making approximately 450 short subjects and 33 features. Among the latter number are two sound films, *Abraham Lincoln* (1930) and *The Struggle* (1931), of relative unimportance in Griffith's total oevre, but still worthy of attention. Among the shorts, the more important are

- *The Fatal Hour* (released on August 18, 1908), with Griffith's first prominent use of cross-cutting;

- *A Corner in Wheat* (released on December 13, 1909), based on the novel *The Octopus* and the short story *A Deal in Wheat,* both by Frank Norris, utilizing cross-cutting to dramatize the plight of the workers in comparison to the life of the "wheat king";
- *The Lonedale Operator* (released on March 23, 1911) with, arguably, the most impressive use of cross-cutting and of the last-minute-rescue motif often associated with Griffith;
- *An Unseen Enemy* (released on September 9, 1912), in which Lillian and Dorothy Gish make their screen debuts;
- *The Musketeers of Pig Alley* (released on October 31, 1912), a precursor of the modern gangster film; and,
- *The Mothering Heart* (released on June 21, 1913), in which Lillian Gish displays, for the first time, the emotional intensity of which she is capable.

The contract makes reference to the need for rehearsal and, from that point onwards, Griffith never relaxed his rule that rehearsing his actors was just as important as shooting the scene itself. As Blanche Sweet recalled, rehearsals at Biograph would not be limited to just one film.

> We had a system, if anything could be called a system in those days. If it was raining or snowing, and we couldn't do exteriors, then we would take the day to stay inside and rehearse several ideas, not just one, but several, so that we would have a backlog on which to draw.[5]

The final clause of the Biograph contract indicates the major reason for Griffith's leaving the company: he was not to receive recognition for his work. It was a humbling demand for a man who, for the first time in his life, had found something at which he could excel and for which he deserved acknowledgment. Griffith's decision to leave Biograph in the fall of 1913 was based also on the company's refusal to permit him to produce feature-length films. He had made one, *Judith of Bethulia,* with Blanche Sweet in the title role, based on the narrative poem and play by Thomas Bailey Aldrich. Released in March 1914, after Griffith had left Biograph, this four-reel biblical drama was hailed by the critics, but its impact is hard to understand today, largely because of its stylized acting and the rough edges to the production. Its battle scenes are badly staged, but they served as a training ground for Griffith, and when he was required to present similar spectacles in *The Birth of a Nation* and *Intolerance,* it was obvious that he had learned from his mistakes.

The Biograph Company was not prepared to permit Griffith to produce another film as lengthy and as expensive as *Judith of Bethulia.* The director had two choices. He could join Adolph Zukor's newly formed Famous Players Company, or he could join entrepreneur Harry Aitken, who controled two production companies, Reliance and Majestic, together with the Mutual distribution setup. Griffith chose the latter, perhaps partly because of a latent anti-Semitic attitude towards Zukor. However, Griffith later became part of Zukor's Paramount Pictures organization in 1918 with *The Great Love,* remained with Paramount through *Scarlet Days,* released the following year, and returned to Paramount for an unhappy stay during 1926 and 1927.

Griffith's next four features after leaving the Biograph Company—*The Battle of the Sexes, The Escape, Home, Sweet Home,* and *The Avenging Conscience* (all released in 1914)—are somewhat minor works in his career. They are important because they illustrate that the director had developed a company of stock players, many brought with him from Biograph, who remained with him for several years, including Lillian Gish, Robert Harron, Mae Marsh, Ralph Lewis, Spottiswoode Aitkin, Henry B. Walthall, and Blanche Sweet. Some, such as Miss Sweet, left Griffith upon receiving better offers from outside companies. They were replaced by other players, including Kate Bruce, Josephine Crowell, Jennie Lee, Elmer Clifton, and George Siegmann, a number of whom had also been with Griffith at Biograph but not made the initial move with him to Reliance-Majestic.

The interrelationship between the director and his actors was important. Mary Pickford once commented: "Griffith knew the strength and weaknesses of all his players and devised ways and means of bringing actors out of themselves by his clever psychological handling. He could make an actor surpass himself in dramatic performances."[6]

Griffith's use of actors impressed those in the theatrical community. George Arliss told *Reel Life* (December 12, 1914):

I confess I always have been opposed to motion pictures. They seemed to me crude—a lowering of dramatic standards which might eventually undermine the art of the stage. But after seeing *The Avenging Conscience* and *The Clansman* [*The Birth of a Nation*] I am convinced that film drama may be both powerful and artistic.

Griffith's use of his players is particularly relevant to the success of *The Birth of a Nation*. The film has no star. As Barnet Bravermann wrote in *The Theatre Guild Magazine* (February 1931):

In this picture Griffith showed for the first time that playing in the cinema bears no relation to acting in the theatre, and that the player as an object is no more important than other objects in the films. He also made it clear that the player as film material, as a character, is always an instrument in the hands of the film director, for the elements of time, movement, and image content in *The Birth of a Nation* were so tightly organized that the picture would have suffered had its footage been used to feature any of the players.

First seen at a preview in Riverside, California, on January 1, 1915, when it was known by its working title of *The Clansman, The Birth of a Nation* marked a turning point in American cinema. Taking a novel and a later play by Thomas Dixon, Griffith produced a drama of the Civil War and its aftermath, the Reconstruction period in the South, of such magnitude that for the first time, the American people understood the power and majesty of the motion picture. *The Birth of a Nation* took every cinematic technique known up to that time and used it to perfection. It illustrated the potential of the motion picture to propagandize and gain emotional momentum from a story. The spectacle of its war scenes was on a scale unknown in the American film industry prior to 1915.

The Birth of a Nation dazzled and also frightened the critics. The film was screened at the White House, before President Woodrow Wilson and others, on February 18, 1915 (possibly the first film to be so honored), and the President supposedly remarked (although no contemporary documentation exists), "It is like writing history with lightning. "

To black Americans, the film was seen as an instrument of racial hatred. Not only did Griffith resort to having white actors play black Americans in blackface, but he also depicted the Ku Klux Klan as the heroes in the production.

The film was reissued in 1921, 1926, and 1930 (with music, sound effects, and an opening prologue in which Griffith briefly discusses the film with Walter Huston); each time it was greeted with open hostility from black Americans and, increasingly, liberal white Americans. The attacks on *The Birth of a Nation* continued to recent times. It was picketed at an October 1947, screening at New York City's Republic Theatre. It was banned by the Boston city censor in April 1952, and by the Atlanta municipal censor board in June 1959. In January 1965, the New York State Conference of the NAACP announced it would fight any reissue of the film in its state. In the township where the film was first seen, the Riverside City Council voted to cancel a screening at the local municipal museum in March 1978. In June 1980, vandals attacked the Richelieu Cinema in San Francisco during a screening.[7]

It was foolishly suggested that Griffith attempted in some way to atone for *The Birth of a Nation* by making *Intolerance*. Nothing could be further from the truth. Griffith saw nothing for which to apologize in *The Birth of a Nation*. He recounted the story of the Civil War and Reconstruction as he had been told of it and as he had read of it (as frequent footnotes from published histories in the film's subtitles signify). Certainly, there is no question that *The Birth of a Nation* directly led to the rebirth of the Ku Klux Klan; KKK Imperial Wizard William Joseph Simmons announced the revival of the Klan simultaneously with Atlanta's opening of *The Birth of a Nation* on December 6, 1915.[8] But Griffith made no excuses for the glorification in *The Birth of a Nation* of the original Klan. In the 1930 prologue to the sound version of *The Birth of a Nation*, he told Walter Huston, "... the Klan served a purpose then." Like Thomas Dixon, who is much maligned as a Southern bigot and racist, Griffith had neither time nor respect for the modern Klan. By making *The Birth of a Nation*, Griffith and Dixon may have led to the resurrection of the KKK, but such rebirth pleased neither man.

As late as 1947, Griffith wrote to the British film journal *Sight and Sound:*

I am not now and never have been "anti-Negro" or "anti" any other race. My attitude towards the Negroes has always been one of affection and brotherly feeling. I was partly raised by a lovable old Negress down in old Kentucky and I have always gotten along extremely well with the Negro people.

In filming *The Birth of a Nation,* I gave to my best knowledge the proven facts, and presented the known truth, about the Reconstruction period in the American South. These facts are based on an overwhelming compilation of authentic evidence and testimony. My picturization of history as it happens requires, therefore, no apology, no defence, no "explanations." 9

Those who criticize *The Birth of a Nation* as racist are inclined to ignore that the film is only unusual in its sweeping dramatic emotionalism, not in its depiction of black Americans. In the same year as *The Birth of a Nation* was released, William Fox produced *The Nigger,* based on the 1909 play by Edward Sheldon, which deals quite offensively with "the colored problem." In a 1915 interview, Sheldon commented:

As I have pointed out in the play the negro problem is in my belief due largely to bad whiskey. There is hardly one of the "usual crimes" of the Southern negro, for which the penalty is usually lynching, that has not alcohol as an underlying cause. Take liquor out of the South and the race problem would cease to be. The negro is naturally primitive. Alcohol brings the worst in him to the surface. It makes him worse than the brutes.10

The second Mrs. D. W. Griffith, Evelyn Baldwin, emphasized the unfairness of the criticism that was always attached to Griffith's work:

I think it's a little ridiculous to put the blame on a man who told the story the way he saw it. The day was completely different. The Negro's lot was different in those days. There's no point in getting away from it. I can remember when I was a child, Negroes were not permitted to sit in a theatre, they had to go upstairs. They couldn't sit on a bus, they had to go in the back. They couldn't eat in a restaurant. You know this isn't right, but don't blame the passerby, or someone who tells you about it. And so far as racism, well it depends on how you want to describe racism, I guess. I know when we went to Florida, we had a Negro chauffeur, and a very fine person he was. And every time we got in the deep South we had trouble finding a place for him to stay, a place for him to eat, and one time in a public park in Miami, he was mobbed because he wanted to drink from a water fountain. And the people that mobbed him were very dirty white people, who hadn't washed in some time. This upset Mr. Griffith very much. Is this racism?[11]

What makes Griffith's next masterwork, *Intolerance,* so extraordinary is that it is totally different from *The Birth of a Nation.* The director had already filmed a modern story involving capital and labor, titled *The Mother and the Law,* late in 1914. He left it unfinished while overseeing the premiere screenings of *The Birth of a Nation* and then returned to the studio to turn this simple story into a multistory, multilevel condemnation of intolerance. He completed shooting *The Mother and the Law* and additionally shot three further stories—the Judean Story, culminating in the crucifixion of Christ; the French story of the St. Bartholomew's Day massacre in 1572; and the story of the destruction of Babylon in 539 B. C. —all of which illustrate a basic theme of man's inhumanity to his fellow man and which Griffith edited together as *Intolerance.* Each of the stories was complete in itself, and all but the modern story end in tragedy. These stories were intercut with comparison of one moment in history to another and then combined into one gigantic epic of intolerance. The excitement and drama mount as each story merges with another until the horror and tragedy of each moment in time literally engulfs the audience.

The Babylonian story, with its huge set looming over Sunset and Hollywood Boulevards in Los Angeles, is the best known and the most spectacular of the stories. The Christ story receives scant attention from Griffith, perhaps because it is so well-known to the audience. The French story has a gentle simplicity in the relationship between Brown Eyes and Prosper Latour (played by Margery Wilson and Eugene Pallette), so different from the gutsy comedy of the Mountain Girl and the Rhapsode (played by Constance Talmadge and Elmer Clifton) in the Babylonian drama.

However, it is the modern story that most grips an audience emotionally, thanks in no small part to the performances of the two leading players, Mae Marsh and Robert Harron. In this film and in *The Birth of a Nation,* Mae Marsh gives the two greatest dramatic performances ever seen in American silent films. Playing opposite Mae Marsh, as he did so frequently from Biograph days onward, Robert Harron (1893-1920) proves himself a brilliant actor under Griffith's guidance. Two moments stand out—the first as he kneels with unseeing eyes at the side of his dead father, and the second as he returns to his wife, smilingly looking around the pitiful room and then slowly replacing his smile with unbelieving sorrow as he learns what has happened to their baby.

"A Sun Play of the Ages," as *Intolerance* was subtitled, uses the image of Lillian Gish as "The Woman Who Rocks the Cradle" to symbolize continuity through the decades. It is a curiously wooden device holding together four stories that are brilliantly juxtaposed and fluidly edited for dramatic impact.

Although hailed as a masterpiece by the trade press, *Intolerance* did not do well financially and was criticized rather unfairly by the popular press. Typical of the reaction of the latter is the following review by James Metcalfe in *Life* (September 21, 1916):

> Grand in spectacular effect is *Intolerance,* the picture play that Mr. Griffith gives us as the successor to *The Birth of a Nation.* In it he has carried the picture play to the limit of its possibilities so far as doing practically everything that can be done with the motion picture. He has run the gamut from the homeliest modern domesticity to the tremendous orgies and barbarous battles of the Babylonians and Persians, all mixed in with the Huguenot persecution and the life of Jesus Christ. He has even attempted to include an idea. Unfortunately, the idea is that the intolerance coming down the ages is the same intolerance on which professional reformers and prohibitionists thrive in our time and country. Mr. Griffith could have presented more forcibly the undeniable truth of his argument if his great pictures had been more simply arranged and strung on a more logical thread. Like most moving-picture producers, he has become intoxicated with the mechanical possibilities at his command, and in the gorgeousness of his production has completely forgotten the artistic possibilities and argumentative power of concentrated simplicity.

Intolerance illustrates admirably the big things the moving picture does and equally the big things it doesn't do under its present inspiration.

Released in 1916 at a time when Europe was at war and there was discussion of preparedness in the United States, it is not surprising that *Intolerance* was criticized for its antiwar stance. At its British premiere at the Theatre Royal, Drury Lane, on April 7, 1917, Griffith appeared in person and took the opportunity to applaud President Wilson's intervention in the European war: "I am happy to think my country will soon be taking part with yours in this greatest fight for freedom."

Surprisingly, *Intolerance* was also attacked for its intolerance. The *Philadelphia North American* (December 30, 1916) wrote of

. . . certain grossly vicious features . . . [including] propaganda for legalized debauchery and using it as a vehicle of libel against a class which comprises some of the cleanest-souled, most unselfish and self-sacrificing women of the nation. . . . A second and most dangerous argument presented is that for legalized or legally tolerated houses of prostitution. This is done by cunning inference. . . . Finally, this insult is hurled in the faces of the pure motherhood of the land: "When a woman ceases to attract men, she sometimes turns to reform as a second choice." It is done with palpable intent to incite popular resentment against social workers, because—drawing the inference from the whole film—they are dangerous foes of the saloon and the brothel.

The financial loss Griffith and his company suffered as a result of the commercial failure of *Intolerance* plus the mixed critical response, might have given him pause to consider his future in the film industry. In reality, he was too busy to pause. He was to set sail for England, but before so doing, there was supervisory work to complete in Hollywood.

Extraordinary as it may seem, throughout the production of *Intolerance,* Griffith was also serving as one of the three production heads of the Triangle Film Corporation. Founded in the summer of 1915 by Harry Aitken, Triangle served as distributor of productions from Thomas H. Ince, Mack Sennett, and Griffith. Both Griffith and

Ince were to supervise the making of one five-reel feature a week; Griffith's company was to be known as Fine Arts and have studios at 4500 Sunset Boulevard (studios that were used for the filming of both *The Birth of a Nation* and *Intolerance*).

The Fine Arts Company is, perhaps, of greater importance because it brought Douglas Fairbanks to the screen in *The Lamb*, released on November 7, 1915. In all, Fairbanks made twelve features and one short for Fine Arts, many of which were written by Anita Loos and directed by her husband, John Emerson. And when Fairbanks left Fine Arts to form his own company in February 1917, he took Loos and Emerson with him. Fine Arts was also responsible for a 1916 production of *Macbeth*, starring the great British actor Sir Herbert Beerbohm Tree—considerably unsuited for films—and a number of mildly pleasing features starring Norma Talmadge, Lillian and Dorothy Gish, DeWolf Hopper, Bessie Love, Seena Owen, and others.

During the course of its life—Griffith disassociated himself from the company in March 1917, at which time the name disappeared from the screen—Fine Arts produced some eighty features. Certainly the majority were made without Griffith's supervision, under the competent, if somewhat unimaginative, direction of Christy Cabanne, John Emerson, Allan Dwan, Paul Powell, Lloyd Ingraham, Sidney and Chester Franklin, Chester Withey, and others. Also certainly, the daily supervision of the Fine Arts output was in the more than capable hands of Griffith's right-hand man, Frank Woods. However, Griffith was, by all contemporary accounts, involved in a number of ways with at least half-a-dozen features. An examination of extant Fine Arts productions reveals many directorial and editing techniques that only Griffith could have provided. He also contributed stories for *The Lamb, The Lily and the Rose* (1915), *Let Katy Do It* (1916), *The Wood Nymph* (1916), *Hoodoo Ann* (1916), *An Innocent Magdalene* (1916), *The Marriage of Molly O '* (1916), and *Diane of the Follies* (1916). A remarkable achievement![12]

Griffith followed *Intolerance* with *Hearts of the World*, one of only three features in which Lillian and Dorothy Gish costar. It is very much a film that illustrates the respective talents of each actress. Lillian is the consummate dramatic performer, suffering as audiences expected Lillian Gish to suffer. Yet, Lillian Gish is an actress who is able to spark an audience to suffer along with her;

her emotions are the viewer's emotions, and her ultimate rescue is a rescue from our own traumatic nightmares. *Hearts of the World* gives full reign for the first time to Dorothy's comedic talents. In the role of "The Little Disturber," complete with black wig, she is, as Harry Carr described her in *Photoplay* (March, 1918), "a little twelve-o'clock girl in a nine-o'clock town." This film is one of the few in which Dorothy's personality seems stronger than that of Lillian's, and it is small wonder that as a result of her performance here, Dorothy starred in a popular series of comedies released by Paramount.

Hearts of the World is a prime example of a classic screen melodrama. In many respects, it is similar to *The Birth of a Nation*, in that it is a love story into which a war intrudes. Mae Marsh is threatened with a fate worse than death at the hands of a renegade Negro in *The Birth of a Nation*, while Lillian Gish faces a similar fate at the hands of a German soldier in *Hearts of the World*. Both the individual Negro and the individual German are the villains, and the director is careful to indicate he is not condemning an entire race or nation, but only elements within the same.

The feature was released in 1918, three years after *The Birth of a Nation* and two years after *Intolerance*. The last two films are screen masterpieces—they belong to the ages—which *Hearts of the World* is not and does not. It is, however, the first of a group of important Griffith features—*True Heart Susie, Broken Blossoms, Way Down East,* and *Orphans of the Storm*—illustrating that Griffith could produce films at a level below masterpiece, but far above the ordinary, while working on a reasonably tight schedule and budget.

The major problem with *Hearts of the World* is that it is a film about war and hatred made by a man whose previous film had preached tolerance, peace, and brotherly love. Why did Griffith make *Hearts of the World?* In part, undoubtedly, because he was an old-fashioned Southerner, with close and sympathetic ties to the United Kingdom. He told the audience for the British premiere of *Intolerance* that he was "very much in love with this land my forefathers left many years ago" and that "the first girl I fell in love with was an English girl. Yes, little Emily in *David Copperfield*."[13] As an Anglophile, it was easy for Griffith to be persuaded by newspaper tycoon Lord Beaverbrook to make what is basically a piece of British propaganda. Griffith was also a snob, and he realized that such a film would—and, indeed, did—bring him into close contact with members of the British aristocracy. The poor boy from Kentucky had finally arrived in high society.

Griffith's supposed initial reason for coming to England was for the British premiere of *Intolerance*. After visiting the battle front in France, he cabled Lillian and Dorothy Gish, Billy Bitzer, and Robert Harron to join him in London. While there, Griffith and Lillian Gish were walking through the city's East End and saw a woman (probably a prostitute) with a curious gait that Lillian demonstrated to Dorothy and that Dorothy uses as part of her characterization in *Hearts of the World*. It may well be argued that with this role, Dorothy Gish was the screen's first flapper.

Griffith did not film very much, if anything, on the battlefield, because, after all, who wants civilians filming in the middle of a war and a battle cannot be staged for the camera under real wartime conditions. Indeed, it is questionable that Griffith wished to film the reality of war. At the time, he complained to *Motography* (October 27, 1917) that "viewed as drama, the war is in some ways disappointing."

The French village sequences were filmed at two English villages, Stanton in Worcestershire and Shere in Surrey, with some additional scenes shot in Hollywood, directly under the Babylonian set of *Intolerance*. The battle scenes were filmed at the Lasky Ranch. He told a reporter from *Exhibitor's Trade Review* (May 24, 1919), "It takes 10,000 eyes to see a modern battle—and no living creature has that many eyes. Only the motion picture camera has 10,000 eyes. Thus only the motion picture camera can 'see' the war."

Critics were easily taken in by Griffith's fake war. James Metcalfe in *Life* (April 18, 1918) wrote:

> Beyond comparison more impressive are the war scenes in Mr. D. W. Griffith's elaborate moving-picture play, *Hearts of the World*. Here the camera drama demonstrates possibilities at its command that are impossibilities to the theatrical stage. The latter can only present imitations of the great things which the photographic lens reproduces literally. Many of the war pictures shown in *Hearts of the World* were taken at the actual front and under fire of the enemy's guns. With remarkable skill they have

been woven into the warp of the play, so that it is difficult to distinguish real scenes from the manufactured ones.

Because *Hearts of the World* is a piece of propaganda, different versions were made for different audiences. The English saw a version in which they were prominent, the French, one in which they were a major ally, and the Americans, one in which they won the war. There was even a "peace version," first seen in New York in August 1919.

Lillian Gish has suggested that Griffith never forgave himself for producing this piece of wartime propaganda. Unlike *The Birth of a Nation*, Griffith did apparently feel a need to atone, which he did with *It's a Wonderful Life*, a 1924 drama depicting the suffering in post-war German society.

Griffith followed *Hearts of the World* with six minor features produced during 1918 and 1919. The first, *The Great Love*, reunited Griffith with leading man Henry B. Walthall, who had been magnificent and full of gentle dignity as Ben Cameron, "The Little Colonel," in *The Birth of a Nation*. Otherwise, *The Great Love* is an insignificant war melodrama that the director probably enjoyed making because of the opportunity it gave him to photograph members of the British aristocracy helping the war effort. *The Greatest Thing in Life* (1918) is also a war melodrama, often cited to refute claims of Griffith's racism because of a scene in which a Southern snob (Robert Harron) kisses the cheek of a dying Negro soldier. The next film, *The Girl Who Stayed at Home* (1919) is, again, a war melodrama, but offers the delightful bonus of Griffith discovery Clarine Seymour in the role of "Cutie Beautiful." Both it and the next two features, *True Heart Susie* (1919) and *Scarlet Days* (1919), an unexciting Western, mark the first important appearances in Griffith films by Carol Dempster, who replaced Lillian Gish as the director's leading lady in the twenties.

True Heart Susie and *A Romance of Happy Valley* (released immediately after *The Great Love*) are beautiful examples of Griffith's love of the American countryside—the latter is even set in Kentucky. They also demonstrate the simplicity of great acting in the person of Lillian Gish, who remains faithful to the love of her life, played by Robert Harron, in each film. While not a highly regarded production on its initial release—"It suggests an ideal short story expanded to novel length," commented *Wid's Film Daily*

(June 8, 1919)—*True Heart Susie* has since gained recognition as one of the director's finest works, proving his ability to handle simple scenes and situations with the same ease as he could handle a battle scene in *The Birth of a Nation* or *Intolerance*.

The same may also be said of Griffith's next feature, *Broken Blossoms,* which received its world premiere at the George M. Cohan Theatre on May 13, 1919. As evidence of Griffith's importance, it was part of a repertory season at the theatre that included *The Mother and the Law* and *The Fall of Babylon*, both culled from *Intolerance,* and the peace version of *Hearts of the World. Broken Blossoms* possibly represents Lillian Gish's greatest screen characterization: that of Lucy Burrows, a child of the London streets who finds brief happiness through a platonic friendship with a Chinese immigrant played by Richard Barthelmess. Like *Intolerance, Broken Blossoms* preaches tolerance and brotherly love, but on a less grand, more human scale.

As Julian Johnson wrote in *Photoplay* (August, 1919):

> It is the first genuine tragedy of the movies. . . . The visualizing of this bitter-sweet story is, I have no hesitation in saying, the very finest expression of the screen so far. There seems to be no setting or accessory which is not correct in its finest details. The composition is a painter's. The photography is not only perfect, but, with caution, is innovational, and approximates, in its larger lights and softnesses of close view, the details of bright and dark upon the finest canvases in the Louvres of the world. . . . Miss Gish has been allied with the delicate flowers upon the Griffith tapestries for a long, long time, but here she is called upon to play more than a delicate flower. She must, and does, characterize a little creature of infinite pathos. She has to be both Lillian Gish and the Mae Marsh of old rolled into one sorrowful little being, and her success in this strange combination of motives and beings is absolute.

After *Broken Blossoms,* Griffith again took a pause, directing three features of little importance in his total career: *The Greatest Question* (1919), *The Idol Dancer* (1920), and *The Love Flower* (1920). Each highlights a different leading lady associated forever with the director—Lillian Gish, Clarine Seymour, and Carol Dempster.

In 1920, Griffith directed his last masterpiece of the decade, *Way Down East*. He took a hoary old melodrama from the 1890s and created an epic that marked the culmination of all of his film techniques. He combined the spectacular drama of a young girl's facing death on an ice floe with the simplicity of country life. The rescue of that girl (Lillian Gish) from the ice floe by David Bartlett (Richard Barthelmess) was the last-minute rescue for which Griffith had become renowned, taken to its ultimate degree. He also created characterizations of small town life as no other director has done before or since. He created pathos on a grand scale, as when Anna Moore is turned out from the Bartlett household into the snow. He took an intentionally maudlin scene of Anna Moore baptizing her dying baby and made the cinema the art form for the common man.

Way Down East had tremendous impact on both the critics and the public. It also influenced the avant-garde. The great French feminist director, Germaine Dulac, told *The Moving Picture World* (December 4, 1920):

> I have seen *Way Down East*. Like everybody, I have been carried by the emotion when in the final drama, the heroine, small suffering little creature, slips on an iceberg toward an implacable whirlpool, but perhaps I have most quivered when Lillian Gish holds on her breast, with love, the child who is to die. This scene, so simple, so true, made with perfect movements, without any overacting, is one of those most beautiful examples of the parallelism of which I have spoken. The action lived dominated by the action perceived. Mighty symbolism, without any false arbitrary means, drawn from truth itself.

By 1920, changes were taking place in the Griffith empire. The director left California to return to New York City and a new studio in Mamaroneck. *Photoplay* (August, 1920) reported that Lillian Gish was "tired of seeing her name always in the supporting cast, although exhibitors all over the country were fond of billing her above the production, much to the displeasure of Mr. Griffith's business office." It was obvious that Griffith's greatest actress and discovery was soon to leave him, which she did, after one more feature, *Orphans of the Storm* (co-starring sister Dorothy) in 1921. After a reported falling out with the director, Robert Harron left the company and, within a few months, was dead from a self-inflicted and still unexplained gunshot wound.[14]

Despite these changes, during the next decade Griffith continued turning out films that impressed both the public and the critics. Certainly, he made some bad errors of judgment with certain films and certain casting decisions—notably Carol Dempster, although Griffith's choice of her for leading lady and Lillian Gish replacement is exonerated by Dempster's performances in *Isn't Life Wonderful* (1924) and *The Sorrows of Satan* (1927). For every disappointing Griffith feature, such as *One Exciting Night* (1922) or *Sally of the Sawdust* (1925), there is *The White Rose* (1923), reuniting Griffith with Mae Marsh, or *America* (1924), an impressive drama of the Revolutionary War.

In March 1916, *Photoplay* published a photograph of Griffith standing beside the great theatrical impresario David Belasco. The picture was captioned "Elijah and Elisha—Perhaps!," and *Photoplay* pondered, "Today Mr. Belasco, the imaginative visionary of modern drama, is growing old. Will his figurative ermine of poetry and spectacular power fall upon Mr. Griffith? In a word, is the scepter of imagination passing from stage to screen?"

Certainly, Griffith took the mantle from David Belasco, and he achieved more in terms of imagination and invention than the grand old man of the theatre was ever capable of doing. While Belasco is largely forgotten, Griffith is still a name with which to conjure, still a figure of study and of controversy. Unlike Belasco, who was old-fashioned even in his own time, Griffith was a poetic visionary. If Vachel Lindsay is the first major poet to acknowledge the screen, Griffith is the first poet created by that medium—some, indeed, might argue its only.

Aside from wanting to be a playwright, Griffith also wanted to be a poet. In the January 10, 1907, issue of *Leslie's Weekly,* he published a poem titled "The Wild Duck," which ends

> Poor little wild duck! Poor little wild duck!
> In the evening when the wind blows out to the sea!
> Ah me! Ah me! Ah me!
> In the evening when the wind blows out to the sea.

How extraordinary that a man who could write something quite this bad produced so much poetry in his film work. Poetic beauty was something that Griffith most wanted from the screen.

In 1948, he talked with Ezra Goodman.

> What the motion picture lacks is beauty—the beauty of moving wind in the trees, the little movement in a beautiful blowing on the blossoms in the trees. That they have forgotten entirely. They have forgotten that no still painting—not the greatest ever—was anything but a pallid still picture. But the moving picture! Today they have forgotten movement in the moving picture—it is all still and stale. The moving picture is beautiful, the moving of wind on beautiful trees is more than a painting. Too much today depends on the voice. I love talking pictures properly done. Sometimes the talk is good, often very bad. We have taken beauty and exchanged it for stilted voices. In my arrogant belief we have lost beauty.[15]

The beauty that the cinema has lost is the tragic beauty of "the hopeful geranium" and Mae Marsh in *Intolerance;* of Lillian Gish's "virginal beauty" in *Orphans of the Storm;* of the tears in the eyes of Adolphe Menjou's Satan as Mavis (Carol Dempster) rejects his offer of immediate fame and success in *The Sorrows of Satan;* of the homecoming scene in *The Birth of a Nation* and its antecedent in *The Informer* (1912); of the countryside, where even policemen become human, compared to the New York Jewish ghetto in *A Child of the Ghetto* (1912).

In a 1928 address to the newly formed Academy of Motion Picture Arts and Sciences, Griffith said

> When motion pictures have created something to compare with the plays of Euripides, that have lasted two thousand years, or the works of Homer, or the plays of Shakespeare, or Ibsen, or Keats' "Ode to a Nightingale," the music of Handel, Bach and Wagner, then let us call our form of entertainment an art, but not before then.

Griffith was too much of an egotist not to know that he and his films had given the motion picture the position and prominence to call itself an art form. Egotist or not, he was right.

Notes

1. Isaac Goldberg, ed., *The Theatre of George Jean Nathan: Chapters and Documents Towards a History of the New American Drama,* reprint (New York: Simon & Schuster, 1926), pp. 19-21. Nathan also had a close, possibly romantic, relationship with D. W. Griffith's greatest star, Lillian Gish, in the twenties.

2. Interview with Mrs. Ray Deibel, July 23, 1975, at Contented Acres, Centerville, Kentucky. Mrs. Deibel has a map in her possession showing her farm in the ownership of the Griffith family in 1879. It was then called "Lofty Green Farm."

3. For a detailed history of Griffith's stage career, see Russell Merritt, "Rescued from a Perilous Nest: D. W. Griffith's Escape from Theatre into Film," *Cinema Journal,* Vol. XXI, No. 1 (Fall 1981), pp. 2-30.

4. D. W. Griffith papers in the Museum of Modern Art.

5. Interview with Anthony Slide, November 14, 1970.

6. Letter to Barnet Bravermann, June 18, 1943, in the files of the Museum of Modern Art.

7. A good study of contemporary black reaction to *The Birth of a Nation* is Russell Merritt, "Dixon, Griffith, and the Southern Legend," *Cinema Journal* (Fall 1972), pp. 26-45.

8. For more information, see Maxim Simcovitch, "The Impact of Griffith's *Birth of a Nation* on the Modern Ku Klux Klan," *The Journal of Popular Film,* Vol. I, No. 1 (Winter 1972), pp. 45-52.

9. *Sight and Sound,* Vol. XVI, No. 61 (Spring 1947), p. 32. The same issue contains an article by Seymour Stern titled "Griffith Not Anti-Negro."

10. "Author of Fox Play Discusses Its Basic Idea," *Motion Picture News* (March 20, 1915), p. 51.

11. Interview with Anthony Slide, June 12, 1975. Blanche Sweet offered one example of D. W. Griffith's racism during a conversation on May 10, 1972. While making an Indian picture at Biograph, the actress expressed her admiration for the physique of an Indian extra dressed only in a loin cloth. Griffith turned to her in disgust and called her a "Nigger lover. "

12. For more information, see Anthony Slide, *The Kindergarten of the Movies: A History of the Fine Arts Company* (Metuchen, NJ: Scarecrow Press, 1980).

13. *The Moving Picture World* (May 26, 1917).

14. Harron had just completed starring in the feature *Coincidence* for Metro, and the producer was faced with the task of exploiting a film whose star was dead. Back in 1920, the only way of so doing was to release the film without mention of Harron's name.

15. *Picture News Weekly* (March 28, 1948).

7

Sound and Music

Thomas Carlyle wrote that "Silence is deep as eternity, speech is shallow as time." It is a pertinent comment when arguing for the aesthetic purity of the silent film. However, there was and is no such thing as a silent film. Music has always been an integral part of a silent film presentation. For example, when the Lumière films were first presented in England, on February 20, 1896, at London's Regent Street Polytechnic, they were accompanied by a harmonium borrowed from the chapel next door.

Only one serious argument has been made for the presentation of silent films without musical accompaniment, and that was by Vachel Lindsay in *The Art of the Moving Picture*. Lindsay insisted,

> The perfect photoplay gathering-place would have no sound but the hum of the conversing audience. If this is too ruthless a theory, let the music be played at the intervals between programmes, while the advertisements are being flung upon the screen, the lights are on, and the people coming in. ...To ask for music with photoplays is like asking the man at the news stand to write an editorial while he sells you the paper[1]

Films were initially accompanied by either a single pianist or a player piano. Of the latter, Carli Elinor wrote:

> When the instrument stopped, an usherette would walk down the aisle and you would see her putting on a new roll— maybe her favorite tune, disregarding the mood of the scene on

the film; or if there were not many rolls to choose from, the same one would be played over and over again. In those days music to pictures was an incidental matter regarded by the house manager as so much necessary noise to be obtained as cheaply as possible.[2]

If the film theater also offered vaudeville, a trio consisting of pianist, violinist, and drummer would accompany the acts, but they would leave the pit and rest while the films were screened.

Gradually, the player piano was replaced by an automatic machine designed for theatrical use, which provided semi-orchestral and sound effects. It was controled by the operator; thus, music could be synchronized with the action on screen. Among such popular instruments were the Peerless orchestrion, the En-Symphonie, the Wurlitzer pianorchestra, and the fotoplayer. The manufacturer of the last, the American Photo Player Company, issued catalogs of piano rolls for use with moving pictures and listed under headings such as "heavy music," "pathetic," "sentimental," "dramatic," and "oriental."

The use of pipe organs in theaters has been dated back to 1898,[3] but generally, the idea gained popularity after 1910. The major supplier of organs was the Rudolph Wurlitzer Company, and Wurlitzer became almost a generic name for theater organs. The Robert Hope-Jones organ that Wurlitzer installed in the Vitagraph Theater was praised by J. Stuart Blackton.

We early concluded that an orchestra could not give the proper atmosphere nor the artistic accompaniment which we felt our special features demanded. In this instrument, there is no disturbing element of scratchy string tone or blatant brass effects, which are usually found in an orchestra. . . . As the instrument is controlled by one musician, the effects and changes are made instantaneously, which, in our opinion, helps to improve the picture.[4]

Certainly major theaters such as New York City's Rivoli, Criterion, Roxy, Rialto, and Capitol had large orchestras accompanying the silent films on the screen, many consisting of more than forty players and often with musical directors who became well-known names in film music composition. At the same time, and contrary to popular opinion, the majority of motion picture theaters in the United States used organ accompaniment rather than orchestras during the Silent Era.

As early as 1910, theaters experimented with lavish music and sound effects to accompany films. When the Orpheum Theater (Chicago) presented *The Penitent of Florence* in the spring of 1910, not only was an organ with musical chimes used, but choir boys singing both in front and behind the screen were also heard.

The first music composed specifically for a film was a score by Camille Saint-Saëns, published as his Opus 128, for the 1908 Film D'Art production *L'Assassinat du Duc de Guise / The Assassination of the Duke de Guise.* This score helped pave the way for later French film scores by other major composers, notably Arthur Honegger and Erik Satie. In the United States, the first score written for a film was composed by pianist/organist Walter Cleveland Simon for the 1911 Kalem production *Arrah-Na-Pogue,* based on a play by Dion Boucicault. Simon's four-piece orchestral score was his first work for Kalem and later he was to compile musical cue sheets for the company's productions.

The Edison Company was the first to start providing musical suggestions to accompany its films. These music cue sheets became a regular feature of the company's house organ, *The Edison Kinetogram,* beginning with the issue of September 15, 1909. The Vitagraph Company began providing cue sheets in 1910. Within three years, generic musical cue books became available, beginning with the *Sam Fox Guide* in 1913 and followed by publications from Schirmer and Photoplay Music. Most of the music included in these volumes was preexisting material, but the *Sam Fox Guides* did include specially composed music by J. C. Zamecnik, who had studied composition under Anton Dvorak. A similar series, *Kinobibliothek,* was compiled in Germany by Guiseppe Becce. The best known of such works is Erno Rapee's *Motion Picture Moods for Pianists and Organists,* a 678-page volume published in 1924 by G. Schirmer.

When Zukor's Famous Players Company released the Sarah Bernhardt vehicle *Queen Elizabeth* in the United States, it boasted a specially composed score by Joseph Carl Breil (1870-1926), as did Zukor's *The Prisoner of Zenda* (1913), *Tess of the Storm Country* (1914), and possibly other titles. Breil later composed and compiled music for releases from the Triangle Film Corporation, but he is best known as the composer of the original score for D. W. Griffith's *The Birth of a Nation,* first heard at the Riverside, California, preview on January 1, 1915, and later at the New York City premiere on March 3, 1915. Breil's love theme for the film was later to become known as "The Perfect Song," which became the signature for the *Amos 'n Andy* radio and television series.

Breil did not, however, compose the score for the official world premiere of *The Birth of a Nation* at Clune's Auditorium in Los Angeles on February 6, 1915. That score was compiled and composed (mainly the former) by Clune's general music director, Carli Densmore Elinor (1890-1958). Elinor described his work at Clune's:

> My effort was to surround the photodramas with appropriate music and to reach greater artistic perfection. I concentrated on "synchronous" music, which means happening at the same time. This type of music taken by itself would be doubtfully intelligible except as a medley of musical scraps, but if taken in connection with the play to which it is adapted, leaves little to be desired. It supplies emotional atmosphere. By means of varied devices of tonal art, the music provides a tonal mood for each emotion visualized on the screen.

Elinor also arranged the score for Griffith's *Hearts of the World.* "Sweetest Bunch of Lilacs" was his musical choice for the love scenes between Lillian Gish and Robert Harron. Dorothy Gish's theme was "It's Delightful To Be Married," made popular a few years earlier by vaudeville and revue star Anna Held. Elinor later became musical director for the California Theater in Los Angeles; here, among other things, he was responsible for compiling the musical cue sheets for Goldwyn features.

Popular composer Victor Herbert wrote an original score for the 1916 Thomas Dixon production of *The Fall of a Nation.* The film was a plea for militarism and strongly anti-German and, in what was almost a battle of the film scores as much as a battle between two features with opposing viewpoints, Thomas H. Ince's production, *Civilization,* released in the same year, included an original score by Victor Schertzinger (1890-1941). Later, Schertzinger wrote the score for the Billie Burke feature *Peggy* (1916), and became a highly successful and very competent film director. His last production as both director and composer, *The Fleet's In,* released by Paramount in 1941, includes such perennial, popular favorites as "Tangerine," "I Remember You," "Arthur Murray Taught Me Dancing in a Hurry," and the title song.

Men such as Breil and Schertzinger raised the standard of film music. Thanks to their efforts, early audiences no longer accepted such musical clichés as "The William Tell Overture" for action sequences or "Hearts and Flowers" for the love scenes.

The history of early American cinema is littered with experiments at combining sound and picture. Some received brief public attention. Most were received with universal disdain. Virtually all synchronized the camera and projector with phonograph cylinders or discs.

The first major American combination of the phonograph with the moving picture was done by the National Cameraphone Company, active from 1908-1910. Founded by E. E. Norton, a former mechanical engineer with the American Gramophone Company, Cameraphone operated a manufacturing plant in Bridgeport, Connecticut. The chief problem encountered by the Cameraphone was the impossibility of simultaneously recording picture and sound; the company had to make a record of the sound first and then have the performers mime to their recording in front of the camera.[5]

At the same time that Cameraphone was presented, the Cinephone and Fotophone systems were also brought out in the United States. *The Moving Picture World* reported that the Gaumont Chronophone system was also popular with audiences in the United States, although it had not been seen or heard at any New York City theater.[6] It appears that such a statement was somewhat premature, because the Chronophone was first demonstrated in Paris before the Academie des Sciences on December 27, 1910, and in London before the Royal Institution on May 10, 1912. The Chronophone was certainly a major advancement over the Cameraphone because sound and picture could be recorded simultaneously. "Many people, including Thomas A. Edison have realized this difficulty," reported *Film Reports* (May 6, 1911), "but none have yet solved the problem satisfactorily, except Mr. Gaumont, who last year succeeded completely by a new patented system, of realizing this wonderful improvement. He has since been busy making subjects and has lately launched the new Chronophone on the French market, where it is having wonderful success, the French papers being full of praise for the improvement."

On May 7, 1910, *The Moving Picture World* editorialized:

> In our opinion the singing and talking picture is bound sooner or later to become a permanent feature of the moving picture theater. . . . We would say that the future of the singing and talking photograph is at this moment fuller of promise than ever it was.

Unfortunately, the promise was not to be fulfilled by Thomas Edison.

As early as 1889, Edison's associate W. K. L. Dickson was experimenting with the synchronization of the phonograph and the motion picture. There is a story, doubtless apocryphal, that when Edison returned from a trip abroad on October 6, 1889, he was met with a screening of a film showing Dickson raising his hat and saying, "Good morning, Mr. Edison, glad to see you back. I hope you are satisfied with the Kineto-Phonograph."[7] Edison was not satisfied, and these early sound films were not seen publicly until April, 1894, in a Kinetoscope Parlor in New York City. The only surviving "sound" film from this period shows W. K. L. Dickson playing a violin into a large recording horn while two men beside him dance a waltz together.[8]

Edison's laboratory and studio staff took up the problem of sound films again in 1911 and were able to devise a system whereby the sound could be picked up from a distance of twenty feet or more, thus permitting some movement for actors in the films.

Robert Grau foresaw the possibility that the "talking picture" would capture on film the great names of the legitimate stage and of opera:

> The advent of the "talking" picture, with all the enhancement which it promises to bring, should result in a general uplift together with much benefit to the masses who must naturally appreciate any effort which will make it possible for them to see and hear for ten cents that which has heretofore cost from fifty cents to two dollars.[9]

The reality was to be far removed from the high ideals that the critics saw for the new Edison invention.

There was initial enthusiasm, as is usual with any new amusement. The first screening in New York City on February 17, 1913, was greeted with fifteen minutes of sustained applause from an audience that saw a program beginning with a lecture and ending with a pianist, violinist, and soprano performing "The Last Rose of Summer."

A reporter wrote

> After the lecturer had been talking for a while, he dropped a dinner plate to the floor. It fell with a crash and the fragments were seen rattling about. There was no appreciable lapse of time between the action and the sound. You could hear the pieces clatter as they rolled about, and, as before, there was no feeling of illusion, but a perfectly natural concurrence of sound and motion. Whistles and horns were blown and some dogs that were called in opened their mouths and barked. There were short barks and long ones, but that did not matter. What might be called the registry of effects was in each case simultaneous or as nearly so as would appear under natural conditions. The lecturer wound up with a eulogy of Edison, in which he said: "Consider the historic value of a kinetophonic production of George Washington, if it were possible to show it now, and you will realize the splendid opportunities of future generations to study the great men of today. The political orator can appeal to thousands while remaining at his fireside; the world's greatest statesmen, actors and singers can be seen and heard in even the smallest hamlet, not only today, but a hundred years hence. In fact there seems to be no end of the possibilities of this greatest invention of the wizard of sound and sight, Thomas A. Edison." [10]

M. R. Hutchinson was the chief Edison engineer responsible for the production of sound films, which were photographed by Lewis Physioc and directed by Allan Ramsay. For the first time in the history of the motion picture in America, the director was not able to talk his actors through a scene, so the director devised a sign language to communicate with the actors during filming.

A detailed description of the technical aspects of the presentation of the Edison sound films is provided by Hugh Hoffman.

The Edison outfit consists of a giant phonograph, an Edison projector, and a synchronizing mechanism. The phonograph is operated by a small motor, for reasons which will appear presently. A large wax cylinder record is used, measuring about four inches in diameter. Some of the phonographs are equipped for disk records. An ordinary phonograph horn is used. The phonograph is located just behind the curtain, and in vaudeville theaters is set below the level of the stage. For operation, the trap door is opened, the phonograph operator sets his horn, starts his motor, waits for his cue, which is in the picture itself, and then throws in a clutch or switch which starts the phonograph. The trap door arrangement is probably used to save the time that would be required to set the phonograph properly, thus avoiding a stage-wait.

The projector used is the regular Edison Kinetograph which is too well known to need description, except that on the take-up pulley there is bolted a gear wheel that is connected to the synchronizer by a chain belt. The main trick is in the synchronizer, one of the most beautiful little pieces of mechanism that ever was made. A mere glance at it is sufficient to convince one that it is an example of the highest type of the machinist's art. It bulks to about the size of a small cigar box, and the mechanism is encased in a metal envelope. The synchronizer is bolted to the off side of the machine table and is propelled by two different forces; on one side by the moving picture machine, which is turned by hand, and on the other by a belt from the phonograph motor. The synchronizer is all gears, and if these gears are not traveling at the same rate they will bind and stop the projector. There is a warning brake that tells the operator to slow down or hurry up, as the case may be. It operates by centrifugal action, like a governor. In addition to this there is a traveling bevel gear, or differential, between the two sets of gears, which is operated by turning a knob. This arrangement enables the operator to catch up or drop behind if there is the slightest variation between the phonograph and the lips of the actor. The operator must keep his eyes on the picture all the time. He also has a telephone receiver on his head which is connected by wire to the phonograph, and this enables him to hear it at any distance.

The same motor that propels the phonograph also drives the phonograph side of the synchronizer. This is done by a belt that travels from it to the operating room and back again. The belt is a strong, black waxed silk cord about the size of a heavy fish line. In theaters it passes up through the ceiling, across the dome roof, or inner dome roof, over to and through the proscenium wall, and by various angles it reaches the phonograph from underneath the stage. At every corner, this belt passes around pulleys that are encased in metal, making them dust and water proof. Two belts are usually installed so that in case one breaks the other is handy. In the case of small picture theaters, this belt would probably be rigged close to the ceiling. It is not necessary, with the Kineto-phone, for an operator to be a mechanical or an electrical expert, but he must not be a greenhorn by any means. Its operation requires a reasonable amount of common sense and during the time of operation it requires that the operator shall concentrate all of his faculties upon the work.

In case of a patched reel (i.e., a reel with splices and missing footage), if the cut-out is not more than a few inches it is easy for the machine operator to drop back enough for the phonograph to catch up. In case of serious or long breaks, the Kinetophone Company provides an extra subject for substitution and the broken reel is taken out of commission until the broken scene is replaced with a new one. One of the principal claims of the Edison Company is that their field of reproduction is practically unlimited, because their records and films are made at the same time and by the same machinery.[11]

The Edison films were not released through the General Film Company to theaters but were exclusively distributed by the American Talking-Picture Company, which was created by the United Booking Office of America. The latter was owned by vaudeville entrepreneurs B. F. Keith and E. F. Albee and, obviously, was intended to provide talking pictures as part of a vaudeville bill. Audiences tired very quickly of the novelty. The Edison films had no major stars and usually consisted of items that would have been considered of little entertainment even in the smaller vaudeville theaters. Audiences were unwilling to sit through filmed acts that were inferior to live entertainment and the showdown came in March 1913, when the films were soundly booed at New York's Colonial Theater.

Variety (March 21, 1913) gleefully reported: "The talking picture film has been forced upon vaudeville audiences in New York for several weeks, excepting at Hammerstein's. This house, not exhibiting them at all, has been doing the biggest business of any variety theater in town." The Kinetophone quickly disappeared into oblivion.[12]

The British Vivaphone system, promoted in 1913, was similar to the Kinetophone and made available in the United States and Canada by Albert Blinkhorn. The process was explained by Hugh Hoffman in *The Moving Picture World* (June 28, 1913):

> The synchronizing device is located in the operating room. It is a sheet metal box that stands on edge. It is about two inches thick, fifteen inches long and a foot high. There is an electric light inside this box that shows a red bulls-eye when lighted, to the phonograph operator, who is located on or near the stage. On the machine operator's side of this box is an upright slit through which the light shows in its ordinary color. Outside the box, on the machine operator's side, is an upright pointer about the width and length of a lead pencil, which in its normal upright position always covers the slit in the box and stops off the light. Attached to this pointer are two miniature windows about the size of a postage stamp; one on each side of the pointer. These little flag windows or window flags are on a level with the light slit in the box. One window is colored red and the other green. These window flags indicate whether or not the machine and phonograph are in time with each other. When machine and phonograph are in time, the pointer covers up the slit and there is no light. If they get out of time the pointer moves to one side or the other, according to whether the machine is running too fast or too slow. When the pointer moves to the right it brings the little red window across the light slit and produces a red light, which means that the machine is running too slow. If the machine is going too fast the point goes the other way and brings the green window across the light slit, thus producing the green signal, meaning too fast.
>
> There is a particular spot on the film that must be threaded in the machine directly over the aperture for a starting point. Likewise there is a marked starting point on the phonograph disk. The machine operator signals the phonograph man that he is

ready, by turning on the light in his synchronizing box, and that shows the red bulls-eye to the stage. The moment the phonograph starts, the synchronizing box begins to tick slowly, like a clock. At the first tick the machine operator starts his picture. A special handle is required for turning the machine. This handle is electrically connected, by wire, to the synchronizing box, in a way that affects the pointer and its little colored windows. It is the operator's business to see that the pointer stays perpendicular, which means that he is in time with the phonograph.

The only connection between the phonograph and the synchronizer is an ordinary double bell wire. This wire is attached to a skeleton casting, bearing a magneto. One end of the casting rests upon the solid part of the phonograph, and the other end fits over the pin in the center of the disk record. The revolutions of the disk establish a make-and-break circuit that travels through the magneto back to the synchronizer and causes it to tick. The handle of the machine also establishes a make-and-break circuit with the synchronizer at the same time. The phonograph travels at the same speed always. If the machine goes too fast the extra magnetic force generated by the speed pulls the pointer to one side. If the machine goes too slow the phonograph magneto, by its greater excitement, pulls the pointer the other way. On reasonably short film patches the operator can slow down until the phonograph catches up. On bad breaks a new subject should be used.

What gave the Vivaphone some popularity was that it used both a standard phonograph and a standard projector.

Another sound-on-disc system was Webb's Electrical Pictures, presided over by George R. Webb with films directed by J. W. Ashley, first seen at New York's Fulton Theater in May 1914. The 35-minute program included minstrel showman Billy Burke singing, "Get Out and Get Under," and vaudeville comedian Nat Wills. So inadequate was the music in the film that the theater orchestra had to help "flesh out" the numbers.

Variety's Sime Silverman opined (May 8, 1914)

In communities where the Edison didn't show (if there are any such) the Webb pictures will be an attraction. In all other places the show will have to make a strong fight to gain a play at the box office, although from the Webb subjects a program might be gathered that will start something in the talk line among the natives. This, however, could hardly be accomplished with the first bill laid out.

In 1914, the Selig Polyscope Company, in association with the Cort-Kitsee Company, filmed a series of short films of the immensely popular, Scottish-born vaudeville performer Harry Lauder. The process used was, again, sound on disc and patented by Dr. I. Kitsee. It was not because the process was good, but because the subject was Harry Lauder that the films were first seen in New York City at the Palace Theater, home of American vaudeville. Lauder's manager, William Morris, presented the program, which consisted of four songs: "She's Ma Daisy," "Saftest o' the Family," "Parted on the Shore," and "Wee Deoch and Doris."

Variety's Sime Silverman complained (May 8, 1914) that the phonograph horn was placed in such a position that the sounds did not appear to come from Lauder's mouth—a constant complaint about these early experimental films—but continued, "For those who like Lauder and for those who haven't seen him, the Lauder Talker is a big act for vaudeville, and it gives the house the privilege of billing the Lauder name."

In 1912, Edward H. Amet (1864-1947) experimented with making sound on disc films at his ranch in Newhall, California. (In the 1890s, Amet was involved with George K. Spoor.) There is no evidence that Amet's work was ever shown commercially.[13]

A little known but important pioneer in film sound was Orlando E. Kellum (1880-1942), who patented "A Talking Picture Mechanism" in 1912, and more importantly, in 1919, "A Method of Producing Assembled Synchronous Kinetograph and Phonograph Records." Kellum first demonstrated his work in New York City in October 1913. "He did show perfect synchronism, obtained in a very ingenious way," reported *The Moving Picture World* (November 1, 1913). "His machine is a wonder. He deserves the highest success and he will attain it if he will only give the public something worth while." Among Kellum's filmed subjects were humorist Irvin S. Cobb; vaudevillians Ruby Norton, Miller and Lyles, Sam Moore and His Singing Saw, and the Van Eps Trio; labor leader Samuel S. Gompers; Secretary of the Treasury William Gibbs McAdoo; and actor Frederick Warde.

In the Kellum system, electrical impulses from a commutator connected to the phonograph turntable were sent by wires to a series of electromagnets in the synchronizing device used for either the camera or the projector. The electromagnets were linked by pistons to a crankshaft that rotated the projector mechanism in exact synchronization with the phonograph.

Kellum's plans to build a studio in the Edendale district of Los Angeles early in 1916 did not materialize, but in 1921, his sound system was used by D. W. Griffith for two sequences in *Dream Street*. One featured Tyrone Power, Sr., and the other had leading man Ralph Graves singing the title song. With accompanying Kellum sound shorts, *Dream Street* opened at New York City's Town Hall on May 2, 1921. The "sound version" of *Dream Street* was also seen in Brooklyn and Chicago.[14]

Kellum's system and the other processes discussed here all used sound on disc or cylinder, which was the basis for the Vitaphone process. Indeed, Kellum sued Warner Bros., owners of the Vitaphone process, for patent infringement in 1931, and the case was settled out of court. The modern sound film is based on the sound-on-film process developed in the twenties and outside the focus of this book; however, some developments did transpire earlier.

In 1910, Eugene Lauste claimed to have filmed sound and picture on the same strip of film. As early as 1919, Professor Joseph Tykociner of the University of Illinois developed a sound camera, and he demonstrated it on campus in 1922. Dr. Lee De Forest patented the Audion tube in 1907, which made the amplification of electrical impulses possible. Theodore Case began experimenting on sound recording in 1911 and was joined by E. I. Sponable at his laboratory in Auburn, New York, in 1916. These two men were largely responsible for the development of sound-on-film motion pictures.[15]

Several nonmechanized attempts were made to synchronize the silent film with the human voice. Prior to 1910, many teams of actors toured the country, providing spoken dialogue for their silent colleagues on the screen. The Actologue Talking Picture Company, which operated out of Denver, kept many such groups gainfully employed. A 1908 article in *The Moving Picture World* discussed this novelty in some detail.

The most successful idea in the talking picture field is the plan recently introduced by Will H. Stevens, of New York City, and which consists of a small cast of versatile actors who speak the lines which are apropos to the various characters from behind the screen, and who imitate the different sounds descriptive of the varied situations in the picture.

The above system was termed "humanovo "and was a phenomenal success from the start. Many different companies were sent out, each with one or more reels of film, and in most cases playing week stands. The Humanovo, like all successful undertakings, soon had its imitators, and up to the present moment there are at least a dozen different concerns engaged in the promotion of moving talking pictures.

The putting out of this new form of talking picture is by no means as simple as one might at first imagine, and it requires a thoroughly competent and long-experienced stage director to select suitable people and to rehearse the varied subjects. Many inexperienced and incompetent people have naturally drifted into the business, but their efforts are always immediately recognizable by the marked insipidity and amateurishness of their productions. In the staging of the talking pictures there are many important details to consider, and the smallest detail is oftimes the most important. It is, of course, imperative that the author of the dialogue for the different parts be a writer of ability, with an all-round experience of foreign travel and a good knowledge of human nature. He must also be of an imaginative nature and quick of eye, as the overlooking of some small situation is sometimes apt to spoil the entire story. The writer must now be assisted by a rapid and able stenographer who can take down the lines as fast as the composer speaks them off. In the framing up of the impromptu dialogue for the talking picture, the reel is usually run off a few times to enable the producer to become familiar with his subject.

The lines and business are then crudely recorded in shorthand and are afterwards typed and modified, and the characters are sorted out to suit the different talkers. The actors are then rehearsed, and after a few suggestions and alterations, the company is ready for the road.[16]

The Humanovo Company was owned by Adolph Zukor and boasted of twenty-two road companies, each consisting of three actors touring with various films produced by the French Pathé Company, notably a version of *The Two Orphans* (later filmed by D. W. Griffith as *Orphans of the Storm*). When the Humanovo was presented in New York City at the 23rd Street Theater on August 31, 1908, *The New York World* reported that police had to be called to clear a way through the crowds awaiting admission between 8 p.m. and 10 p.m. The same newspaper (September 1, 1908) claimed:

> These pictures have become such a craze that travelling theatrical companies are having difficulty in finding theaters for their attractions to appear in as the managers of many of the finest playhouses in the city have turned them into permanent homes for the so called "Talking Pictures," finding that line more profitable than the presentation of the ordinary theatrical production.

As late as 1924, the Gaumont Company in England released *The Prince and the Maid,* directed by Ludwig Czerny, with lyrics by Adrian Ross and music by Hans Ailbout. A quartet of singers toured with the production and from positions in the orchestra they followed the score as it appeared at the bottom of the film frame.

Live narration of films dates back at least to 1898, when a lecturer appeared with the New York presentation of *The Passion Play at Oberammergau.* Between 1909 and 1912, W. Stephen Bush in *The Moving Picture World* offered regular "tips" for lecturers who appeared to explain and amplify what was taking place on the screen, although he did warn in the issue of November 15, 1911: "Do not . . . attempt to lecture on a film unless you feel in your heart and soul that there is a need for it and that you are competent to fill that need."

On the whole, producers accepted that there was such a need and published lecture material for circulation with the film. For example, Selig published a twenty-page pamphlet to accompany its 1911 production of *Cinderella,* starring Mabel Taliafero, which included a complete lecture and suggestions for the musical accompaniment. Written by Cecil Metcalf, the lecture included lengthy introductory remarks, which noted that the film cost $21,310 to produce, contained 99 scenes, and was eight weeks in production. As the lecturer made his final opening remarks, he was told to move to one side of the stage and signal the projectionist to begin. The lecturer amplified upon every title in the film. Following the first title, "Once upon a time there was a little girl named Cinderella who lost her mother," the lecturer commented, "Cinderella's mother dies. The child entering, comprehends the situation. Cinderella and her father are grief stricken."

To those familiar with early one-reelers, the use of a lecturer *is* understandable. It is often difficult to follow the action on the screen, and these commentaries may have helped early audiences to better appreciate the drama that they were watching. It is also possible that a substantial portion of the audience was illiterate and unable to read the subtitles.

The lecturer became less and less necessary as films developed narrative styles. As films increased in length, it was also easier for producers to tell their stories without telescoping action; thus, the narrative became more understandable to the audience. Eventually, by the mid-teens, spoken dialogue became an accepted part of the subtitles, which were no longer limited to brief descriptions of what was to happen or what had already happened on screen.

Notes

1. Vachel Lindsay, *The Art of the Moving Picture* (New York: Macmillan, 1916), pp. 189-190, 193.

2. Carli D. Elinor, *From Nickelodeon to Super-Colossal: The Evolution of Music-to-Pictures,* unpublished manuscript copy, Anthony Slide collection. Other quotes by Elinor are also taken from this essay.

3. Q. David Bowers, *Nickelodeon Theaters and Their Music* (Vestal, NY: Vestal Press, 1986).

4. Ibid., 185.

5. For more information on the Cameraphone, see "Cameraphone the Latest Wonder," *The Moving Picture World*, Vol. II, No. 17 (April 25, 1908), pp. 369-370; and Carl Herbert, "The Truth about Talking Pictures," *The Moving Picture World,* Vol. IV, No. 12 (March 20, 1909), pp. 327-329. An unpublished article by William F. Haddock in the files of the Film Department of the Museum of Modern Art indicates that Cameraphone subjects were filmed by John Mitchell on the top floor of Daly's theater, New York City, but there is no contemporary evidence for this claim.

Further, Haddock states the Cameraphone system was invented by a J. A. Whitman, a name that does not appear in contemporary reports.

6. "The Singing and Talking Picture: What is Its Future?," *The Moving Picture World*, Vol. VI, No. 18 (May 7, 1910), pp. 727-728. This same article states that the Nickel Theater in Bedford, Massachusetts, showed a Gaumont Chronophone film of Harry Lauder and that the local newspaper praised the clearness of his songs. Information on the European screenings of the Gaumont Chronophone films is taken from *Proceedings of the Royal Institution of Great Britain* (June 1914), pp. 479-490.

7. William Kennedy, Laurie Dickson, and Antonia Dickson, *History of the Kinetograph, Kinetoscope and Kineto-Phonograph* (New York: Albert Bunn, 1895).

8. This film is often erroneously identified as the first "gay" film.

9. Robert Grau, "The Advent of the 'Talking' Picture, and Its Effects on the Theatrical Map," *The Moving Picture World*, Vol. VIII, No. 4 (January 28, 1911), p. 178.

10. Bailey Millard, "Pictures That Talk," *Technical World Magazine*, Vol. XIX, No. 1 (March 1913).

11. Hugh Hoffman, "The Talking Picture," *The Moving Picture World*, Vol. XVI, No. 13 (June 28, 1913), p. 1347.

12. A useful introduction to the subject is Rosalind Rogoff, "Edison's Dream: A Brief History of the Kinetophone," *Cinema Journal*, Vol. XV, No. 2 (Spring 1976), pp. 58-68.

13. The camera with which Amet made sound films is preserved at the Los Angeles County Museum of Natural History, which is also the repository for Amet's papers.

14. The surviving Kellum Talking Pictures are preserved at the UCLA Film and Television Archive.

15. A good general introduction to the subject is E. I. Sponable, "Historical Development of Sound Films," *Journal of the Society of Motion Picture Engineers*, Vol. XXXXVIII, No. 4 (April 1947), pp. 275-422.

16. Sydney Wire, "How Talking Pictures are Made. Scarcity of Picture Actors," *The Moving Picture World*, Vol. III, No. 7 (August 15, 1908), pp. 137-138.

8

The Star System

Because the concept of stardom is synonymous with the motion picture, it is convenient to assume that the American film industry has been creating stars for as long as that industry has been in existence. Such is far from the case. Indeed, for the first fifteen years of its life, the American film industry paid scant attention to the idea of film stars but borrowed personalities from other fields; subjects featured political, sporting, or military figures. Some of the first "stars" of the motion picture during the last few years of the nineteenth century came from the vaudeville stage, "names" such as dancer Annabelle Whitford (filmed by Edison performing her Serpentine Dance), strongman Eugene Sandow (filmed by both Edison and the American Mutoscope and Biograph Company), and famed beauty Anna Held (filmed by Edison). Held is one of the few major vaudevillians who displayed any screen presence, as witness her delightful performance in the 1916 feature *Madame La Presidente,* in comparison to Blanche Ring's lacklustre feature film debut the previous year in *The Yankee Girl.*[1]

One of the earliest dramatic sequences to be filmed (by Edison) was of May Irwin and John Rice enacting the kissing scene from their 1895 stage success *The Widow Jones,* shown to audiences in 1896 under the title *The Kiss.* Writing in *The Illustrated American* (July 11, 1896), Henry Tyrell described this film subject, which runs but a few seconds, as "[a] formidable challenge to the legitimate drama."

The Widow Jones had received wide publicity—it was May Irwin's first starring role—and, hence, interested the Edison Company as a profitable filmmaking venture. Similarly, the popularity of boxer Gentleman Jim Corbett (who defeated John L. Sullivan in 1892) led to his becoming another of the screen's first stars when he was filmed by Edison in the Black Maria Studio on September 7, 1894, fighting Pete Courtney.

By the turn of the century, producers were less interested in using outside personalities in their films, presumably because of cost and other considerations. Friends, relatives, and employees from behind the camera were used in films such as Vitagraph's *The Burglar on the Roof,* filmed in 1897. The film featured company cofounder J. Stuart Blackton in the title role and the wife of the janitor of New York City's Morse Building, where shooting took place.

Two other Vitagraph productions illustrate the attitude of many early producers towards stage performers. When the company filmed a scene from the 1901 Broadway success *A Gentleman of France,* it did not hesitate to announce in its catalog that the production, released as *The Great Sword Combat on the Stairs,* featured the star of the legitimate play, Kyrle Bellew. Around the same time, Vitagraph released *The Adventures of Raffles, the Amateur Cracksman,* featuring J. Barney Sherry in the title role. Sherry was considered too unimportant a stage actor to receive recognition in promoting the film, despite his displaying a propensity for screen acting that later served him well as a prominent member of Thomas H. Ince's stock company.

Producers began to look to the legitimate stage for actors to join their stock companies, but they did not approach major stars, whose salaries were beyond their reach and whose egos might prove uncontrollable in the new medium. Rather, they turned to minor players of the stage's stock and touring companies. Such players were happy to accept the steady income that motion pictures offered, and it is doubtful that many considered the new industry beneath contempt, as legend has it.

Henry B. Walthall was supposedly shocked to discover that fellow actor James Kirkwood had decided to enter films in 1909, although not too shocked also to join the American Biograph Company a few months later. Also in 1909, Hobart Bosworth insisted that the Selig Company not reveal that he was their new leading man. He claimed to be "heartily indignant" upon receiving an offer to play the lead in the company's *In the Sultan's Power.*

However, as Robert Grau has pointed out in his 1914 volume *The Theater of Science,* such expressions of outrage were seldom heard at the time, only later when actors began to reminisce about the early years of the motion picture. As a typical example of a minor player accepting the security of the film industry, Grau chose John Bunny, who commenced his scene career with Vitagraph in 1910.

> Bunny had been an actor for twenty-six years. His average salary was about $100 a week. He had been often promised more than this, but so unstable was the business procedure and often the engagements were so short and so varied that Bunny fairly jumped at the chance to enter the film which he had observed closely, and as he put it himself, "Either I must make good on the screen or else starve to death."

It was not starvation but Bright's disease that killed the comedian at the height of his screen fame in 1915.

Another field from which a number of screen players were recruited was that of illustrated song slides. These slides, projected on stereopticons and popular in the preteens, showed uncredited models depicting scenes from popular musical numbers. Among Mabel Normand's appearances was one in the slides for "Is There Anything Else That I Can do for You?" Alice Joyce was seen in "I'd Rather Be on Broadway with You," and Francis X. Bushman was the lead in "Sailor Boy." Others seen, but unidentified, in song slides included Lillian Walker, Anita Stewart, Norma Talmadge, Priscilla Dean, Florence La Badie, Patricia Collinge, Ethel Grandin, Helene Chadwick, Gertrude McCoy, Anna Q. Nilsson, Raymond McKee, and Claire Whitney.

Interestingly, these slides were often shown as "fillers" between films at nickelodeon presentations.*Views and Films Index* (July 28, 1906) compared the song slide manufacturers—the best known of whom were DeWitt C. Wheeler, John D. Scott, and Edward Van Altena—to photographic artists: "He poses the people, selects and constructs the scenes and makes up a picture show to illustrate the songs, much as the stage manager and his assistants prepare the stage for a dramatic production."

Eventually, film producers used song slides to promote their new stars. Kenneth Casey was featured in one series as "The Moving Picture Boy," while Florence Turner appeared in another as "The Vitagraph Girl." [2]

The trade press was slow to recognize the film star *per se*. Ben Turpin was the first performer to be the subject of a profile in *The Moving Picture World*. In the April 3, 1909, issue, an article appeared titled "Life of a Moving Picture Comedian." In the piece, Turpin wrote

> I have been in the moving picture biz working for The Essanay for two years, and I must say I had many a good fall and many . . . a good bump, and I think I have broken about twenty barrels of dishes, upset stores, and also broken up many sets of beautiful furniture, and had my eyes blackened, both ankles sprained and many bruises, and I am still on the go. This is a great business.

Slowly, *The Moving Picture World* began to devote prominent space to film actors. Pearl White (when she was still associated with the Crystal Company and long before she became a serial star) was the subject of an article on December 3, 1910. Three weeks later, the trade paper devoted a full page to Mary Pickford, one of the first players generally recognized by the public before her name was listed or known. By 1911, the journal had stories on actors and actresses who were temporarily forced to retire from the screen for one reason or another. For example, in the February 4, 1911 issue, readers learned that

> Little Bebe Daniels, the well-known professional child actress, lately appearing in Bison stock, has given up the picture work for the present, and is now attending the Dominican Sacred Heart School. Those who have observed the child's work in the pictures concede for her a brilliant future when she leaves the school and again takes up dramatic work.

The public's desire to know the names of its favorite film players increased. Audiences demanded that theater managers request such names from the production houses. "Pretty soon it will be necessary to project upon the screen the cast of characters as well as the name of the play," a harassed exhibitor told *Munsey's Magazine* in 1909.[3]

Initially, producers were wary of identifying their players—not because it was against the interests of the performers, but rather because (as happened very quickly) it might lead players to recognize their commercial potential. The Kalem Company was the first to accept the value of star names and in January 1910, it began sending out posters and postcards promoting its players to theaters. The identification on posters of players in specific films did not come into general use until 1912.

Other studios quickly reevaluated their policies towards identifying members of their stock companies. Vitagraph established a routine of sending its actors and actresses out to make personal appearances at theaters screening their films. One of the earliest documented appearances was by Florence Turner at the Saratoga Park Moving Picture Parlor in Brooklyn in April 1910. Francis X. Bushman recalled his first personal appearance for columnist Hedda Hopper.

> I started in Pennsylvania, in the mining area [where] there were many Poles and other recently arrived foreigners who worked in the mines—many couldn't speak English. I was booked by a man who ran a picture exchange in Pittsburgh. I took along five pictures in which I starred, and stood on a little elevated place—they didn't have a stage—and I talked to them. When I got down to walk up the aisle—you can believe it or not—people in the audience shrunk aside. They just couldn't understand how I could be there, and up on the screen at the same time. In two months, I covered every town and city in Ohio and Pennsylvania. I got 75% of the gross, and worked from 10 a.m. to 1:30 the following morning.[4]

Frank E. Woods, who reviewed films in *The New York Dramatic Mirror,* began providing readers with information on screen performers. In an article titled "Why Is A Star?" in the October 1919, issue of *Photoplay,* he recalled.

> Several Lizzies wrote to me wanting to know about the Vitagraph Girl or the Biograph Girl, or whether Mr. and Mrs. Jones [characters portrayed by John Compson and Florence

Lawrence in Biograph productions] were really married or not, or if Broncho Billy had a wife, before I took serious notice. Then I answered in the columns of the paper and the lid was off. It was the commencement of the Questions and Answers Department, the predecessor of the most entertaining section of the *Photoplay Magazine,* the Answer Man.

In February 1911, J. Stuart Blackton and Eugene V. Brewster founded *Motion Picture Story Magazine* (later known as *Motion Picture),* which was the industry's first fan publication, although it was initially funded by members of the Patents Group and intended to provide information on films from that source alone. Personalities whose films were selected for promotion in *Motion Picture Story Magazine* were not chosen on the basis of popularity, but by the producers, each of whom was expected to pay $200 a month for a guaranteed number of stories and photographs. Advertisements were an additional cost. It was not a high price to pay in view of the magazine's reported 1912 readership of 500,000, but at least one producer—Selig—was not convinced that it was worth the company's paying for such publicity.

The best known of fan magazines, *Photoplay,* was first published in August, 1911. Both *Photoplay* and *Motion Picture Story Magazine* published nothing more than lengthy synopses of current releases in their early issues, but gradually articles on film personalities became prominent and long serializations on the star's lives began to appear, such as that on Florence Lawrence, published in *Photoplay* from November 1914, through February 1915.

Florence Lawrence (1890-1938) had much to do with the establishment of the star system in America. Beginning her career with the Edison Company in January 1907, she moved to Vitagraph and, by 1908, she was the leading lady of the American Biograph Company, working for director D. W. Griffith and appearing in such important films as *Resurrection* and *The Mended Lute* (both 1909). Biograph was the one company that remained adamant that its players should not be identified by name, thus, Lawrence was known to her fans simply as "The Biograph Girl."

In the summer of 1909, Carl Laemmle was able to lure Lawrence away from Biograph to be the star of his newly formed IMP Company. Naturally, Laemmle did not wish to promote a rival company's films by advertising his new star as "The Biograph

Girl." Instead, he mounted a publicity campaign claiming that Lawrence had been killed in an accident in St. Louis. Once the story was picked up by the trade papers, Laemmle announced the news item was a fake, planted by his rivals in the industry in an attempt to destroy his company and the reputation of his new star.[5]

Lawrence's name was now widely known to the filmgoing public; in fact, when she returned to New York City from St. Louis, there were more people waiting to meet her train than had been present a few weeks earlier to greet President Taft. Happily, and probably accurately, Laemmle was able to advertise Lawrence as "America's most popular moving picture star." When she eventually left Laemmle to join the Lubin Company, her place was taken by Ethel Grandin, whom Laemmle billed as "The Imp of the IMP Company." Miss Grandin has the distinction of being the female star of the first two-reeler ever shot in Los Angeles—Thomas Ince's *War on the Plains,* released on February 23, 1912.

Meanwhile, Lawrence's place at the Biograph Company was taken by Mary Pickford, who was billed as the current Biograph Girl. As letters to *The Moving Picture World* at that time indicate, filmgoers were not taken in and knew the Pickford was not Lawrence, but it was only a short while before the former supplanted Lawrence as the screen's most popular actress.

Although not a great actress, Mary Pickford (1893-1979) was the silent screen's foremost personality, known and loved as "America's Sweetheart." When the *Chicago Tribune* published her photograph in the spring of 1919, it was captioned, "The Most Beloved Face in the World." [6] By 1916, her salary was in excess of $500,000 a year, and the following year is pinpointed by Edward Wagenknecht as the greatest in her career, with starring roles in, among others, *The Pride of the Clan, A Poor Little Rich Girl, The Little American, Rebecca of Sunnybrook Farm,* and *Stella Maris* (produced in 1917 but released in 1918).

Mary Pickford's contemporaries at Biograph included Blanche Sweet, Robert Harron, Henry B. Walthall, Mae Marsh, Dorothy Bernard, Claire MacDowell, Charles Mailes, Wilfred Lucas, and Lillian and Dorothy Gish (who joined the company in 1912). Because the company flatly refused to identify its players, Biograph's British distributor, M. P. Sales, was forced to invent names for the actors. Blanche Sweet became Daphne Wayne, while Mack Sennett was Walter Terry. Some of the chosen names are

curious, to say the least; Robert Harron might have looked like a
Willie McBain, but Mabel Normand hardly fit the billing of Muriel
Fortescue. [7]

When D. W. Griffith left the Biograph Company in the fall of
1913, many of his former actors and actresses accompanied him,
forming a stock company. Even away from Biograph, none of these
players really received his or her due, because throughout the teens,
Griffith refused to "star" any of his players. They were considered
members of an ensemble company and never introduced to the
audience by way of a subtitle, which was the accepted means of
identifying players in films from the early teens onwards. In addition, the major Griffith actresses represented in the early years by
the Gish sisters and Blanche Sweet, and later by Clarine Seymour
and Carol Dempster, had a peculiar ethereal charm and a dramatic
intensity that prevented their becoming stars in the more accepted
sense.

There must be some question about how anonymous the Biograph players were. Certainly, there was no secrecy involved when
they were signed by other companies. In *The Moving Picture World*
of February 25, 1911, there is a lengthy article regarding two
Biograph actresses, Dorothy Bernard and Florence Barker. The
former is described as "one of the most talked-about actresses in
the world," which is a little hard to believe if the names of Biograph
players were unknown. When Mae Marsh resigned from Kalem and
rejoined Biograph, her return was noted in *The Moving Picture
World* of September 21, 1912. In death, Biograph players received
their rewards. When Vernon Clarges, a member of the Biograph
stock company, died on August 11, 1911, *The Moving Picture World*
published an obituary notice that included the titles of several of his
Biograph films.

It seems certain that by 1912, the names of Biograph players
were known to American audiences. In its issue of October 5 for
that year, *The Moving Picture World* names Henry B. Walthall as
the leading man of *Friends* and *Two Daughters of Eve*. In its issue
of November 9, Blanche Sweet is noted as the star of *The Painted
Lady*. Both Sweet and Walthall are mentioned in the February 22,
1913, review of *Oil and Water*. Finally, on April 22, 1913, *The
Moving Picture World* announced a change in the Biograph policy:
"This week posters were issued bearing photographs and names of
about a score of the members of the acting department of that

organization." But this was really too late, because the bulk of the Biograph players, along with D. W. Griffith, was about to depart from the company.

The first influx of major stars to the motion picture arena came in 1912 with Adolph Zukor's creation of the Famous Players Company. With his slogan "Famous Players in Famous Plays," Zukor provided the filmgoing public with an opportunity to see some of the greatest stage performers of the era, although in reality, all had been at the height of their fame many years earlier. In fact, one of the reasons why Zukor's films were successful may have been because audiences were familiar with these stars and the roles that they were portraying. Audiences knew what to expect and felt comfortable with the plays.

James O'Neill, James K. Hackett, and Mrs. Minnie Maddern Fiske each re-created the plays with which they were most easily associated—*The Count of Monte Cristo, The Prisoner of Zenda,* and *Tess of the D'Urbervilles*—in films that were as creaky as the legitimate vehicles of these players had become. *The Count of Monte Cristo* (1912) was the first to be filmed, and it is reasonably well directed (by Edwin S. Porter), with an intelligent use of locations that offsets the painted scenery. However, the Selig Company rushed into production with its own, shorter version of *The Count of Monte Cristo,* starring Hobart Bosworth, and Zukor temporarily shelved his version, releasing *The Prisoner of Zenda* (1913) as the first "Famous Play," which is everything a badly filmed stageplay can be, with the actors all looking old and unattractive, the camera static, and the scenery artificial.[8]

Undoubtedly, it was the stature of Zukor's associate, theatrical impresario Daniel Frohman, that encouraged this group of stage performers to enter films, and it was Frohman who saw the potential that the motion picture offered to those from the legitimate stage. In an editorial in *The New York Dramatic Mirror,* Robert Grau wrote:

> It was Frohman himself who first predicted better plays for the stage and larger audiences in attendance as a direct result of a photoplay era which has influenced playwrights to a greater simulation of realism, despite the limitations of a four-walled playhouse as compared with the vast resources of the photo-playwright, with all the world for his stage.[9]

While she had refused to appear on the vaudeville stage, Mrs. Fiske felt the motion picture would immortalize her performance as Tess. And after his appearance in the film version of *The Prisoner of Zenda,* James Hackett found an increased audience for his stage performances in the role. James O'Neill told *The New York Dramatic Mirror* (July 23, 1912)

> I have had many years' experience before the footlights and have seen many grand productions, but never in all my travels have I been surrounded with so many congenial people, been furnished with the accessories and allowed the lavish expenditure of money as during these weeks taking that picture.

Among the stage personalities who entered films in the teen years were William and Dustin Farnum, Elsie Janis, Constance Collier, Sir Herbert Beerbohn Tree, Edna Goodrich, Charlotte Greenwood, Lenore Ulrich, Fannie Ward, Maclyn Arbuckle, Jane Cowl, Lou Tellegen, Weber and Fields, Charles Ruggles, Raymond Hitchcock, William Gillette, Fritzi Scheff, E. H. Sothern, H. B. Warner, and Holbrook Blinn. Some, such as Blinn, Ruggles, and Warner, became successful character actors in films, but most failed. "It rained stars, like hailstones," wrote William S. Hart, "and like hailstones, they melted under the California sun." [10]

Maude Adams and Laurette Taylor were eagerly sought by the motion picture industry but declined the invitation; Taylor made her screen debut eventually in 1922 in the film version of her stage success *Peg o' My Heart.* A few stage actresses made a lasting impression on screen: Ethel Barrymore made her debut in 1914, Elsie Ferguson in 1917, and Alla Nazimova in 1916. (Ethel's brother Lionel was frequently on screen after making his debut, under D. W. Griffith's direction, in 1911.)

Some performers failed through no fault of their own. "Marie Doro has what is easily the most appealing and sensitively beautiful face on the stage," wrote Kenneth Macgowan. "Her cheeks seem made for the play of shadows. Her eyes are infinitely wistful. The fact that very few patrons of the movies carried these impressions away with them can be laid to just one thing—stupid stories and poor direction."[11]

Mary Garden and Marguerite Namara were unsuccessful film entrants from the opera stage. After her failure, Mary Garden pronounced, "[a] great actress had no place in motion pictures."12 Only one opera star, Geraldine Farrar (1882-1967), enjoyed a healthy career in films from 1915-1921.

D. W. Griffith might argue that film performers were "people of great personalities, true emotions, and the ability to depict them before the camera. Stage emotions will not do; some of the greatest of actors appear 'stilted' and 'stalky' in front of the camera."13 But it was also obvious, as noted by Kenneth Macgowan, that "so long as the ten-cent public of the movies is curious to see the two-dollar celebrity of Broadway, and so long as a famous name is the only advertising value that producer and public can gamble on, the artist of the voice will be the artist of the picture."14

In discussing the arrival of new actors from the stage, it is often forgotten that quite a few performers now regarded as screen actors and actresses were originally of the stage—notably Marguerite Clark, Sydney Drew, Robert Warwick, Mary Miles Minter, William S. Hart, and Gladys Hulette. The opportunity that the motion picture offered to actors such as these may well have influenced them and their colleagues to point out such alternative possibilities to their theatrical employers, to demand better working conditions and salaries, and ultimately, may have led to the 1913 formation of Actors Equity Association.

In the December 1915, issue of *Theater Magazine,* William Brady confessed that the film "competition is beyond us," and he began concentrating more of his efforts away from the stage and into film production through the World Film Corporation (founded in 1914). The theatrical syndicate of Klaw and Erlanger had already entered films in association with the American Biograph Company.

Conversely, film producers began looking for means to exploit the theater. The Lubin Company signed Marie Dressler during one of the down periods in her career to star in *Tillie's Tomato Surprise* (1915). It also gained screen rights to a handful of plays by Charles Klein (*The Third Degree, The Lion and the Mouse,* etc.) that were not considered terribly valuable at the time but were to prove so to Warner Bros. when it acquired the properties years later.

As a result of Lubin's desire for a star-studded cast, the company lost one of its best-known stock players, Lottie Briscoe, who refused to play a secondary role on screen. That decision in 1915 basically ended her career. As publicist Norbert Lusk recalled

Humble pie did not appeal to the palate of Lottie Briscoe. She refused to have anything to do with any all-star cast, packed her belongings and trudged to the station in red-heeled shoes, lugging a heavy suitcase and passing out of pictures forever. I detail her departure because of a double significance. Miss Briscoe was a leading star without a manager, secretary, press agent, maid, or second-hand car.[15]

Lottie Briscoe was not the only screen performer to refuse to take lower billing to a stage star. *Variety* (May 21, 1915) reports this as the reason that Francis X. Bushman severed his contract with Essanay. A couple of years earlier, the same trade paper noted (November 21, 1913)

Film actors are scrapping for the spotlight. Printing the cast of the leading principals of the multiples [multi-reel films] and leaving the rest of the film mummers out of the lists is causing trouble. The film directors and executives are now going through the experiences of Broadway impresarios of regular productions in attempts to pacify players who want their names mentioned first as well as those who insist that if so-and-so's name is in big type theirs must be, too.

By the mid-teens, many players had their own production companies—not just major stars such as Mary Pickford, but lesser players including Helen Gardner, Florence Lawrence, Gene Gauntier, and Marion Leonard. Stars proliferated in all areas of film. William S. Hart and Tom Mix headed the Western field, comedy was headed by Chaplin, drama by Norma Talmadge and Olga Petrova (possibly the only feminist star developed by motion pictures), and light comedy was represented by Viola Dana and Madge Kennedy. Wallace Reid was possibly the most successful of the light dramatic leading men. Among the popular romantic teamings on screen were Francis X. Bushman and Beverly Bayne, Mae Marsh and Robert Harron, May Allison and Harold Lockwood, Bert Lytell and Alice Lake, and Sessue Hayakawa and his wife, Tsuro Aoki. There were dozens of child stars, including Mary Miles Minter, Clara Horton, Baby Marie Osborne, Helen Badgley, Francis Carpenter, Virginia Lee Corbin, and Thelma Salter.[16]

By January 1917, the highest paid star on screen was Douglas Fairbanks (1883-1939) with an annual income of $780,000. Somewhat half-heartedly, Fairbanks had left a successful stage career to join the Fine Arts Company, for whom he made his film debut in *The Lamb* in 1915. On the whole, Fairbanks' features from the teens do not fully develop the heroic, swashbuckling character with which his name is associated, and it was not until *The Mark of Zorro* in 1920 that Fairbanks really came into his own.

In February 1920, *Photoplay* published a comparison of movie star salaries in 1916 and 1920. In 1916, Frank Keenan drew $1,000 a week from Thomas Ince, Francis X. Bushman was paid $750 a week, and Billie Burke received $40,000 for starring in *Peggy*. By 1920, salaries had risen considerably. Metro paid Nazimova $13,000 a week, while Elsie Ferguson and Geraldine Farrar were each paid $10,000 a week. Theda Bara was drawing $4,000 a week at the end of her contract with William Fox. Mae Marsh was receiving $5,000 a week from Goldwyn. Except for James Kirkwood and Henry B. Walthall, whose salaries were said to be in the $1,000-a-week range, most leading men earned $750 or less a week. Mary Pickford, Charlie Chaplin, and William S. Hart were in the category of one million or more dollars a year, followed by Norma Talmadge and, surprisingly, Anita Stewart, with incomes of $500,000 or more.

With the increase in salaries came an increase in subsidiary demands from the stars. On March 17, 1919, Adolph Zukor was informed by memorandum of demands from Elsie Ferguson and her attorney while Miss Ferguson was working at Paramount's new Astoria studios:

> Miss Ferguson would like a suite of three rooms—an ordinarily spacious dressing room, a reception room and a little room in between, to be used as an office. Now that Miss Ferguson has her own press agent and also has a great many appointments to be taken care of by her personal secretary, Miss Rector, she really has need of space for desk and typewriter and some few bits of office equipment. Concerning the dressing room itself, Miss Ferguson simply asks that [sic] plenty of closet space and a three sided mirror almost full length, in order that she may be able to adjust her gowns more readily than at present. Make-up facilities, similar to those which she now has, are entirely acceptable.

Miss Ferguson would particularly like to be consulted as to
the placing of the electric lights in her dressing room.

With the reporting of the luxurious life of the stars, and as
salaries climbed, the number of actors and actresses working in
films was bound to increase. An examination of the 1918 edition of
The Motion Picture Studio Directory reveals the following statistics. Among the male screen performers there were 356 leads, 161
juveniles, 53 heavies, 329 character players, and 158 comedians.
Among the female contingent, there were 468 leads, 208 ingénues,
187 character players, 148 comediennes, 10 heavies, and 72 child
performers.

As to whom was ultimately responsible for the star system—
the public or the producer—the answer must lie somewhere between the two. Certainly, the producers decided—sometimes
mistakenly—which actor or actress had potential. Yet for every
Douglas Fairbanks that they recruited from the stage and who made
good on screen, there was a Sir Herbert Beerbohm Tree (who, when
asked for his opinion on his American film debut in the 1916 version
of *Macbeth,* was found to be asleep — a bad omen foreshadowing
the public's reaction to the production). There are at least two
examples in the teens of bit players for whom audiences expressed
an immediate liking, curiously, after each had played the same role
in filmed versions of Charles Dickens' novel *A Tale of Two Cities.*
Norma Talmadge was selected for stardom as a result of her playing
a woman on the way to the guillotine (with Maurice Costello as
Sydney Carton) in Vitagraph's 1911 production, as was Florence
Vidor in the same tiny role in Fox's 1917 version starring William
Farnum.

"The star is inevitable," wrote Randolph Bartlett in 1919.[17]
From 1910 to the present, that statement has held true.

Notes

1. Both of these films are preserved in the UCLA Film and Television
Archive.
2. For more information, see John W. Ripley, "Romance and Joy,
Tears and Heartache, and All for a Nickel," *Smithsonian* (March 1982),
pp. 76-82. Contemporary articles on song slides include: "Song Slides:

How They Are Produced," *Views and Films Index* (July 18, 1906), p. 10; and "The Song Slide Situation," *Views and Films Index* (March 7, 1908), pp. 13-15. Because of piracy among song-slide manufacturers, who claimed that one set of slides could cost as much as $500 to produce, there were discussions in 1908 regarding the creation of a protective organization similar to the Motion Picture Patents Comany.

3. William Allen Johnston, "The Moving-Picture Show, the New Form of Drama for the Millions," *Munsey's Magazine* (August 1909), p. 638.

4. Unpublished interview with Hedda Hopper, August 20, 1957.

5. As evidence of Florence Lawrence's popularity, she was the recipient of some of the earliest "fan" letters (preserved in the Florence Lawrence Collection at the Los Angeles County Museum of Natural History). Such letters are of the most innocent nature. John H. Flynn, Jr., of Woburn, Massachusetts, wrote to the American Biograph Company on December 17, 1908, asking the identity of the young lady in *The Reckoning*, *The Ingrate*, and *After Many Years*, explaining, "My reason for asking the above information was the outcome of a wager that I did not have courage to form an acquaintance with this young lady." Leland Ayers wrote from San Francisco to "Dear Stranger" on December 17, 1909: "I missed you in the AB Company and I wondered what became of you until tonight for the first time I saw you in *Love's Stratagem* in the I.M.P. Co. . . . I am just 16 so their [sic] is no danger of flirtation I jest [sic] like you and I would feel highly honored if you would answer this crazy letter."

6. Edward Wagenknecht, *Stars of the Silents* (Metuchen, NJ: Scarecrow Press, 1987), p. 12.

7. A complete listing of such names can be found in Anthony Slide, *The Griffith Actresses* (New York: A. S. Barnes, 1973).

8. *The Count of Monte Cristo* and *The Prisoner of Zenda* are preserved in the Paper Print Collection at the Library of Congress.

9. Robert Grau, "Stage Versus Screen," *The New York Dramatic Mirror* (April 15, 1916), p. 1.

10. Gerald D. MacDonald, "From Stage to Screen," *Films in Review*, Vol. VI, No. 1 (January 1955), p. 15.

11. Kenneth Macgowan, "Stage Stars Who Made Good on Screen," *Dramatic Mirror* (February 15, 1919), p. 229.

12. Ibid.

13. D. W. Griffith, "What I Demand of Stars," *Motion Picture Classic* (February 1919), p. 40.

14. Macgowan, ibid.

15. Norbert Lusk, "I Love Actresses!," *New Movies* (April 1946), p. 29.

16. For a detailed study of child stars of the teens, see Anthony Slide, *Aspects of American Film History Prior to 1920* (Metuchen, NJ: Scarecrow Press, 1978), pp. 16-25.

17. Randolph Bartlett, "The Star Idea Versus the Star System," *Motion Picture Magazine* (August 1919), p. 37.

9

The Role of Women

The importance of women to the American silent film industry cannot be overemphasized. Women thrived and, in many cases, dominated the motion picture world as screenwriters, editors, fan magazine writers, directors, and, of course, stars. As early as October 3, 1908, the trade paper *Views and Films Index* editorialized, "Women's chances of making a living have been increased by the rise of the cinematograph machines."

In 1923, Myrtle Gebhart—a frequent contributor to film magazines—wrote an article on Business Women in Film Studios for *The Business Woman.* She noted

> Excluding acting, considering solely the business possibilities, the positions are held by women in the Hollywood studios as typists, stenographers, secretaries to stars and executives, telephone-operators, hair-dressers, seamstresses, costume-designers, milliners, readers, script-girls, scenarists, cutters, film-retouchers, film-splicers and other laboratory work, set-designers and set-dressers, librarians, artists, title-writers, publicity writers, plaster-molder, casting-director, musicians, film-editors, executives and department managers, directors and producers.

The film industry was wide open to women because it had yet to become departmentalized and because unions—always male-dominated—had made no impact in the new industry. There was no union or guild to prevent a women from being a cutter one week and a director the next. There was no guild to prevent any woman from writing a script, submitting it to a producer, and most important of all, getting it read.

Simultaneously with the growth of the nickelodeon, women became theater managers and, sometimes, owners. One theory has been advanced that women were encouraged to enter the field of theater management because they would bring respectability to a fledgling industry singularly lacking in esteem.[1] The sight of a female manager at the door of the nickelodeon would offer a note of security not only to women patrons, but also to parents concerned about permitting their children to enter these new halls of entertainment.

Miss Alta M. Davis, manager of the Empire Theater in Los Angeles, was quoted by *The New York Dramatic Mirror.*

> It seems to me there is a great field in the movie business, as yet practically unexplored by my own sex, for women of the progressive type who are not satisfied to let the masculine element of every community dominate, plan, manage and originate everything—and, of course, reap all the benefits that naturally accrue to those who have initiative, a quality possessed by women as well as men.
>
> It is a known fact that women and children form the greater part of every moving picture audience, and it is but natural that a woman manager should be better qualified than a man to judge the kind of pictures the majority of her patrons like, when most of them are of her own sex.
>
> After all, the meat in the coconut of successful management, so to speak, is in obtaining the right kind of pictures—pictures that appeal to the greatest number.[2]

Some of the earliest film exchanges were also operated by women. Handling projectors, carbons, condensers, tickets, and announcement slides as well as films, the T. A. Mack Exchange in Chicago was a prominent business until its demise in 1915. It was operated by Theresa McCaffrey, affectionately known in the industry as "Miss Mack." In 1911, the United Film Company's offices in Troy, New York, were managed by a woman named E. M. Murphy, and in the early teens, the educational division of the General Film Company was headed by Katherine F. Carter, who formed her own company, the Katherine F. Carter Educational and Motion Picture Service Bureau, in 1914.

In its issue of November 13, 1909, *The Moving Picture World* hailed Frida Klug as "the only lady so far to our knowledge to grapple with the intricacies of the film importing and renting business." Klug represented a number of Italian producers. Agnes Egan Cobb served as sales manager for Eclair and other producers in the early teens.

"When we see a woman tackling the selling end of the business and getting away with it our hats must come off to that woman," commented *The Moving Picture World* (April 25, 1914).

At least one studio, the Kalem lot in Los Angeles, was managed by a woman—Miss M. E. Gibsone—from 1914-1917.

Lillian W. Brennan was a staff reviewer at *Film Daily* in the twenties, following in the footsteps of at least two female reviewers with other trade periodicals in the teens. Women reviewers were also active on fan magazines: Hazel Simpson Naylor (*Motion Picture Magazine*), Mary Boyle (*Photoplay*), Adele Whitely Fletcher (*Motion Picture Magazine*), Mary Jane Warren (*Motion Pictures Today*), and Delight Evans (*Screenland*).[3]

In 1916, Margery Ordway worked as a camerawoman with Morosco. In 1920, Louise Lowell was inaccurately hailed as "the first and only camera-maid in the world."[4] She was on the staff of *Fox News,* specializing in aerial photography. One of the first prominent still photographers in Hollywood was Ruth Harriet Louise, who began her career at M-G-M in the early twenties at the suggestion of her brother, director Mark Sandrich.

On a more mundane level, a number of stenographers became secretaries to stars and directors and enjoyed a moment of fame in a 1922 *Photoplay* article.[5] Among the ladies featured were Margaret Neff, secretary to Valentino; Josephine Chippo, secretary to child star Wesley Barry; Marjorie Jordan, secretary to Marshall Neilan; Nellie Bly Baker, secretary to Charlie Chaplin; and Gladys Rosson, secretary to Cecil B. DeMille. These secretaries/stenographers were also expected to double as "script clerks" (later known as script girls) after that position was introduced to filmmaking by Famous Players-Lasky in the teens.

Outside of the comedy and Western genres—and that is not to say that women were not prominent in comedies—women dominated the acting field during the Silent Era. They were preeminent in dramas and serials. They were also generally self-created by the film industry. Only a handful of major female stars from the stage enjoyed success on screen, whereas a larger number of male stage actors were successful. The new audiences, created by and for the motion picture, wanted new female stars; on the whole, they did not want existing stars from the legitimate stage. That the audiences were more interested in females is evidenced by the terms used to identify the earliest players. There is the "Kalem Girl," the "Vitagraph Girl," and the "Biograph Girl." Maurice Costello never achieved the prominence of Florence Turner and was, therefore, not dubbed the "Vitagraph Boy." There is no "Biograph Boy," despite Robert Harron's being perfectly suited to the title.

The greatest dramatic actresses of the silent screen were Lillian Gish (1893-1993) and Mae Marsh (1895-1968). They both entered films in 1912 and were both D. W. Griffith discoveries. Lillian Gish came close to surpassing her work with Griffith in later features after she left his company in 1921. Mae Marsh did not; her reputation must rest on her performances in *The Birth of a Nation* and *Intolerance*. But so great is the drama in those characterizations that her estimation is perfectly safe.

The only blatantly feminist screen actress of the decade was Olga Petrova (1884-1977)—described by *Photoplay* (October 1916) as "a patrician of the voiceless stage"—who was born Muriel Harding in England. She adopted not only a Continental name, but also a Continental accent when she arrived in the United States in 1912 to star in a William Harris and Jesse L. Lasky cabaret production at the Follies Begere. She began her screen career in 1914 with *The Tigress,* directed by Alice Guy Blaché, who also directed her second feature, *The Heart of a Painted Woman,* in 1916. Madame Petrova starred in 26 features, all of which were stories of women with strong characters, strong minds, and strong abilities. In *The Light Within* (1918), for example, she plays a doctor of bacteriology who discovers a cure for meningitis and anthrax.

She told Frederick James Smith in *Motion Picture Classic* (September 1918) "I do want to bring a message to women—a message of encouragement. The only women I want to play are women who *do* things. I want to encourage women to do things —to take their rightful place in life."

After retiring from the screen, Petrova wrote a 1922 play, *Hurricane,* advocating birth control; later, she published her autobiography, *Butter with My Bread.* "What is little? What is great?" she wrote. "Let me put it this way, I did achieve what I set out as a child to get, my own bread, my own butter, my own house in which to enjoy it. That—to me— is the height of what I will accept and acknowledge as greatness."[6]

If Lillian Gish and Mae Marsh are the greatest dramatic actresses and Olga Petrova the first feminist actress created by the silent screen, then its first great personality was Mary Pickford (1893-1979). Born Gladys Smith in Canada, Mary Pickford entered films with D. W. Griffith in 1909 after David Belasco changed her name and starred her on stage in *The Warrens of Virginia.* Pickford quickly rebelled against Griffith s dictatorial methods and insisted on adopting a natural style of acting for the screen, a style that became one of her many trademarks.

If the silent era is considered the age of innocence (which it surely was not), then no other actress symbolizes that imagined age more than Mary Pickford. She was "America's Sweetheart," a title bestowed on her not by some Hollywood publicist, but, as she once pointed out, by the American people. To state that Pickford was the silent screen's greatest personality is a minor claim; she was much more. By 1917, she was recognized as the most famous woman in the world. Although she might have been loathe to acknowledge the feminist movement as such, there is little question that the strong characters she portrayed and the power that this actress wielded did much to help the cause of women universally.

The Pickford curls were possibly her best-known feature and were crucial to her portrayals of little girls in the teen years in films such as *Poor Little Peppina* (1916), *The Poor Little Rich Girl* (1917), *A Little Princess* (1917), and *Amarilly of Clothes-Line Alley* (1918). When, eventually, she cut her curls and bobbed her hair in the mid-twenties, so powerful was the Pickford persona that she gave an immediate legitimacy to a hairstyle synonymous with the "Flapper" era.

In features such as *Rebecca of Sunnybrook Farm* (1917), *Daddy Long-Legs* (1919) and *Pollyanna* (1920), Mary Pickford was sweetness personified. Yet there was much more to her life and to her screen personality. If her characters were sweet, they were also tough, and if necessary (as witness her 1926 feature, *Sparrows*), they could be quite ruthless. Similarly, as a businesswoman, Mary Pickford was both tough and ferocious, with an intelligence and negotiating skill equal to those of any of her male counterparts. A businessman such as Adolph Zukor might recognize his coup in 1913 in signing Pickford to a starring contract, but within two years, she was the greatest asset of his company. She dictated the terms of her contract to him, and she raised the salaries that film stars might demand to dizzy heights.

When Pickford's salary became so large that it was difficult for a producer to garner an adequate return on his investment, she became her own producer. With D. W. Griffith, Douglas Fairbanks, and Charlie Chaplin, she created United Artists in 1919. The fact that she was the only women in the quartet, together with the prominence of her partners in film history, clearly indicates Mary Pickford's true importance to the cinema. She was the only woman in the industry to control her own production company, her own studio, and her own distribution setup.

In private life, Miss Pickford's early years were dominated by her mother, Charlotte. Against her mother's advice, she married fellow actor Owen Moore in 1911. In 1920, she divorced Moore and married the most important dramatic actor of the silent screen, Douglas Fairbanks. The two reigned as King and Queen of Hollywood at their Beverly Hills home of Pickfair, where they entertained leading figures from the worlds of literature, show business, politics, and the arts. As Fairbanks' career declined, so did the marriage, but the couple found time to star together in one feature, a 1929 adaptation of Shakespeare's *The Taming of the Shrew.* Eventually, Pickford divorced Fairbanks and married for a third and final time; her last husband was Charles "Buddy" Rogers, her leading man in the 1927 comedy *My Best Girl.*[7]

Screenwriting was another area dominated by women. In the early teens, Mary H. O'Connor and Beta Breuil were story editors at Vitagraph, with Hettie Gray Baker and Louella Parsons holding similar positions with Bosworth and Essanay, respectively. Eleanor Gates formed her own production company in 1914 to film some of the short stories that she had written for the *Saturday Evening Post.*

Gene Gauntier (1891-1966) joined Kalem in 1907 and worked there not only as the company's leading lady, but also as its only scriptwriter for many years. Her adaptations included everything from Civil War dramas to domestic comedies, from *Ben-Hur* to the Bible (*From the Manger to the Cross*). She also wrote and directed a 1910 one-reel film, *Grandmother,* and when she left Kalem in 1912, she founded her own company, Gene Gauntier Feature Players.

Anita Loos (1893-1981) began her career by selling scripts to the American Biograph Company, starting with *The New York Hat* (1912), which D. W. Griffith directed and which featured Mary Pickford. She began a successful writing partnership in 1916 with John Emerson, whom she married in 1919 and whom, unfortunately, she tended to malign unfairly in published autobiographical works. She wrote some subtitles for *Intolerance,* probably the humorous ones relating to Constance Talmadge as the Mountain Girl, and made her mark with a group of teens scripts for Douglas Fairbanks. Her fame has not diminished, thanks to her self-promotion and the many revivals of adaptations of her 1925 novel, *Gentlemen Prefer Blondes.*[8]

A number of major screenwriters entered films in the late teens. Lenore J. Coffee (1896-1983) began her illustrious career by simply submitting a script to actress Clara Kimball Young, who was complaining that she was in need of a good one. Sonya Levien (1888-1960) wrote her first script, *Who Will Marry Me?*, in 1919. Jane Murfin (1893-1955) also began her screen career in 1919 after an earlier career as a Broadway playwright; she successfully combined scriptwriting with producing in the twenties. June Mathis (1892-1927) gained prominence with her screen adaptation of *The Four Horsemen of the Apocalypse* (1921), which made Valentino a star; but she had written more than eighty scripts prior to that, beginning her career in 1916. Two screen writers associated with Cecil B. DeMille in the teens were Jeanie MacPherson and Beulah Marie Dix. Other prominent female screenwriters of the era include Bess Meredyth, Oiuda Bergere, Olga Printzlau, Clara Beranger, Margaret Turnbull, Eve Unsell, Marion Fairfax, and Sada Cowan. "All of them normal, regular women," noted *Photoplay* (August 1923). "Not temperamental 'artistes,' not short-haired advanced feminists, not fadists. Just regular women of good education and adaptability who have caught the trick of writing and understand the picture mind." The article continued, "The field of scenario writing is unique in its possibilities for women." The article added that the average weekly wage of the more prominent female screenwriters was between $500 and $1,000.[9]

Cutting or editing may not have been the most exciting or adventuresome career in the early silent years, but it was a field that appealed mainly to women. Typical of such cutters was Katherine Eggleston of the Mutual Film Corporation. According to *The Moving Picture World* (December 20, 1913), she "views the different scenes of the picture after it is completed and arranges them with an eye to clearness of story-construction and dramatic value, establishing sequence and ridding the picture of all that does not contribute to its effectiveness."

One of the best known and highly regarded film editors, Margaret Booth, began her career as an assistant cutter with D. W. Griffith while he was making *Orphans of the Storm*. From Griffith, she went to the Paramount Laboratories, but did not begin to make a name for herself until the mid-twenties, when she joined Metro-Goldwyn-Mayer, where she remained until 1968.

The actors, the screenwriters, and the cutters—it was from these ranks that America's first women film directors emerged after the way was paved by a French woman named Alice Guy.[10]

A unique individual, Alice Guy (1875-1968) was not only the screen's first woman director, but she also was one of the medium's earliest-known directors of either sex. A secretary to French film pioneer Léon Gaumont when he was still primarily in the photographic business, Alice Guy was appointed Gaumont's first director in 1896, with the explicit understanding with her boss that directorial duties should not interfere with secretarial chores. From her first film, *La fée aux choux / The Cabbage Fairy,* in 1896, through 1907, Alice Guy directed more than 400 films for Gaumont, including more than 100 sound-on-cylinder productions using Gaumont's Chronophone invention. Her secretarial duties were long forgotten by both Guy and Gaumont.

In 1907, Alice Guy married an Englishman named Herbert Blaché and, that same year, accompanied him to the United States where he opened a New York City office for Gaumont. Between 1907 and 1910, Alice Guy Blaché devoted herself to supporting her husband's work and raising a daughter. In September 1910, she returned to film production with the establishment of the Solax Company, where she served as president and director-in-chief, directing or supervising the production of some 332 films.[11]

She allowed Solax to fold in 1913 when she joined forces with her husband in the formation of Blaché Features. In that Herbert

Blaché had become jealous of his wife's success and began stroking his own ego with the creation of a company bearing his name, this was a bad move for Alice Guy. During the remainder of the decade, she directed more than twenty features, initially for Blaché and then for other producers, but she was constantly laboring in her husband's shadow, despite having the greater talent. Alice Guy Blaché's directorial career ended in 1920; two years later, she divorced her husband and returned to France, never again to work in films.

Her career is important not only in terms of the quantity of films that she produced—she made more short subjects than D. W. Griffith—but also in the publicity that she received, which led to the establishment of a place for women as directors. "She is doing successfully what men are trying to do," noted a 1912 fan magazine writer. "She is succeeding in a line of work in which hundreds of men have failed." [12]

Alice Guy was also very much aware of the role that she was playing. In 1914, she published an important article on "Woman's Place in Photoplay Production," writing in part:

It has long been a source of wonder to me that many women have not seized upon the wonderful opportunities offered to them by the motion-picture art to make their way to fame and fortune as producers of photodramas. Of all the arts there is probably none in which they can make such splendid use of talents so much more natural to a woman than to a man and so necessary to its perfection.

There is no doubt in my mind that a woman's success in many lines of endeavor is still made very difficult by a strong prejudice against one of her sex doing work that has been done only by men for hundreds of years. Of course this prejudice is fast disappearing, and there are many vocations in which it has not been present for a long time. In the arts of acting, music, painting, and literature, woman has long held her place among the most successful workers, and when it is considered how vitally all of these arts enter into the production of motion pictures, one wonders why the names of scores of women are not found among the successful creators of photodrama offerings.[13]

The films of Alice Guy Blaché indicate the versatility of subject matter that a woman director could handle. There is not a genre of the era that she did not tackle. The length of her career—some 24 years—illustrates that she moved with the times and adapted her directorial techniques to changes within the industry. Although her films are certainly not on a par with those of D. W. Griffith, they are the equal of those made by most male directors in the teens.[14]

America s first native-born woman director, Lois Weber (1881-1939), used the motion picture in much the same way as D. W. Griffith to present her personal philosophy on a variety of subjects. She was one of the first committed filmmakers, male or female, who saw the possibility of advocating social change through the cinema. Among the topics with which she dealt in her films are racial prejudice, in *The Jew's Christmas* (1913); the power of positive thought over disease, in *The Leper's Coat* (1914); Christian Science in *Jewel* (1915) and *A Chapter in her Life* (1923); political corruption and religious hypocrisy in *Hypocrites* (1915); opposition to abortion in *Where Are My Children?* (1916); the right of women to birth control in *The Hand That Rocks the Cradle* (1917); opposition to capital punishment in *The People vs. John Doe* (1916); and the inadequacy of teachers salaries in *The Blot* (1921).

Her efforts were not always appreciated. "The world is sad enough without anyone's writing photoplays to make it sadder," wrote *The New York Dramatic Mirror* (November 17, 1917) of Lois Weber's work. In June 1918, *Theater Magazine* editorialized against Weber's use of exploitive titles, demanding to know, "When will the public, without any volition, other than its inherent sense of decency, protest against the producer whose product is introduced to them by means of indecent, suggestive titles?"

Like Alice Guy Blaché, Lois Weber lived and worked in the shadow of her husband; but in Weber's case, the husband, Phillips Smalley (who also acted in the couple's films and elsewhere), did not seek the limelight. As far as can be ascertained, Lois Weber simply needed the assurance of her husband's presence and was happy to give him associate directing credit in return.

Also like Alice Guy Blaché, Lois Weber directed and starred in sound-on-cylinder films for the Gaumont Company before joining Edwin S. Porter's Rex Company in 1909. Here, she and Smalley wrote, directed, edited, and starred in the company's releases. When Rex became part of Universal in 1912, the couple went with it.

Aside from a short period with Bosworth from 1914-1915, Lois Weber remained with Universal until 1919, becoming its most important director. She directed Anna Pavlova in *The Dumb Girl of Portici* (1916) and was hailed by the dancer as "the greatest woman producer in the world." [15]

In 1919, Weber formed her own company, Lois Weber Productions, with her own studio at 4634 Santa Monica Boulevard in Hollywood. She directed five features, beginning with *To Please One Woman* (1920), but on the whole, the venture was not a commercial success. Weber's talent faltered as her marriage came apart in the early twenties. She was still, however, subject to considerable press attention and admiration, as evidenced by the following "story" in the *Los Angeles Herald* (February 21, 1921).

Although this photoplay artist is never seen on the screen, she—

Writes her own photoplays.

Puts them in story form.

Chooses and contracts her own players.

Operates a Bell-Howell camera on many of her scenes, and Plans her own lighting effects.

Bosses her own property "gallery."

Sometimes "shoots" with a still camera.

Plunges occasionally into chemicals in her developing laboratory.

Writes her own titles, inserts, prologues.

Knows how to operate a printing machine.

Is her own film cutter, "splicer" and editor.

Plans her own publicity and advertising campaigns for her finished pictures.

Is her own business manager and signs all her checks.

Owns her own studio.

Was the first to "work" her players to the strains of an orchestra.

Was the first woman in filmdom to get $2500 a week (and that was years ago).

"Discovered" Mary McLaren, Mildred Harris, Lois Wilson, Claire Windsor, Priscilla Dean and a half dozen other "stars."

Believes that "the play's the thing" and not the players.

Does her own cooking and raises her own vegetables.

Knows every branch of film business from actual experience as player, director and business manager.

Supervises the marketing and distribution of her photoplays.

Is financially independent of the movie magnates.

Does a man's work, but has never marched in a suffragist parade.

Has made nearly 100 photoplays.

Was one of the first five actresses to leave the speaking stage for picture work.

Who is she?

She is Lois Weber, qualified voter.

Between 1921 and 1926, Lois Weber made no films, but in the latter year, she married Captain Harry Ganz and revived her career with the direction of *The Marriage Clause* (1926), *Sensation Seekers* (1927), and *The Angel of Broadway* (1927). She made one last feature, her only talkie, *White Heat,* released in 1934.

Something of an enigma in the study of women in film because she did not espouse any feminist causes and was strongly antiabortion, Lois Weber, nevertheless, remains a major figure in film history.

Curiously, Universal was the one studio where women directors were most active in the teen years. At one time, Carl Laemmle had a total of nine of them under contract, most raised from the ranks of his writers, editors, or actresses. In the last group were Cleo Madison, Ruth Stonehouse, Lule Warrenton, and Grace Cunard. Elsie Jane Wilson followed her husband, Rupert Julian, as a director at Universal in 1917. From the ranks of the screenwriters came Ruth Ann Baldwin (who was also an editor), Jeanie MacPherson, and Ida May Park. Miss Park, married to director Joseph De Grasse, is probably the most important in this group. She began her directing career in 1917 with *The Flashlight Girl* and directed Universal's most important dramatic star, Dorothy Phillips, in *Fire of Rebellion* (1917) and *The Grand Passion* (1918). Interestingly, she contributed a chapter on film directing to a 1920 volume on *Careers for Women.*[16]

Outside of Universal, there were a number of women in the teens who directed the odd feature. As already noted, Gene Gauntier directed one film in 1910. At Selig, actress Kathlyn Williams directed, wrote, and starred in a 1912 two-reeler, *The Leopard's*

Foundling. Mabel Normand directed a number of comedy shorts at Keystone, including several starring Chaplin. Lillian Gish directed one feature, *Remodeling Her Husband*, starring sister Dorothy and released in 1920. In 1916, screenwriter Julia Crawford Ivers directed *The Call of the Cumberland* for Pallas. The second Mrs. Sidney Drew, Lucille McVey, appears to have been responsible for the construction of many of the couples' comedies at Vitagraph and Metro and continued as a director after her husband's death in 1919.

Frances Marion (1890-1973) was a screenwriter generally noted for her prolific output and the trite nature of many of her scripts, quite a few of which seem to have been plagiarized from other sources. She was active in films from the early teens and also directed three features: *Just Around the Corner* (1921), *The Love Light* (1921), and *The Song of Love* (1923). *The Love Light,* filmed in 1920, is of most interest because its leading lady is Mary Pickford, with whom Marion had first worked as an actress in 1915 and for whom she wrote many screenplays. As a Mary Pickford vehicle, it is one of the actress's weaker films, but as a piece of filmmaking, it cannot be faulted.

Vitagraph's scenario department head, Marguerite Bertsch, directed a handful of films for the company in 1916 and 1917. Also at Vitagraph, actress Helen Gardner co-directed *The Still, Small Voice* in 1915, and in 1921, Lillian Chester (billed as Mrs. George Randolph Chester) directed *The Son of Wallingford*. Nell Shipman worked as an actress and writer at Vitagraph in the teens and later directed and starred in a number of features. Margery Wilson, who played "Brown Eyes" in *Intolerance* and was William S. Hart's leading lady in five features, turned to directing in 1920 with *That Something* and directed two further features in the twenties.

She did not make the grade as a director, but at least one Lasky contract player, Camille Astor, was promoted to assistant director in 1916 on the feature *The Sowers*.

With the suffragette movement and acceptance of women as directors, it was natural that at least one feminist film company be formed. Funded by local Los Angeles society women, the American Woman Film Company was formed in May, 1917. That same month, an automobile accident injured 24 members of the company while on location at Chatsworth, and the American Woman Film Company failed to produce a single film.[17]

"We are here, sisters, and we're so stubborn that we're going to make our mark," wrote Myrtle Gebhart in 1923.[18] Quite obviously, many women in the film industry already had done that.

Notes

1. This theory was initially advanced to me by Eileen Bowser, former curator of the Film Department of the Museum of Modern Art.

2. "Great Field for Women," *The New York Dramatic Mirror* (February 10, 1917), p. 24.

3. C. S. Sewell, "Reviewing Pictures," *The Moving Picture World* (March 26, 1927), p. 324.

4. "The First Camera-Maid," *Photoplay* (February 1920), p. 80.

5. Lois Hutchinson, "A Stenographer's Chance in Pictures," *Photoplay* (March 1923), pp. 42-43, 107.

6. Letter to Anthony Slide, 1972.

7. Mary Pickford's biography, *Sunshine and Shadow*, was published by Doubleday in 1955. A good double biography is Booton Herndon, *Mary Pickford and Douglas Fairbanks* (New York: W. W. Norton, 1977).

8. Anita Loos' autobiography, *A Girl Like I*, was published by the Viking Press in 1966.

9. "How Twelve Famous Women Scenario Writers Succeeded," *Photoplay* (August 1923), pp. 31-33.

10. The remainder of this chapter is a summary of material from Anthony Slide, *Early Women Directors* (reprint : Da Capo Press, 1984).

11. Only a handful of Solax films have survived; the majority of those are preserved at the Library of Congress.

12. H. Z. Levine, "Madame Alice Blaché," *Photoplay*, Vol. II, No. 2 (March 1912), pp. 37-38.

13. Alice Guy Blaché, "Woman s Place in Photoplay Production," *The Moving Picture World* (July 11, 1914), p. 195.

14. For more information, see *The Memoirs of Alice Guy Blaché,* trans. Roberta and Simone Blaché, edited by Anthony Slide (Metuchen, NJ: Scarecrow Press, 1986).

15. H. H. Van Loan, "Lois the Wizard," *Motion Picture Magazine,* Vol. XI, No. 6 (July 1916), p. 41.

16. Filene, Catherine, ed., *Careers for Women* (Boston: Houghton Mifflin, 1920.)

17. For more information, see "Women Start Something," *The Moving Picture World* (May 27, 1916), p. 1515; and "Twenty-Four Film Actors in Wreck," *The Moving Picture World* (June 17, 1916), p. 2037.

18. "Myrtle Gebhart, Business Women in Film Studios," *The Business Woman,* Vol. II, No. 2 (December 1923), p. 68.

10

New Technologies

While certain crucial matters connected to the technical development of the motion picture, such as the 35mm standard width film, were determined at its birth, a number of innovations took place during the next twenty years. Some were tried and dismissed as irrelevant. Others were put to one side for use much later in the cinema's history. Most helped the successful growth of the motion picture, even if their introduction was not always noticed by the filmgoing public.

The 35mm film width was determined by W. K. L. Dickson and George Eastman in 1889. Panchromatic film was not introduced until 1913 and not manufactured by Eastman-Kodak on a regular basis until 1923. In the late 1880s, a standard was set for four equidistant perforations to each frame of film. This standard was adopted for the Lumière camera, patented in 1895, and the Mutograph camera, created by Herman Casler and W. K. L. Dickson for the American Mutoscope and Biograph Company in 1899. The latter used the same design principles as an earlier camera that used film of 68mm width.

The most popular camera throughout the world up to the First World War was the Pathé camera, similar in principle to the Lumière invention. Billy Bitzer and Karl Brown used Pathé cameras to film both *The Birth of a Nation* and *Intolerance*. The Pathé camera was superseded by a Bell & Howell camera introduced in 1912 and modified in 1921. Bell & Howell, founded in Chicago in 1907, introduced the first gauge for perforating film accurately, an important piece of machinery that helped establish the company as a

leading manufacturer of film-related equipment. The Bell & Howell camera was, in turn, replaced by the Mitchell camera, first used
in 1920 by Charles Rosher to film Mary Pickford in *The Love Light*.

An examination of early films reveals that many companies
used one make of camera to photograph exterior scenes and another
to photograph interiors. Because of a lack of uniformity when film
from the two cameras was spliced together, the frame line would
change at the splice. As a result, individual projectionists had to
readjust the framing at each scene change.

As early as 1908, it was usual to time each scene at rehearsals
in advance of actual filming. The seconds were converted to feet—
one second was the equivalent of one foot of film by 1914, thus
indicating that the average film from that period should be projected
at sixteen frames per second, as opposed to 24 frames per second
for late silent and early sound films. The footage or the number of
seconds per scene was noted on the script and, at the end of each
take, the director confirmed with the cameraman that the scene had,
indeed, run its allotted number of feet of film.

Because projectors were hand-cranked, operators could speed
up or slow down a film, regardless of the producer's intentions. The
faster each reel of film was cranked, the more shows a day an
exhibitor could offer and so increase his revenues. Similarly, at the
last show of the day, the projectionist might speed up the cranking
to get the program over as quickly as possible in order to leave early.
In an effort to prevent this practice, many producers began indicating on the film leader or on the musical cue sheets accompanying
the film the correct speed at which the production should be
screened. There is no evidence that projectionists paid any attention
to these instructions.

There was little art to projecting. At most nickelodeons, the film
ran off the projector not onto a take-up reel, but into a bucket. Often,
as the projectionist cranked with one hand, he could be holding a
newspaper that he was reading in the other.

There were, of course, producers who took exceptional care
with the presentations of their works. D. W. Griffith is an obvious
example, often visiting the projection room immediately after a
screening and re-editing his films even after their release. For the
1919 premiere of *Broken Blossoms,* he devised a presentation that
included a one-act prologue, "The Dance of Life and Death"

(written by the director) and an elaborate lighting system that threw colored lights on the screen as the film was projected.

Griffith's "Method and Apparatus for Projecting Moving and Other Pictures with Color Effects" was granted Patent No. 1,334,853 by the United States Patent Office on March 23, 1920. As a result of these lighting effects, according to *Exhibitor's Trade Review* (April 17, 1920):

> The scenes seemed bathed in a vibrant mauve, while the inner core of the picture itself shimmered with salmon pink. The symbolic blue of the Orient lighted the Chinese scenes, and gave atmosphere to the portions of the story wherein the Chinaman figured. Words cannot do justice to the photographic effects, many of which were like beautiful moving canvasses colored by an impressionistic touch.

Outside of the mainstream of filmmaking, the motion picture was refined for specialized use. Stereoscopic or three-dimensional films were screened at the Astor Theater in New York City, on June 10, 1915. Three reels of film, including footage of actress Marie Doro and of Niagara Falls, were presented by Edwin S. Porter and W. E. Waddell and watched by an invited audience looking through red and green glasses. Portending a criticism applicable to 3-D films throughout their history, critic Lynde Denig in *The Moving Picture World* (June 26, 1915) commented, "the task of holding cardboard glasses in place for half an hour at a stretch is not altogether comfortable."

Research into 16mm for home use began at Eastman Kodak in 1914, but the gauge was not introduced until 1923. In France, 28mm home movie film was introduced by Pathé for use in its Pathé K-O-K projectors in 1912 and brought over to the United States the following year for use in its Pathescope projectors. In 1913, Edison introduced the Home Kinetoscope Projector, which used three parallel rows of film that were a total of 32mm in width. The film for all these gauges was acetate-based safety film, unlike the highly inflammable nitrate film used for professional filmmaking and presentation until 1950.

In the field of medicine, motion pictures of surgical operations, for which special lighting was required, were first taken at Britain's University of Birmingham in 1902. On January 4, 1908, film of an operation performed in France was first shown to American students at the Chicago Night University. New York City hospitals began using films to teach students later that same year, and by 1910, the motion picture was accepted as a means of demonstrating surgical procedures.[1]

News footage, both genuine and faked, is as old as the cinema itself. Some of the first films were actuality subjects, forerunners of America's earliest newsreel, *Pathé's Weekly,* the first issue of which was released on August 8, 1911. It was followed by *Vitagraph Monthly of Current Events* (first seen in 1911), *The Gaumont Animated Weekly* (first seen in 1912), *The Mutual Weekly* (first seen in 1912), *Hearst-Selig News Pictorial* (first seen in 1914), *Kinograms* (first seen in 1919), and *Fox News* (first seen in 1919). World War I was the first major conflict brought first-hand to the American people through the efforts of newsreel cameramen and the staff of the United States Army Signal Corps.[2]

The earliest films were shot in what was little more than a roofless shed open on one side. The enclosed sides were used to support the primitive sets and as protection against the weather, while the camera was placed opposite the open side. Both the shed and the camera were mounted on a common movable platform so that the open side could always face the sun.

One industry expression that dates from the preteens is the "lot," in reference to the film studio. It originated when films were shot in the open-air on vacant property lots rented by producers. These open-air stages used reflectors and diffusors to control natural sunlight. Diffusors were strips of white cloth hanging on wires stretched across the stage. Depending upon the effect called for by the script, the director, or the cameraman, the diffusors could be moved back and forth.

Because there was no night shooting on open stages, night scenes were tinted blue in the finished film. Balboa's scenario editor, Clifford Howard, recalled:

> Technically this particular tinting was known as "moonlight"; and a part of a scenario writer's training was to remember to append the notation "Moonlight" to every scene in his script in which the action was required to take place supposedly in the dark, whether in a storm out on the plains or in the quiet depths

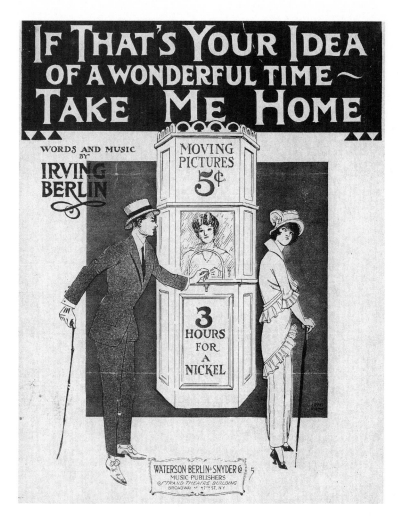

A 1914 Irving Berlin song indicates the contempt in which the motion picture was held.

WHEN A FELLER NEEDS A FRIEND

While a cartoon from the *Chicago Tribune* of 1913 illustrates the universal popularity of the motion picture and its stars.

of a dungeon. For lamplight effect the scenarist wrote "Amber";
and the laboratory man would tint the film accordingly.[3]

Glass-enclosed studios were introduced as early as 1910. *The
Moving Picture World* (December 31, 1910) compared the sunlight
streaming through the glass studios to the heat from a "battery of
steam radiators." These studios were constructed of steel frames
with both the roof and the upper sides made of continuous glass
paneling. Night scenes could now be filmed at such studios using
either electric arcs or mercury vapor lamps. The latter, with their
green lights, were considered the better choice, both from an
economical and a creative viewpoint.

Cooper-Hewitt mercury tube lighting was used at the American
Biograph Company as early as 1905. Some of the earliest studio
lighting equipment was manufactured by the New York City-based
Kliegl Bros., whose lights became known as Klieg lights.

Universal built its first indoor studio (a converted garage) in
1915 when unseasonably wet weather slowed production on the
serial *The Master Key*. The company acquired all of the available
studio lighting in Los Angeles, consisting of five Kleig side arcs
and one 35-amp spotlight, and imported twenty banks of Cooper-
Hewitt lights from New York City. The Winfield-Kerner Company
studio lamp was introduced in the spring of 1915 and was the most
popular form of studio lighting until 1918, when the Sunlight Arc
Company introduced the Sun Arc. Harry D. Brown noted in 1926.

> From 500 to 1000 kilowatts are used on the average interior
> set today, and as much as 5000 have been used on others. From
> an approximate total of 30 kilowatts back in 1914—used by all
> the studios—the Hollywood film industry today has a capacity
> for approximately 30,000.[4]

Initially considered exclusively the cinematographer's domain,
lighting gradually became equally part of the art director's function.
In 1924, art director Wiard B. Ihnen and D. W. Atwater of the
Westinghouse Lamp Company wrote:

> Lighting is the very essence of the motion picture. Figura-
> tively, it is the palette of the art director and occupies the same
> relation as pigment does in a painting. It is the medium. It might

be argued that action is the medium of the movie, but if the analogy of the painting is followed out, action is the subject matter expressed in terms of light. Light should be one of the first thoughts in visualizing a scene. It is just as important as the actor and, in fact, sometimes it takes the place of the actor. It is often possible to heighten the dramatic value of the scene by suggesting the actors with a play of light rather than by actually showing them.[5]

Art directors as such were first used on films in the early teens. They were designated "technical directors" because they were part of the technical crew, expected not only to prepare blueprints of the sets, but also to find the necessary props or set dressings, and often design and rent appropriate costumes. Not until the twenties was the art director so described with his activities divorced from those of the set dresser and the costume designer. At least one art director, Harold Grieve, quit the industry because he felt that his job should entail all three activities.

The following commentary from a 1914 volume on film production provides a succinct description of what later came under the art director's jurisdiction, but was then closely supervised by the director.

On the receipt of the scenario, the producer, or director as he is sometimes called, makes such additions as he thinks necessary, and notes the details of the scenes and properties required for the play. After the lists of scenes and properties have been made, orders are given to the scenic and property departments for the making of the various sets. Costumes are selected and in the case of an outdoor scene, the producer determines on the proper locality for the action.[6]

The man generally acknowledged to be the screen's first art director was Wilfred Buckland (1866-1946), who was associated with the great theatrical producer David Belasco for many years. A friend of the de Mille family, Buckland was brought to Los Angeles by Cecil B. DeMille to work on *The Squaw Man* in 1913. From that year through 1920, he worked not only on DeMille features, but also on virtually all of the films from the Jesse L. Lasky Feature Play Company and, later, the Famous Players-Lasky amalgamation. He was largely responsible for the general use of indoor lighting through the importation of Klieg lights from the New York City stage. He helped expand the relationship between the director and the art director and proved that the latter is as much responsible for the look of the film as any other member of the company.

Many of Buckland's sets have an artificial theatricality to them, a result of his stage training. It is also probably no coincidence that both Belasco and DeMille were showmen in the old-fashioned theatrical sense. The outrageous DeMille sets created by Buckland, such as those for *Male and Female* (1919), are far divorced from twentieth century reality, having their origins in the theater of Victorian melodrama. Despite such criticism, however, there is a tremendous scope to Buckland's work—from the simple sets that relied on lighting and shadows for effect, as in *The Cheat* (1915), to the towering pseudo-French settings for *Joan the Woman* (1916).

Buckland's last major contribution to films was the castle setting for Douglas Fairbanks' 1922 production of *Robin Hood*. Buckland's end was particularly tragic. At the age of eighty and fearing that his own death was near, he shot and killed his mentally retarded son, a former patient at the Camarillo State Hospital for the Insane, and then turned the gun on himself. "I am taking Billy with me," he wrote in a note to his executor, Cecil's brother and fellow director William de Mille.

In 1922, Buckland set the groundwork for the way in which the work of the art director could expand.

> One of the greatest faults in our methods of studio production is the fact that we usually overburden the art director by turning him into an architectural draughtsman who grinds out some sketches for picture after picture, often handling as many as eight or 10 productions at once. It is only by permitting the art director to concentrate his energies and thoughts entirely upon a single production at a time that he can give his best to it and can conduct experiments. . . . And it is only thus that we will progress along artistic lines in our films, outside of the acting itself.
>
> Another step that will ensure every progress will come when the cinematographer and the art director realize the necessity for their closest collaboration, not only during the actual filming of a picture, but in advance preparations in the building of sets,

placing of lights and planning of composition effects. Not only can they thus obtain results that will be novel and pleasing but also they will prove to heighten the dramatic values of the photoplay and force the attention on the high lights of the story itself.[7]

The most magnificent set created by an art director in the teens is certainly the Babylonian set for *Intolerance,* the work of Walter L. Hall. Working from Hall's blueprints and sketches, the set was constructed under the supervision of Huck Wortman.[8]

A highly stylized art director, whose American career began in 1914 with *The Dollar Mark,* Ben Carré (1883-1978) entered films with the French Gaumont Company in 1907. He worked in close collaboration with Maurice Tourneur (1873-1961) and was responsible for the imaginative fairy tale sets of such films as *The Blue Bird* and *Prunella* (both from 1918) for which the director was noted.[9]

The general policy regarding costuming during the teens was that actors and actresses were required to provide their own clothing for contemporary stories and that producers would furnish period clothing. Virtually all of the major studios operated wardrobe departments, and Western Costume first began supplying necessary period attire in the early teens. Legend has it that William S. Hart was Western Costume's first customer.

Kathlyn Williams, who was regarded as one of the best-dressed actresses of the screen, noted that performers had to expect to pay as much as three times the cost of a stage wardrobe because films had more scenes and, subsequently, more costume changes. Mary Pickford recalled, "We used to save our old clothes for the pictures. Any old thing would do. I knew a leading woman when I first went into pictures who used to change her dress carefully when she came down to the studio, donning her second-best clothes even if she was playing the part of a millionaire's wife."[10]

Having to provide one's own clothing could result in serious problems for an actress, as Blanche Sweet recalled in connection with the 1914 D. W. Griffith feature *The Escape.*

Mae Marsh and I are in old, dilapidated clothes, and we had gone and picked them out—not at a thrift shop, nothing as good as a thrift shop, but something worse. I had a temperature and I didn't know what I was doing half the time, and my grandmother called the doctor. The doctor came—and scarlet fever! I don't know where you get scarlet fever, but it was evidently the old clothes I had on.[11]

With most creative editing done in the camera, the task of cutting room workers was simply a matter of joining pieces of film together. Designated as "cutters" rather than editors, their work received almost negligible attention during much of the Silent Era. The tools of their trade were a pair of rewind arms, a pair of scissors, and a primitive viewing device; the standard piece of editing equipment, the moviola, did not come into use until 1924. With no machinery to help splice film together, cutters scraped the edge of the frame, applied cement by hand, and then held the two pieces of film together, again by hand, until they bonded.

Early editors were not confined to the editing rooms in the teens but were often expected to be on the sets, watching films being shot in order to obtain a first-hand knowledge of the scenes that they were going to have to cut. They also served as glorified script girls. In 1918, *Photoplay* named the most prominent cutters as Frank Lawrence, formerly of Vitagraph and then with Universal, Arthur Ripley of Fox,[12] Del Andrews of Triangle, Billy Shea of the Fairbanks company, Anne Bauchens with Lasky, and James and Rose Smith with D. W. Griffith.[13]

James and Rose Smith worked with Griffith from his entry into directing at the Biograph Company. James, or Jimmie, Smith attended St. Joseph's Parochial School with Robert Harron, and the two boys joined Biograph together—Harron as a messenger boy and Smith as a shipping clerk. Rose Smith worked at Gaumont and Eclair in New York City before joining Biograph. The couple married in 1916 while cutting *Intolerance*.[14] To the Smiths may, perhaps, go the blame for the curious manner in which Griffith features are cut—with preceding medium or close shots repeating the action seen in the earlier long shots (or vice versa).

The power and emphasis that editing could accomplish were not discovered by an editor but by early film pioneers in the United Kingdom and Germany, and then by Edwin S. Porter in the United States, all of whom cut their own films. Later, Mack Sennett illustrated the use of editing for fast, comedic effect, while D. W. Griffith used editing to build dramatic tension.

Interestingly, as editing became a craft in its own right, those early pioneers who had introduced it to motion pictures failed to keep up with new techniques. While Griffith was moving the camera closer to his actors, Porter insisted on showing his players full body as late as 1913. The trade papers, which tended to be slow in accepting change, criticized the films of Griffith and others, but praised Porter. In an article titled "Too Near the Camera," *The Moving Picture World* (March 25, 1911) noted.

> The Rex releases are examples, to our mind, of the proper thing to do. Here Mr. Porter works on a large stage, and places his camera at a considerable distance from his actors. The result is that he avoids abnormality of size, and when you see the pictures on the screen, they express the proper sensuous impression of size.[15]

Ben Carré claimed to have been the first art director to add color to a set—in 1910—largely to help the actors create a mood. But color was added to the black-and-white of silent films much earlier, as far as the audiences were concerned, and it also was added for mood effect.

Tinting (the coloring of the entire frame) and toning (the changing of the black areas to a contrasting or harmonizing color) were staple, artificial devices used in silent films as an escape from black, white, and gray. In its basic form, it was used to color night scenes (which were shot in daylight) blue. But there were many other tints available with such romantic names as "peachblow," "verdante," or "caprice." The last, according to Eastman Kodak, was an "audacious magenta," symbolizing "the mood of fickleness, impulsive action, rash adventure." From a few standard tints in the early years, a total of sixteen were eventually offered by Eastman Kodak in the late twenties.

In the early years of the century, stencil coloring was introduced by Pathé under the name Pathécolor but not made accessible to American producers. Working at the Pathé laboratories in France, hundreds of women used pantographs to trace the outlines of each color section from an enlarged projected frame. The final result, after the dyes were spread over the film by using the stencils, was both impressive and gaudy.

The first major color system introduced to the motion picture was Kinemacolor, invented by Edward R. Turner and F. Marshall Lee. It was a two-color additive system involving photography through red-orange and blue-green filters with projection through the same colored filters at a speed of 32 frames per second. The process was first demonstrated in London on May 1, 1908, and quickly acquired for exploitation by the American-born Charles Urban (1867-1942).

Urban is one of those little-known figures in film history whose career is quite fascinating. He came to London to manage the local office of Edison's agents and, in 1898, founded the Warwick Trading Company, which distributed the films of Britain's earliest pioneers, including G. A. Smith and James Williamson. He also developed a lightweight projector, the Urban Biograph, recognized as "the most efficient instrument of its class," according to the British trade paper *Cinema* (January 1, 1914). For many years, he also presented film programs as part of the music hall entertainment at London's Alhambra Theater and, in 1903, founded the Charles Urban Trading Company, sending cinematographers, notably Joseph Rosenthal, throughout the world to film actualities. With the demise of Kinemacolor, Urban returned to the United States, where he became involved in educational films in the late teens and also marketed a home movie projector, the Spirograph.

The Kinemacolor process was first screened publicly by Urban at London's Palace Theater on February 26, 1909, with the initial film showing a young cadet waving the Union Jack. In 1911, Urban was commanded by King George V to film the spectacular Durbar in Delhi, India, in Kinemacolor. The process was first seen in the United States at Madison Square Garden on December 11, 1909, and the following year, the Kinemacolor Company of America was created to exploit the new invention. In 1912, this company established a studio at 4500 Sunset Boulevard in Hollywood, a studio that later became known as the Fine Arts Studio, where D. W. Griffith filmed *The Birth of a Nation* and *Intolerance*. (Kinemacolor had announced plans to produce its own version of *The Clansman* there in 1913.) The company eventually ceased operations in 1915 without making any major contribution to film history.

Apart from the process not being in full color, Kinemacolor had a more mundane problem: viewers complained that the color hurt their eyes. The edges of images showed one color infringing upon another. "Nothing was quite in focus," commented director/screen-writer Victor Heerman.[16] In an effort to persuade audiences to the contrary, Felix Feist of the Kinemacolor Company insisted.

> Kinemacolor relieves the eyesight. It furnishes to pictures the colors of nature. Kinemacolor projection is new. Natural colors on the screen are so different from the ordinary pictures that the viewer wishes to see everything at once; to see if all the objects on the screen are really correctly colored. The result is that the eyes roam all over the screen instead of being focused on the action, as the patrons have learned to do with the black and white pictures.
>
> Try rolling your eyes around when looking at a bare wall in daylight and you'll get eyestrain without any trouble. When you go and see Kinemacolor don't try to see everything at once. Give your attention to the action of the picture, enjoy yourself, don't try to find an error in the coloring. The colors are all right, they are nature's colors, photographed as they actually appear; we do not add anything or take anything away, so they must be right.
>
> When people accustom themselves to looking at natural color moving pictures, as they did accustom themselves to look at black and white ones, this foolish idea of eyestrain will be forgotten, because it is a foolish idea.[17]

The Technicolor two-color process did not receive public recognition until 1922 with the release of *The Toll of the Sea*. It was another ten years before the three-color Technicolor process was demonstrated publicly with the release of the Walt Disney cartoon *Flowers and Trees*. However, Technicolor did produce one, almost experimental, feature in the teens, *The Gulf Between*, supervised in 1917 by C. A. Willat and starring Grace Darmond and Niles Welch. The process, invented by Dr. Herbert T. Kalmus (1881-1963), was then an additive one, similar in many ways to Kinemacolor. *The Gulf Between* was first screened at a private showing at New York City's Aeolian Hall on September 21, 1917. It was no great compliment when Peter Milne in *Motion Picture News* (October 6, 1917) called it "unquestionably the finest natural color picture ever produced."

Did contemporary audiences really care to see films in color rather than black-and-white? The answer appeared to be in the affirmative, although it was two decades later before color became an accepted part of screen entertainment. *The Moving Picture World* published an editorial on the subject that provides a valuable indication of the attitude of producers towards the topic.

Occasionally a reel is seen that is appropriately toned or tinted or both, and it is a relief to the eye and frequently brings applause to a picture that would have passed in silence if in cold black and white. We have heard manufacturers remark when this subject was mentioned that the people were already getting enough for their money. Rather a narrow-minded attitude, is it not?

Toning, of course, is a considerable added expense, as the photograph has to be developed in black and white, carefully washed and then treated with other chemicals which alter the color of the silver deposit; also the work has to be done by skilled labor. Tinting alone is both simple and inexpensive. Where both are used together and in colors appropriate to the subject the result is almost as satisfying as hand coloring or natural color photography. We have in mind some Great Northern subjects that were double toned and tinted, and the impression conveyed was that we were looking at the actual scene. The same can be said of some of the Gaumont scenic films and an occasional Eclair.

Pathé, of course, leads the world in artificial coloring, and some of their mechanically colored films d'art rival the hues of Kinemacolor, although, judging from the records of the patent office, we expect soon to see stencil colored films from an American manufacturer. But pigment coloring is of course vastly more expensive than toning and the latter suffices in most cases. Tinting is sometimes used as a cloak for poor photography but the photograph must be perfect if it is to be toned.

Of the American manufacturers, Selig, Edison and Vita-graph occasionally send out toned pictures, in some of which the various scenes were differently toned, appropriate to the subject. Lubin has also, lately, sent out some very fine toned and tinted subjects which have greatly helped to establish a new standard of quality for the Lubin product. Thanhouser, Nestor and others have shown that they have the knowledge and the facilities for this work and no doubt they have had pleasing comments from their customers when they, if seldom, departed from the black and white.[18]

The development of screenwriting during the silent era is the history of both the script and the subtitle. From a one-page affair read by the director to his actors prior to shooting in the preteens, the script developed into a sophisticated form by 1920, often indicating both action and appropriate subtitles in its pages. Subtitles similarly developed from sometimes ungrammatical, unwieldy descriptions, to pertinent signposts to the plot, often attractively and individually decorated.

A number of definitions are in order in any discussion of silent screenwriting. The first is the unhyphenated name "subtitle," the word most commonly used during the Silent Era to describe linking titles. They were never referred to as inter-titles but were sometimes called "captions," particularly in the twenties.

A script is and always has been precisely that. The word scenario was sometimes used in place of script, but it was not an acceptable term. A scenario was merely a plot outline or story written for the screen from which the script was produced. Indeed, at one point, the Copyright Office refused to permit copyrighting of scripts that were labelled scenarios on the basis that they were not completed dramatic compositions.[19]

Much misinformation has been disseminated regarding early producers not using scripts. The reality was that scripts were used, but they were not always provided to the players. Even D. W. Griffith, who supposedly made *The Birth of a Nation* and *Intolerance* without the aid of any paperwork, had a daily shooting script that he prepared the night before in collaboration with Frank E. Woods, but he did not share it with his players. They learned what was expected of them at rehearsals.

Mack Sennett and other slapstick comedy producers worked on a similar basis, but their scripts often gave only the basic outlines of the plot with notations for one comedian or another to perform various "bits of funny business" where appropriate to the action. Those humorous moments were conceived on the set, often on the spur of the moment, depending on what props or other devices were available to the actors.[20]

The distribution of early scripts was very much a matter of who needed to know. Until actors gained enough prominence to demand script approval, it was not considered necessary for actors to know too far in advance what the next film was to be.

Initially, directors or producers were responsible for reading submitted scripts and selecting and editing them for filming. As the work of the director expanded with the increasing length of films, production companies devised the idea of a scenario editor, sometimes referred to in the teens as a "critic." Roy McCardell is generally acknowledged to be the first in-house screenwriter. He was hired by the American Mutoscope and Biograph Company in 1898, but it was not until around 1908 or 1909 that staff writers became established at production companies, and even then producers remained willing to buy scripts submitted by freelance writers (and nonwriters). Players would often submit ideas for scripts as a means of supplementing their income, and if those ideas or scripts were not accepted by their own companies, they would offer them elsewhere. For example, when Mary Pickford was with American Biograph, she submitted scripts to the Selig Polyscope Company.

The field was wide open to anyone with ideas. Roundsman Daniel Fogarty (of New York City's 22nd Police Precinct) wrote an article in 1905 suggesting a film on the life of a New York City policeman and was immediately approached by F. F. Proctor's Enterprises, offering to put a "machine and an operator . . . at your service any time that you care to accept it." Police Commissioner William McAdoo was also happy with the notion of the New York City police being the subject of scripts.

> The picture idea is an admirable one, particularly if the case of Patrolman Enright was enacted, along with the chasing of the thief, the killing of Enright, the wounding of Patrolman Bachman and, finally, the capture of the thief. I believe also that the scene of a patrolman rescuing a man or woman from drowning would appeal very strongly to the public and show forcibly the courage and bravery of the men who make up this force.[21]

Early subtitles were numbered sequentially to help the cutter assemble the film. At first, subtitles with dialogue contained not only the quoted sentence, but also the name of the individual speaking the lines. Titles in foreign language productions were subject to criticism if producers failed to hire someone with an adequate knowledge of English to translate them. "The grammar was bad, but the spelling as a rule even worse," wrote W. Stephen Bush in *The Moving Picture World*.[22] Subtitles were also criticized for their use of slang expressions. In 1916, *The Moving Picture World* commented.

> If the reputable newspaper bars vulgar speech from its columns as a matter of good breeding and out of respect for its readers why cannot the producer of motion pictures keep the literature of the gutter out of the titles on his films? . . . The language of our titles ought to be clean and decently grammatical.[23]

The early subtitle was basic in its simplicity. Modern audiences often have difficulty in following early one-reel productions because of a lack of descriptive subtitles, but today's audiences are not used to this medium. "People get used to reading pictures," wrote W. Stephen Bush in 1913. "There is a grammar of pantomime which is easily learned by a little practice."[24] The same simplicity of titling was welcomed at the end of the silent era when Dorothy Richardson wrote in *Close Up;* "The test of the caption is its relative invisibility. In the right place it is not seen as a caption; unless it lingers too long upon the screen."[25]

Disagreeing with Bush and Richardson was director Charles Gaskill, who wrote in 1913.

> The interscript (subtitle, caption, heading, reading matter, et cetera) in a motion picture is precisely the reverse of the illustration in a story book. Its office is also more. It must be used not only to define the action; it must indicate the logic, the poetry, the sentiment, the philosophy and other abstract qualities found in the picture—it must illuminate. Just as many mistakes are made in trying to avoid an interscript as in trying to pad out a story with them.
>
> Nowhere in a motion picture is the hand of the intelligent, understanding artist more evident than in the quality of its interscripts, their placing and phrasing. Likewise, nowhere else in the picture is bad taste more likely to appear—for most "manufacturers" really treat the art as a manufacturing business,

and often some little girl or quite ignorant woman or man is placed in charge of the manufacture of interscripts. . . .

It may be stated as a principle that the interscript should be used to carry the action over a hiatus, when it will serve to intensify the power of the story, when it will augment and vivify the sentiment and poetry of the story, whenever its presence proves a grace in the story, whenever its use will grip the point intended by the action of the story.

Too much attention has been paid to the scarecrow erected by the smart Aleck critics who have, without a particle of sense or reason, declared that a word should never be used in a motion picture unless it is necessary to "help" the action. Millet's title does not help the "action" of his painting one jot:[26] it illuminates the logic of the picture; namely that the meek and humble, who make the beds for the rich and idle, must be thankful for the opportunity! It turns the picture into a dissertation on religion and political economy. It is not necessary to confine the illustration to Millet either—motion pictures are full of evidences of this sort.

Instead of leaving the matter of inserts or inscripts to feeble-minded persons because they are feeble-minded, and therefore will be understood by a feeble-minded audience, the manufacturers should employ the most cultured, intelligent and intellectual writers to do this work. The only reason advanced by them for not doing so, as I understand the matter, is that they are afraid the thinking person will "go over the head of the audience!" Which, of course, is the veriest rot. The real artist never goes over the head of any one. In the ratio that he does is his title to artist faulty. Anyway, it is far better to go over heads than to lie under feet.[27]

With the need to improve the subtitle, the idea developed to decorate it with scenes illustrating the phrases. Such decorative titles originated in 1916 with Irvin Willat, head of the photographic and art department at Triangle Kay-Bee. One of his first efforts was *Civilization's Child;* a typical subtitle of which was described by *The Moving Picture World* (December 30, 1916): "the efforts of a ward politician to get an unprotected girl into his clutches was symbolized by a realistic picture of a spider endeavoring to entice an unsuspecting little fly into the meshes of his web."

By 1917, *The Moving Picture World* surmised that "beautiful art titles contribute quite as much to the subtitles as does the power of repose and expression in the performance of the principals."[28]

Within a year, major producers established special departments to produce these decorative titles and subtitles. The making of such titles was explained by Loren E. Taylor of the West Coast studios of Famous Players-Lasky.

> The title sheets come to us from the scenario editorial department, typewritten, and we are then required to design "atmospheric" backgrounds, which means that they must be so harmonious as to keep the audience in the atmosphere of the story. In other words, there must be no jarring note which would take the spectator's mind from the story and spoil its continuity for him.
>
> The lettering is either painted or printed, as the case may be. The background is painted and photographed. A non-actinic color is employed for that part which is to be covered by lettering later on a second exposure. By using actinic shades in certain degrees the exact color values are obtained for the screen, giving results either solidly subdued or vivid.[29]

Some of the most beautiful titles and subtitles of the period are those for Cecil B. DeMille productions, which are also hand or stencil-colored.

By the end of the decade, sophistication had also developed regarding actors speaking dialogue. If a film was set in a foreign-language country, it was not unusual to have the actor "mouth" dialogue in the language of that country—at least in the closeups. As early as 1915, actors were provided with full dialogue scripts and expected to learn their lines for delivery in front of the camera. Audiences might not be able to hear the actors, but they could lip-read.

William S. Hart rehearsed dialogue in advance, claiming: "I consider that dialogue is indispensable and, what is more, that the right lines and the right emphasis are equally indispensable."

Cecil B. DeMille stated: "I use dialogue exactly as if I were staging a play. The dialogue is written in my manuscripts by the author, and even the choice of words, pronunciation and enunciation are insisted upon, to get the 'just right' time and facial expression."

Somewhat less rigid was Mack Sennett: "In the making of our comedies, spoken dialogue is a regular accompaniment of the action. As a rule, this dialogue is given to the actor by the director, and is carefully followed, although a portion of it is 'ad lib' and impromptu on the part of the players."[30]

Critics still complained that scripts were written by individuals lacking in dramatic sense. Cinematographers complained that one reel out of every five-reel feature that they shot was nothing but subtitles.[31] However, by the end of the decade, there was little argument that the writing of scripts and the writing and manufacture of subtitles had reached a level that could not be bettered in the twenties.

Notes

1. For more information, see articles in *The Moving Picture World* issues of January 1, 1908, February 29, 1908, April 18, 1908, and 2, 1910. The uses to which the motion picture might be put in the aid of science is also the subject of Leonard Donaldson's *The Cinematograph and Natural Science: The Achievements and Possibilities of Cinematography as an Aid to Scientific Research* (London: Ganes, 1912).

2. The best and, indeed, the only book-length study of the history of the newsreel in the United States is Raymond Fielding, *The American Newsreel, 1911-1967* (Norman, OK: University of Oklahoma Press, 1972).

3. Clifford Howard, "The Cinema in Retrospect," *Close Up* (December 1928), p. 35.

4. Harry D. Brown, "The Evolution of Studio Lighting," *The American Cinematographer,* Vol. VI, No. 10 (January 1926), p. 13.

5. Wiard B. Ihnen and D. W. Atwater, "Toward a Closer Co-operation between Producer and Engineer in Motion-Picture Lighting," *Transactions of the Illuminating Engineering Society* (October 1924), p. 8.

6. John B. Rathbun, *Motion Picture Making and Exhibiting* (Chicago: Charles C. Thompson Company, 1914), p. 60.

7. George Landy, "Wilfred Buckland Expunds Theories," *The American Cinematographer,* Vol. III, No. 5 (August 1922), p. 6.

8. Walter L. Hall's work is discussed by Karl Brown in *Adventures with D. W. Griffith* (New York: Farrar, Straus and Giroux, 1973).

Wortman's work is discussed in *Photoplay* (February 1917), which carries a story on page 17 headed "Here's the Chaldean Who Built Babylon."

9. For more information on the early figures of Hollywood art direction, see the Thames Television/Victoria & Albert Museum catalog, *The Art of Hollywood,* edited by John Hambley and Patrick Downing and published in 1979.

10. Grace, Kinglsey, "Clothes," *Photoplay,* Vol. VII, No. 6 (May 1915), p. 100.

11. Interview with Anthony Slide, November 14, 1970.

12. Arthur Ripley later became a screenwriter and director noted for his work in collaboration with Frank Capra and Harry Langdon in the twenties.

13. Helen Starr, "Putting It Together," *Photoplay* (July 1918), pp. 52-54.

14. Gene, Copeland, "The Story of Rosie and Jimmie Smith," *Photoplay* (January 1920), pp. 76-78.

15. Other articles critical of filmmakers "cutting off the feet" of their actors include: "The Factor of Uniformity," *The Moving Picture World,* Vol. V, No. 4 (July 24, 1909), pp. 115-116; and H. F. Hoffman, "Cutting off the Feet," *The Moving Picture World,* Vol. XII, No. 1 (April 6, 1912), p. 53.

16. Interview with Anthony Slide, May 17, 1976.

17. "All Eyes Are on Kinemacolor," *Motography* (July 12, 1913), p. 6.

18. "Toning and Tinting as an Adjunct to the Picture," *The Moving Picture World,* Vol. VIII, No. 11 (March 18, 1911), p. 574.

19. "Don't Say Scenario!," *The Motion Picture News* (March 21, 1914), p. 29.

20. Tom Stempel's article on "The Sennett Screenplays" in *Sight and Sound* (Winter 1985-86), pp. 58-60, is based on his examination of scripts in the Mack Sennett Collection at the Academy of Motion Picture Arts and Sciences. In claiming that this collection proves that Sennett always used scripts, he does not acknowledge that the early years of Sennett's career are not represented here. The scripts often end without resolution of the plot, simply suggesting appropriate ad-libbing on location.

21. Letter from William McAdoo, dated September 19, 1905, and other papers formerly the property of D. J. Fogarty in the author's possession.

22. W. Stephen Bush, "Perfection in Titles," *The Moving Picture World,* Vol. XVIII, No. 1 (October 4, 1913), p. 25.

23. " 'Slang' in Titles," *The Moving Picture World,* Vol. XXIX, No. 1 (July 1, 1916), p. 63.

24. W. Stephen Bush, "Perfection in Titles," p. 25.

25. Dorothy M. Richardson, "Captions," *Close Up* (September 1927), p. 56.

26. A reference to Millet's painting "The Angelus," which would have little meaning without the appended title.

27. Charles L. Gaskill, "Function of the Interscript," *The New York Dramatic Mirror* (January 8, 1913), p. 31.

28. "Subtitles de Luxe," *The Moving Picture World,* Vol. XXXII, No. 7 (May 19, 1917), p. 1123.

29. Lawrence Williams, "The Making of Photoplay Titles," *Motion Picture Magazine,* Vol. XVII, No. 2 (March 1919), p. 86.

30. "There Is No 'Silent' Drama," *Photoplay* (September 1915), pp. 73-76.

31. "Why Is a Subtitle?" *The American Cinematographer* (December 15, 1921), p. 12.

11

Genres

To suggest that one genre was more important than another in silent film production is an exercise in futility. As pioneer producer Siegmund Lubin so aptly put it in 1913, "Today we make that kind of film, and tomorrow another kind."[1] There were, however, different genres and different cycles of films popular at various times during the teens. Two genres—the serial and slapstick comedy—were introduced in the teens. Additionally, a special type of heroine, the vampire or "vamp," flourished during that one time period in film history.

> Those of us who are familiar with the productions of the articulate stage know very well that every time we go to see a show we sit before the curtain in a thrill of anticipation, waiting for the magic moment to come, feeling certain that we shall get an excitement of some sort or other. The orchestra plays, the footlights go on and the curtains part. But what do we see if it is the screen? A sneering, hip-wriggling, cigarette-smoking vampire. She exercises a wonderful fascination upon every man that is brought anywhere near her, and so far as I have been able to judge, the only reason for this strange fascination is the combination of the three attributes I have already mentioned. They are good enough to apparently kill any man at fifty yards.[2]

Thus wrote director Maurice Tourneur of that peculiar phenomenon of the teen years, the screen vamp. She was first seen in a one-reel Selig production, *The Vampire,* released on November 10,

1910, based on the painting by Sir Edward Burne-Jones (who was familiarly referred to in Selig publicity as "Ed") and the well-known verse by Rudyard Kipling. Neither the film nor a record of its cast or director survives, but Selig publicity states.

> A picture with a high conception of the great lesson taught by the master work of this great artist and finished with a correctly posed reproduction of the painting completing one of the most sensational films ever released and destined to be a feature subject on every program.

Kalem was the next company to exploit the vamp with a three-reel feature also titled *The Vampire,* directed by Robert Vignola and released on October 15, 1913. Alice Hollister stars as Sybil, an adventuress/vampire, but the highlight of the production is the once-famous "Vampire Dance," a quite ludicrous affair, performed by Bert French and Alice Eis.[3] Director Vignola and the Kalem Company returned to the theme the following year with the two-reel *The Vampire's Trail,* released on August 3, 1914, and again starring Alice Hollister with Alice Joyce and Tom Moore.

The greatest exponent of the vamp character was Theda Bara (1892-1955), who was born Theodosia Goodman in Cincinnati, Ohio, and whose screen name is an anagram of "Arab Death." She was first seen on screen in January 1915, in William Fox's production of *A Fool There Was,* based again on the Kipling poem and also on the 1909 play by Porter Emerson Browne, which had served as a vehicle for Katherine Kaelred. Audiences watched fascinated as the vampirish Miss Bara kissed her victims with such passion that their very souls seemed to be sucked from their bodies. What now seems hilarious was once the height of sophistication to the basically unsophisticated film audiences of the teens. Miss Bara's command to "Kiss me, my fool" was greeted not with guffaws, but with shock.

A Fool There Was is the only teens feature in Theda Bara's career to survive in its entirety, and it indicates that here was no great actress. Nevertheless, the film launched Theda Bara on a career at Fox that included starring roles in *Romeo and Juliet* (1916), *Camille* (1917), *Cleopatra* (1917), *The She Devil* (1918), and *Salome* (1918). It also encouraged Bara imitators—notably Louise Glaum, who entered films in 1911, and Valeska Surratt from the legitimate stage and vaudeville. However, the vogue of the vamp was brief, and by the twenties, Miss Bara was reduced to parodying her earlier characterizations.

Chance played little part in the introduction of the serial or series film. Film producers quickly realized that fans would return week after week to see favorite stars in recurring roles and that such fans would be more interested in the stars and their fictional predicaments than in the quality of the productions. Producers also speedily grasped the benefit of a tie-in with newspapers, thus assuring considerable free publicity. Newspaper owners went along with the scheme because they knew that serializing a story in their journals concurrent with the film's release would result in increased circulation figures; filmgoers would want to read the stories of the serials as well as see them.

Serials endured into the fifties, but during the sound era, they were considered a staple of children s entertainment. Such was not the case during the teens, when serials were enjoyed as much by adult audiences as by children. Serials were not, however, considered on par with feature-length productions and were paid scant attention by the trade papers, while the popular press basically ignored them.

The Edison Company produced America's first serial in 1912. It was titled *What Happened to Mary?*, starred Mary Fuller, and was released in collaboration with the magazine *Ladies World*. Six one-reel episodes, each complete in itself, were released at the rate of one a month. (In the United Kingdom, the story was serialized in *Home Chat*.) So successful was the series that a sequel, *Who Will Mary Marry?* written, as was the first, by Bannister Merwin, was produced the following year. In the initial chapter, "A Proposal from the Duke," Mary was involved with an impoverished Duke, played by Ben Wilson. Edison's publicity suggested, to the delight of Miss Fuller's fans, "As Mary is now a millionairess, it is natural to suppose that she will be sought after by men of various stages and ages—the duke is the first but you must not miss any of the others!"

The first true serial, with episodes ending to be continued the following week, was Selig's *The Adventures of Kathlyn,* the first episode of which was released on December 29, 1913. Produced in association with the *Chicago Tribune,* which was in the middle of a circulation war with other local newspapers, each two-reel episode was adapted by Gilson Willets from the story by Harold

MacGrath and directed by Francis J. Grandon. The star was Kathlyn Williams, "the girl without fear," and week after week she escaped death from lions, tigers, and other animals provided by the Selig Zoo. In reality, Miss Williams (1888-1960) was a far better actress than her work in this serial might suggest; there is always a maturity and intelligence to her portrayals.

The Adventures of Kathlyn established the popularity of the serial genre and companies rushed into further productions. Eager for a successor to *Who Will Mary Marry?*, Edison produced *Dolly of the Dailies*, the first episode of which was released in January 1914, again starring Mary Fuller and directed by Walter Edwin. That same year, Mutual produced *Our Mutual Girl*, a fifty-two episode serial with each chapter one reel in length, which told the story of a simple country girl, played by Norma Phillips, who finished up a year later as a wealthy society lady. Lubin also entered the serial field in 1914 with *The Beloved Adventurer*, directed by and starring Arthur Johnson.

Pleased with the financial success of *The Adventures of Kathlyn* and the subsequent increase in its circulation, the *Chicago Tribune* sponsored another serial, *The Million Dollar Mystery*, produced by the Thanhouser Company. Twenty-three episodes long, the serial ran concurrently with the film version in the *Tribune* in the United States and in *Reynolds News* in the United Kingdom. The plot, written by Harold MacGrath and Lloyd Lonergan, told of a secret society called "The Black Hundred" and its attempts to gain control of a lost million dollars. There was a kidnapped heiress played by Florence La Badie, a villainous countess essayed by Marguerite Snow, and a handsome and heroic newspaper reporter played by the capable James Cruze. In the first chapter, the players were introduced, and the audience told of the parts they were portraying—rather similar to a modern preview trailer. In the final chapter, the entire cast was brought back again, linked hands, and said farewell as a curtain descended upon which was written "Goodbye" in orange blossoms. *The Million Dollar Mystery* was said to have cost $125,000 to produce and brought in $1,500,000 for its backers. A sequel was obviously in order.

As part of an even more aggressive promotion of the genre, the *Chicago Tribune* conducted a scenario contest, with the winner receiving a cash prize of $10,000 for the best serial story. The winner was Roy L. McCardell, who (by a curious coincidence) was the only professional writer competing. His story was titled *The Diamond from the Sky* and produced by the American Flying A Company at its Santa Barbara studios. The story of the diamond heirloom of the Stanley family was promoted in studio publicity as "Emphatically the greatest film ever produced, a ceaseless cataract of action—The Serial Wonderful!" Thirty-two episodes told of the endeavors of the villains, played by William Russell and Charlotte Burton, to secure the heirloom from Irving Cummings and the gypsy heroine, played by Mary Pickford's sister, Lottie. First released on May 3, 1915, the serial was directed by Jacques Jaccard and William Dean Tanner. The latter subsequently changed his name to William Desmond Taylor and his shocking murder in 1921 ended the career of Mary Miles Minter, with whom the director was romantically linked.

The Kalem Company entered the serial field in 1914 with a series of two-reel dramas starring Alice Joyce. The first was titled "The Show Girl's Glove," and the entire series was published in the British women's magazine *Home Notes*.

That same year, Kalem began releasing its most famous serial, *The Hazards of Helen,* which was seen in 119 one-reel episodes through 1916. The serial was the brainchild of director J. P. McGowan, who directed the majority of the episodes. (Later episodes were directed by Paul Hurst, Leo D. Maloney, Robert Vignola, and James Davis.) The original Helen was Helen Holmes (1892-1950), who commenced her career with Keystone in 1912 and was introduced to McGowan (to whom she was married at one time) by Mabel Normand. *The Hazards of Helen* was notable for its Western and railroad[4] stunts and is so fast-paced that the audience has little time to ponder the vagaries of the plot or to become bored. A 1915 fan magazine article gives some indication of the stunts performed by Helen Holmes.

> In Helen's Sacrifice [the first episode of the serial] she rode a horse over a fifty-foot cliff, and leapt from her saddle onto the footplate of a fast speeding locomotive. In The Girl at the Throttle she averted a terrible railway disaster by driving an engine at sixty miles an hour. In The Stolen Engine she leapt from the footplate of one engine to the cab of another travelling in the same direction on a parallel track. In The Black Diamond Express she made an exciting dash through the clouds in a

monster biplane. In The Escape on the Limited she drove a steam railcar at breakneck speed, and in The Girl Telegrapher's Peril she leapt from a trestle into the river below.[5]

When Helen Holmes and McGowan left the company in the summer of 1915, it was decided to continue the serial with another Helen—Helen Gibson (1894-1977), who was every bit as active as her predecessor if not quite as attractive. When either Helen Holmes or Helen Gibson was unavailable, Kalem had no compunction about other actresses, such as Anna Q. Nilsson or Elsie McLeod, playing the title role.

Kalem actress Marin Sais (1890-1971) was perhaps the busiest serial practitioner. She was seen in *The Girl Detective* (1915), *Stingaree* (1916), *The Further Adventures of Stingaree* (1917), and starred in *Mysteries of the Grand Hotel* (1915), *The Social Pirates* (1916), *The Girl from Frisco* (1916-1917), and *The American Girl* (1917).

Additional series from Kalem include a group of three-reelers released in 1915 that showed the application of the Ten Commandments to contemporary conditions and was produced in association with the Christian Science movement and the sixteen-episode *The Virtues of Marguerite,* starring petite Marguerite Courtot.

Another important producer of serials was Universal, whose first offering in the genre was *Lucille Love, Girl of Mystery,* released in fifteen episodes beginning April 14, 1914. As the serial chapters were released, the story was published in the *Chicago Herald* and the British *Weekly Dispatch.* "Who was Lucille, girl of mystery with the beautiful face hidden by a black mask?" demanded the publicity handouts. Apparently, "she was the daughter of a well-known officer in the army, but tiring of a life of adventure, had decided to settle down in the peaceful calm of wedded life, and was now touring the world in search of a husband." This world tour brought Lucille Love in personal appearances to many theaters at home and abroad. It soon became apparent that there was a large number of Lucille Loves touring the world, but the film Lucille Love bore a striking resemblance to Universal star Grace Cunard (1893-1967).

Teamed with Miss Cunard as leading man and director for this and future Universal serials was Francis Ford (1882-1953), whose brother John also appeared in small parts in some episodes of *Lucille Love, Girl of Mystery.* Cunard and Ford formed an ideal screen partnership. Besides starring in the serials, they also wrote their own scenarios, edited and titled the productions, and quite often shared directing honors.

The second serial from Universal, *The Trey o' Hearts,* released in fifteen episodes in the summer of 1915, was the work of writer Louis Joseph Vance and director Wilfred Lucas. Cleo Madison starred in the dual role of identical twins, innocent Rose and villainous Judith. Trick photography made it difficult for the audience, as well as leading man George Larkin (who later starred in the Kalem series *Grant, the Police Reporter*), to tell one from the other. Later in 1914, Universal released *The Master Key,* directed by and starring Robert Z. Leonard. Ella Hall was the leading lady in this story of the search for a lost mine. As a publicity gimmick, Universal offered serial fans the Master Key bracelet, which was advertised as "the fad of the hour. Snap it on your sweetheart's wrist. You wear the key that unlocks it."

The second Cunard/Ford serial, *The Broken Coin,* was released in twenty-two episodes beginning June 21, 1915. It was the story of a broken coin that would, when pieced together, show the map to a lost fortune. Carl Laemmle appeared on screen as a newspaper proprietor who sends out his chief reporter, none other than Miss Cunard, on the quest for the treasure.

The Broken Coin introduced a new serial star in the person of Eddie Polo (1875-1961), who was billed as "The Hercules of the Screen." Among his claims to fame were that he could lift three men simultaneously; that he was the first man to leap with a parachute from the Eiffel Tower; that he was the first man to prove parachute jumping from a plane was feasible at any height; and that in *The Broken Coin,* he easily caught Grance Cunard in his arms after she jumped fifteen feet from a balcony. Polo stayed with Universal for eight years, leaving in 1922 to form his own serial production company.

He was featured in one of the last Cunard/Ford serials, *Peg o' the Ring,* released in fifteen episodes from May 1, 1916. This circus story had Grace Cunard in the title role of Peg, whose mother had been bitten by a leopard shortly before her daughter's birth. This mishap resulted in Peg's acquiring the unfortunate habit of scratching and tearing at anything in sight on certain nights. (Could this be the earliest screen incarnation of the Werewolf legend?) Miss Cunard was not entirely happy with the production and, at one point, she walked out and was replaced by Ruth Stonehouse. The Cunard/Ford partnership ended with the sixteen-episode *The Purple Mask,* first seen in December 1916.

Another popular serial partnership at Universal was that of Ben Wilson and Neva Gerber, who starred in two 1917 serials, *The Voice on the Wire* and *The Mystery Ship.* The former, directed by Stuart Paton, concerned "The Black Seven," a secret society with "advanced theories of life and death."

Liberty, a Daughter of the U. S. A. introduced Marie Walcamp as a Universal serial star in the summer of 1916. Set in Mexico, the twenty-episode serial, as was so often the case, had an heiress as its heroine. Miss Walcamp's other major Universal serial was *The Red Ace* (1917).

Essanay entered the serial field in January 1916, with *The Strange Case of Mary Page,* a fifteen-episode crime story written by Frederick Lewis and directed by J. Charles Haydon. Edna Mayo was the heroine with Henry B. Walthall, looking a little too old and serious for a serial hero, as her lover. Each episode revolved around the evidence offered at a murder trial.

From Vitagraph came a three-episode parody of the serial genre in 1915 with *The Fates and Flora Fourflush, or The Massive Ten Billion-Dollar Vitagraph Mystery Serial,* starring Clara Kimball Young. The parody was directed by Wally Van, who also directed another Vitagraph serial, *The Scarlet Runner* (1916). The company's first genuine serial was *The Goddess,* released in fifteen episodes beginning May 10, 1915, starring Earle Williams and Anita Stewart under the direction of Ralph Ince. Vitagraph's main contribution to the genre was seven serials featuring William Duncan and released between 1917 and 1921: *The Fighting Trail* (1917), *Vengeance and the Woman* (1917), *A Fight for Millions* (1918), *Man of Might* (1919), *Smashing Barriers* (1919), *The Silent Avenger* (1919), and *Fighting Fate* (1921).

In 1916, Billie Burke starred in *Gloria's Romance,* a twenty-episode serialization of a modern romantic novel, released by George Kleine. Described as "The Serial Supreme," it was a supreme failure. Harry Houdini entered films in 1919 with a serial titled *The Master Mystery.* Arthur B. Reeve was the author of this story of a robot that destroys everything in its path, with heroines Marguerite Marsh and Ruth Stonehouse about to suffer a similar fate, except for the quick intervention of the hero.

One of the more charming of the later serial players was Irene Castle (1893-1969), already famous as a dancer with her husband, Vernon, when she entered films with the serial *Patria*. The heroine was an attractive young girl who thwarts enemy spies (led by Warner Oland) and saves America from invasion. Milton Sills, making his first major screen appearance, plays the Secret Service agent hero. The serial was produced by William Randolph Hearst's International Films for release by Pathé. Intended as prowar propaganda at a time when America was neutral, the serial was banned for a while. When it was eventually released in 1917, much of the war scare had died down, and the film was not a tremendous success.

As is obvious, the majority of serial stars of the teens were women. It was not until the twenties that men began to dominate the field and not until the sound era that the serial heroine was displaced totally by the hero. Such change of sex for the serial stars clearly indicates a change in audience make-up from general adult audiences in the teens to boys at Saturday matinées in the thirties and later.

The two most famous silent serial stars were Ruth Roland (1894-1937) and Pearl White (1889-1938). Both women were extremely attractive and should have enjoyed, but did not, careers in legitimate features. In terms of production values, acting and action sequences, there is little to distinguish one lady's films from those of the other. Pearl White always dresses very sensibly and simply—her costumes change little through the years. Ruth Roland, on the other hand, is fond of overelaborate costumes that do little to flatter her figure and, at times, make her appear almost frumpy.

Ruth Roland was the "Kalem Girl" and was first seen in serials in that company's *The Girl Detective,* released in the fall of 1914. After completing eight episodes of the series, she left Kalem for Balboa in December 1914, and was replaced by Cleo Ridgely, who was the wife of *The Girl Detective*'s director, James Horne.

At the Balboa Amusement Company, located in Long Beach, California, Ruth Roland starred in the *Who Pays?* series opposite director-to-be Henry King. The series is important because it was the first time the genre was used for social commentary. Each episode of the series, released by Pathé early in 1915, posed an ethical or sociological question. King was involved in some way with the direction, which was credited to Harry Harvey; later in 1914, he began his directorial career officially at Balboa.[6]

Who Pays? was followed by Ruth Roland's first Pathé serial, *The Red Circle,* the first of the fourteen episodes of which were released in December 1915. In 1919, Miss Roland became her own serial producer, releasing through Pathé, with *The Adventures of Ruth,* directed by William Parke and written by Gilson Willets.

Pearl White commenced her screen career with Powers in 1910. By the time she left the Crystal Film Company early in 1914, she was a popular leading lady in its comedies, looking considerably more buxom than she appeared in her serials.

In 1914, Miss White joined Pathé, where she had worked some years earlier as a minor player, and began work on the company's first serial, *The Perils of Pauline.* Badly written and directed (by Louis Gasnier and Donald MacKenzie), the twenty-episode serial was a sensational success. It was produced with the financial backing of William Randolph Hearst, who is said to have titled the serial and who, of course, gave it maximum publicity in his newspapers.

The following description of chapter one, "Twixt Earth and Sky," from the original campaign book, vividly brings the serial to life.

> Stanford Marvin died leaving a huge fortune to be shared between Harry, his son [Crane Wilbur], and Pauline, ward [Pearl White]. If, however, Pauline died within a year without marrying Harry, Raymond Owen [Paul Panzer], Marvin's secretary, inherited everything. Owen set himself out to encompass Pauline's death and whilst snap-shooting her in the basket of a balloon, arranged for someone to create a panic by rushing into the crowd. Then Owen cuts the ropes. "My God! " gasped Harry, in horror. "The balloon has escaped, and Pauline is alone in mid-air!"

The Perils of Pauline was followed by Pearl White's greatest serial success, the thirty-six episode *The Exploits of Elaine,* directed by Louis Gasnier and George B. Seitz, and released beginning in December 1914. The serial was also published in the Hearst newspapers and in the British *The News of the World.*

In this adaptation of the detective stories of Arthur B. Reeve (the American equivalent in popularity if not intellectual ability of

Arthur Conan Doyle), Arnold Daly plays Craig Kennedy, the famous detective, Creighton Hale is Jameson, his likeable young assistant, and Pearl White is Elaine Dodge, who pursues her father's assassin and is forever at the mercy of Sheldon Lewis, "The Clutching Hand." Other villains whom Miss White encounters in the serial are Lionel Barrymore as Marcus del Marr and Edwin Arden as Wu Fong.

So successful was *The Exploits of Elaine* that two sequels, *The New Exploits of Elaine* (1915) and *The Romance of Elaine* (1915), were produced. There was even a popular song, still remembered, written in praise of Elaine and her exploits.

> Elaine, Elaine, I love you all in vain.
> Elaine, Elaine, you've set my heart aflame.
> Of all the girls you're the sweetest I've seen,
> Always to me as sweet as sweet sixteen.
> I dream of you all through the livelong day,
> And then when I see you, you fade away.
> Elaine, Elaine, please come down from the screen,
> And be my Moving Picture Queen!

Pearl White made seven further serials, all of them immensely successful, and she also starred in a number of features for Pathé and Fox that were not very successful. In 1922, she made her final serial, *Plunder,* for her old director, George B. Seitz and her old company, Pathé. The following year, she sailed for France to star in three features, the final one being *Terror/The Perils of Paris* (1924). She travelled extensively and entertained lavishly in an apartment in Paris and a chateau at Biarritz. Her lesbian activities were the sensational gossip of French society. Undoubtedly the most popular star of the serial genre and one of the best-loved actresses of early American cinema, Pearl White made all of her films in either Paris or the New York City area. She never set foot in California.[7]

Mack Sennett was a Canadian who introduced slapstick comedy to American cinema. He was the creator of the comic cop, the custard pie in the face, and the pratfall; his Keystone Kops and his Mack Sennett Bathing Beauties have an enduring familiarity to the American public. His films were generally crude and lacking in production values, but they fulfilled a need, as did Abbott and

Costello and the Three Stooges in later decades. A man of little business acumen and with no understanding of the higher aesthetics of filmmaking, Mack Sennett introduced stars as varied as Marie Dressler and Bing Crosby to the screen. Among those whom he helped make famous were Mabel Normand, Ford Sterling, Gloria Swanson, Phyllis Haver, Chester Conklin, and Charlie Chaplin.

The man considered to be the Father of American Film Comedy was born Michael Sinnott in the Canadian farming town of Richmond, which is midway between Montreal and Quebec, on January 17, 1880. In 1902, Sinnott came to New York City, changed his name to Mack Sennett, and got a job in burlesque. Six years later, after achieving no real success on the stage, he went to work as an actor for the American Biograph Company. He made his first slapstick film appearance in *The Curtain Pole,* released on February 15, 1909, and directed by D. W. Griffith. The raison d'etre for the film was a comic chase, and *The Curtain Pole* perhaps gave Sennett his first inkling of the potential of such action.

In 1911, while working with Biograph in California, Sennett was promoted to directing, and that same year he directed his first comedy, *Comrades,* with Del Henderson, Vivian Prescott, Grace Henderson, and Sennett himself. In July 1911, Sennett directed his first film with Mabel Normand (1894-1930), *The Diving Girl,* which also featured a group of women in bathing costumes—precursors of the Mack Sennett Bathing Beauties. Except for a short period with Vitagraph during 1910 and 1911, Normand remained with Sennett until 1918, when she became one of the first stars of Goldwyn Pictures Corporation.

In 1912, Sennett joined Charles O. Baumann and Adam Kessel to form the Keystone Film Company, which gave its name to the most popular form of slapstick comedy. It released its first two films, *Cohen Collects a Debt* and *The Water Nymph,* on September 23, 1912. Mabel Normand, Fred Mace, and Ford Sterling were the company's initial stars, joined in 1913 by Roscoe "Fatty" Arbuckle and his wife, Minta Durfee, Chester Conklin, and Charlie Chase. Charles Chaplin (1889-1977) made his film debut with Keystone in *Making a Living,* released on February 2, 1914, and introduced the Tramp character in his second Keystone short, *Kid Auto Races at Venice,* released on February 7, 1914. During the year he was with Keystone, Chaplin made thirty-five films, writing and directing all but the first twelve of them. Among the films was the first

Chaplin feature, *Tillie's Punctured Romance,* released on November 14, 1914, which introduced Marie Dressler to the screen. It was also Sennett s first feature, and he did not make another one until 1917, when he formed the Mabel Normand Feature Film Company for the production of *Mickey.*

Keystone disappeared in 1917 when Sennett began producing comedies for Paramount release. Around the same time, he added new stars, including Louise Fazenda, Marie Prevost, and Phyllis Haver.

He explained his comedy philosophy to the British fan magazine *Pictures and the Picturegoer* (March, 1925).

> There are two characters on the screen that the audience feel vicious toward. These are the policemen and the man in the top hat. For some extraordinary reason, they feel abused if you let a man in a top hat escape unscathed. They want something done to him. I imagine the reason for this is something deeper than the mere fact that a top hat looks funny falling off. After all the joke of life is the fall of dignity. And the top hat is the final symbol of dignity.

Unfortunately, audiences were becoming more sophisticated and demanding a little more from their screen comedies than the fall of dignity. Sennett returned to short-film production with the coming of sound, and in 1933, he declared bankruptcy. He died in poverty on November 5, 1960.[8]

Sennett's contemporary, Hal Roach, was quite dogmatic in his opinion of Sennett's demise.

> Sennett would put nobody under contract. He said this is the Mack Sennett Studio—I'm Mack Sennett. If they don't want to work for me, I'll get somebody else, and they'll be stars. If Sennett had put the people under contract, look who he'd have had. He would have had Chaplin, Arbuckle, Al St. John, Ford Sterling, and so on. They were all his people. Mack was a very rough character. He didn't want anybody running his business. He didn't want anybody under contract.[9]

Hal Roach (1892-1992) entered films in 1912 with the Bison Company, but his successes date as much from the sound era as from the silent years. In 1915, he formed the Rolin Film Company, whose star attraction was Harold Lloyd (1893-1971). Lloyd was initially seen in a Chaplinesque imitation as "Willie Work." A new characterization, "Lonesome Luke," was introduced in 1915, but the familiar Lloyd character with the glasses was not seen until 1919 in the two-reel short *Bumping into Broadway,* in which Lloyd's leading lady is Bebe Daniels (just prior to Cecil B. DeMille's signing her to a contract). The Harold Lloyd character, with a Horatio Alger quality, enthusiasm to succeed, a positive outlook on life, and the skills needed for winning the girl, heralded the demise of the slapstick comedian.

Aside from Sennett, slapstick comedy was limited to smaller companies such as Henry M. "Pathé" Lehrman's L-KO Motion Picture Company, whose leading lady, Alice Howell (1888-1961), was notable for her grotesque "scrub lady" make-up and penguin walk. She belonged to a school of comedy that included the grotesque Gale Henry, usually partnered with Max Asher in Joker Comedies and the Lehrman Sunshine Comedies, featuring lions and scared Negroes. Vitagraph's Larry Semon (1889-1928), with his white, clownlike make-up, and films with titles such as *Hindoos and Hazards, Huns and Hyphens,* and *Big Boobs and Bathing Beauties* (all released in 1918) is also typical of the genre.

Light, domestic comedy was dominated by Mr. and Mrs. Sidney Drew, first at Vitagraph and then at Metro (until Drew's untimely death in 1919). Similar comedy was also offered by Mr. and Mrs. Carter De Haven.

A cross between domestic and slapstick comedy was produced by Al Christie (1882-1951), who was associated with David Horsley's Nestor Film Company. Christie brought the Nestor Company to Hollywood in October 1911, making it the first company to locate within the geographical boundaries of Hollywood with the rental of a building at Sunset Boulevard and Gower Street. The choice of the name "Nestor" is perhaps a subtle reference to the company's fights with the Motion Picture Patents group. In Greek mythology, Nestor is the wise leader who accompanies the Greeks to Troy and returns victorious to his own kingdom after the war. Nestor Film Company wisely left the Patents Company-dominated East Coast and led the exodus of the independents to California.

Nestor comedies featured Eddie Lyons and Lee Moran, supported by leading lady Victoria Forde. Billie Rhodes (1894-1988), who entered films with Kalem in 1913, became the Nestor Girl in 1914, and developed into a fairly successful and competent purveyor of polite comedy. In 1916, Al Christie left Nestor and formed his own company in association with his brother, Charles. "He does not seek to raise the guffaw by resorting to the grotesque or the vulgar," wrote *Pictures and the Picturegoer* (January, 1922). "The secret of this merchant in screen fun is to persuade the world to laugh with his shadow characters on the silver screen, and not to titter *at* them."

A 1914 textbook on the film industry announced that there were six principal subject headings under which films could be listed: Dramas, Comedies, Topicals (i.e., newsreels), Trick Pictures, Educationals, and Industrials.[10] In reality, whatever description might be used for a particular film, there is one subject heading under which a vast number of films from the teens fall—exploitation. Films might exploit a social movement, a singular happening, or an emotional public outburst. There were even exploitation films without any redeeming social or political qualities, created simply to titillate an audience.

As a result of the scandal following the murder of Stanford White by her husband, Harry K. Thaw, Evelyn Nesbitt enjoyed a career in vaudeville and in films, starring in nine features between 1914 and 1919. Audrey Munson was a well-known model, and her body was shown to good effect in Thanhouser's *Inspiration* (1915) and in two American Film Company productions from 1916, *The Girl o' Dreams* and *Purity*. The last film created a furor with its nude poses by Miss Munson.

Mary MacLane created a sensation in 1917 with the accounts of her sexual adventures in *I, Mary MacLane*. The following year, Essanay filmed the book, with Miss MacLane playing herself, under the title *Men Who Have Made Love to Me*.

A 1911 Rockefeller Commission on Vice report with its stories of white slavery and women forced into prostitution paved the way for a flood of films on the subject, including *Traffic in Souls* (1913), *The Inside of the White Slave Traffic* (1913), *The Dupe* (1916), *Evil Hands* (1916), *Protect Your Daughters* (1917), and *Is Any Girl Safe?* (1918).

Equally fascinating and exploitable to the film industry was the question of drug addiction, depicted as tragic in *Slaves of Morphine* (1913) and *The Devil's Needle* (1916), but also characterized as fun-provoking in films such as *The Mystery of the Leaping Fish* (1916), starring Douglas Fairbanks.[11]

An expert in the production of exploitation films was Ivan Abramson (1872-1934), who served as manager of Jacob P. Adler's Company and founded the Ivan Grand Opera Company in 1905 before entering films. The type of film in which Abramson specialized can be gleaned from the titles of some of his teens features: *Should a Woman Divorce?* (1914), *Sins of the Parents* (1914), *The Sex Lure* (1916), *Married in Name Only* (1917), and *A Child for Sale* (1920). Abramson's biggest success came with *Enlighten Thy Daughter,* produced by his own Ivan Film Productions in 1917. It recounts the tragedy of a daughter who is not taught the facts of life and dies as a result of a botched abortion. (Films in the teens were strongly antiabortion but often advocated birth control.) In *The Moving Picture World* (January 6, 1917), Edward Weitzel called *Enlighten Thy Daughter* "a powerful object lesson on the subject," and Abramson remade the film in 1933.

In reviewing *A Child for Sale,* which attacked both striking laborers and profiteering capitalists—Abramson would never bite the hand that fed him, be it the moviegoing public or his backers (including William Randolph Hearst)—critic Burns Mantle made a comment in *Photoplay* (June 1920) that is applicable to all of Abramson s films, stating that they represent "the sincere protest of one who would take a hand in setting the world straight."

As indicated by *A Child for Sale,* the issue of capital versus labor was rehashed frequently on screen. The modern story of *Intolerance* depicts the effects of a long drawn-out strike on workers and is probably based on a 1914 strike against the Colorado Fuel and Iron Company. Certainly, the factory owner in the feature is an obvious fictionalization of John D. Rockefeller, whose Rockefeller Foundation was a major shareholder in the American Agricultural and Chemical Company, the subject of a bitter 1915 labor dispute. (Like *Intolerance, A Child for Sale* also criticized the shallowness of philanthropists, but unfortunately, Ivan Abramson was no D. W. Griffith.)

The film industry could make fun of strike actions as in *How the Cinema Protects Itself against Strikes* (Eclair, 1911), which uses trick photography to move sets and to costume actors, or *Cops on Strike* (Pathé, 1910), in which striking policemen are arrested by newly released prisoners. On the whole, however, labor unrest was not a subject for humor, with the industry perhaps siding more with the workers than with management, but only by a slim margin. Typical of the negative representation of unions is Thanhouser's *The Strike* (1914), in which *The New York Dramatic Mirror* (April 29, 1914) noted: "We are shown the worst elements of organized labor, and none of the better." Workers are shown to advantage in *The Right To Labor* (Yankee, 1910), *A General Strike* (Gaumont, 1911), *The Long Strike* (Essanay, 1911), and *The Long Strike* (IMP, 1912). Both sides were at fault in Vitagraph's *Capital vs. Labor* (1910) and brought together only through the intercession of the church in the form of a young minister who calms the striking miners and obtains concessions from the capitalist.

The final chapter, episode twelve of the 1915 series *Who Pays?*, presents a grim portrait of a capitalist who retaliates against his striking workers by foreclosing on their company-owned homes. One of the workers seeks revenge with a gun but accidentally shoots the capitalist's daughter, who is sympathetic to the strikers. A final title asks: "Who Pays?"

Upton Sinclair's 1906 novel, *The Jungle,* was filmed in 1914 by the All-Star Feature Corporation, but the film achieved little success, despite Sinclair's appearing not only in the film's final reel, but also at each performance of the feature in New York City. One of the most dramatic labor-versus-capital films is Eclair's 1913 production of *Why?*, which ends with the workers burning down the Woolworth Building in New York City. *Why?* might be the first film to advocate anarchy.

The tragedy of child labor was the subject of many films, including *Suffer Little Children* (Edison, 1909), *The Cry of the Children* (Thanhouser, 1912), and *Children Who Labor* (Edison, 1912).

Women's suffrage was generally the subject of ridicule on screen with films such as *Oh, You Suffragette* (American, 1911), *When the Women Strike* (Lubin, 1911), *A Militant Suffragette* (Thanhouser, 1912), and *The First Woman Jury in America* (Vitagraph, 1912). Chaplin indicated his opposition to the cause in *A Busy Day* (1914), in which a militant suffragette, played by the comedian in drag, is drowned at the film's close.

The women's movement was vindicated in Republic's *Votes for Women* (1912), directed by Hal Reid, which found corruption in the male-controlled U. S. Senate and included appearances by two of

America's leading suffragettes, Jane Addams and Anna Howard Shaw. In 1913, the Unique Film Company produced a four-reel feature, *Eighty Million Women Want—?*, with its title taken from Rheta Childe Dorr's book *What Eighty Million Women Want.* It featured Mrs. Emmeline Pankhurst and Harriet Stanton Blatch in a melodrama that mixed political corruption and romance. In *The Moving Picture World* (November 15, 1913), W. Stephen Bush commented.

> Those who have looked upon the Votes-for-Women move-
> ment as the last refuge of old maids and cranks are due for a most
> pleasant surprise and agreeable disillusionment. The heroine of
> the story, though a staunch enough suffragette, is womanly from
> top to toe, and both she and the hero look and act their best when
> they gaze upon the marriage license, which forms the finale of
> the story.

A final film advocating women's rights was *Woman's Work in War Time,* produced by the S. S. Film Company for the New York Woman's Suffrage Party in 1917. Written and directed by a man, Charles J. Davis, Jr., the film was described by *Motion Picture News* (September 15, 1917) as "essentially a propaganda offering setting forth what the women of the country are doing and will do as their share of the war's work."[12]

Within a year of the commencement of the First World War in Europe, a number of films were produced exploiting the issue of America's neutrality and urging an attitude of preparedness. The most influential of these films was Vitagraph's *The Battle Cry of Peace,* based on a 1915 book, *Defenseless America,* by Hudson Maxim. Vitagraph's co-founder, the English-born J. Stuart Blackton, who did not become an American citizen until after the film's completion, was encouraged in the production by Theodore Roosevelt.

First seen publicly in the summer of 1915, *The Battle Cry of Peace* depicts a weak and defenseless America that falls to German-looking invaders who embark on a wholesale campaign of rape and destruction. A "peace at any price" advocate is shot in the street, while his wife kills herself and her two daughters rather than face an uncertain fate at the hands of enemy soldiers. The climax of the film shows the Capitol in ruins. The production was endorsed by many politicians as well as the Daughters of the American Revolution, but it did not win the approval of President Woodrow Wilson. It was also denounced by Henry Ford (whom Vitagraph successfully sued for libel).

A sequel, aimed at showing the role that women might play in a worldwide conflict and titled *Womanhood, the Glory of a Nation,* was released by Vitagraph only days before America's entry into the First World War in April 1917. A third Vitagraph production, *Whom the Gods Destroy,* released in December 1916, was loosely based on Sir Roger Casement's efforts to encourage Germany to help in the fight for Irish independence and was aimed at diffusing Irish-American hostility towards the allies.

Thomas Dixon took up the cause of preparedness with *The Fall of a Nation,* which opened at New York City's Liberty Theater on June 6, 1916, and is perhaps of most interest not because of its storyline, but because of an original musical score composed by Victor Herbert. "The music was inspiring and arranged to fit the scenes of the picture with great care," reported *Motion Picture News* (June 24, 1916).[13]

Those opposing America s intervention in the war were heartened by Thomas Ince's production of *Civilization,* first seen publicly at the Majestic Theater in Los Angeles on April 17, 1916. Unlike *Womanhood, the Glory of a Nation,* it advocates women as peacekeepers in a mythical Kingdom (remarkably Germanic in costuming) that is forced into war by a belligerent monarch. The film also uses allegory with Christ returning to earth in the body of the inventor of a military submarine. President Wilson endorsed *Civilization* with "a message of humanity" appended to the production. Ince and others in the industry argued, with some validity, that *Civilization* helped Wilson's re-election campaign.

Few anti-British films were produced between 1914 and 1917. Edwin F. Weigle photographed *The German Side of the War* (1915) for the *Chicago Tribune,* which appears to have been a very anti-British publication. (It also sponsored the 1921 feature *Ireland in Revolt,* again photographed by Weigle, depicting the horrors of the British occupation of Ireland.)

The other memorable piece of anti-British propaganda is *The Spirit of '76,* produced by Robert Goldstein, who boasted of owning the largest theatrical costume company in the United States. He supplied the costumes for *The Birth of a Nation,* in which, through the Epoch Producing Company, he owned considerable stock. Goldstein decided to enter film production and established the Continental Producing Company in the spring of 1916, capitalized at $250,000 to be used for the production of one film, *The Spirit of '76*. Leading roles were assigned to Adda Gleason, Howard Gaye, Jack Cosgrove, and Jane Novak. The film was shot at the former Rolin Studio on Santa Monica Boulevard in Los Angeles.

Jane Novak recalled, "Everyone in the company was constantly excited and thrilled by what we expected to be one of the greatest films. D. W. Griffith came several times to see our sets and watch a bit of our work. Mr. Goldstein was a small man, very gentle and softspoken—kind to everyone."[14]

Written and directed by Goldstein, *The Spirit of '76* is extraordinarily lurid. Against a backdrop of the American Revolution, it tells of Catherine Montour (Adda Gleason), a half-Indian, who aspires to be Queen of America and who has great influence with George III (Jack Cosgrove). The film closes with Catherine unknowingly in love with her brother, Lionel Esmond (Howard Gaye), and about to marry him when the relationship is revealed. Catherine is unsuccessful in recapturing the King's favor.

A number of historical events are depicted, including Patrick Henry's speech before the Virginia House of Burgesses, Paul Revere's ride, the signing of the Declaration of Independence, and Washington (Noah Beery) at Valley Forge. Even the Tory Walter Butler (George Cheeseborough) is pictured.

Goldstein scheduled *The Spirit of '76* to open at Orchestra Hall, Chicago, in June 1917, almost simultaneously with the beginning of the draft. Despite the city's earlier pro-German stance—the police censor had banned Mary Pickford's *The Little American* as being offensive to Chicago's German population—the film immediately ran into censorship troubles and some particularly vicious anti-British propaganda was ordered to be removed from it. Even with cuts, the film resembled an epic on the scale of *The Birth of a Nation,* running approximately 12,000 feet in length.

Critical reaction was reasonably favorable. Genevieve Harris wrote in *Motography* (June 23, 1917): "To sum up, the picture contains a number of splendid moments and a great deal of narrative neither convincing nor interesting."

According to *Exhibitor's Trade Review* (June 9, 1917), "Contrary to the opinion of the Chicago censors it contains nothing that would dampen the fervor of America at war now. Instead, it inspires patriotism. It has some truly wonderful moments and should cause the red blood of any American to tingle."

The Spirit of '76, including the scenes cut by the Chicago censor, opened at Clune's Auditorium, Los Angeles, on November 28, 1917. Two days later, Federal officers entered the theater and seized the print. Goldstein was taken into custody and charged with violation of the Espionage Act.

On December 4, 1917, a Federal Grand Jury handed down indictments against Goldstein on three counts. The first alleged a violation of Section 3 of the Espionage Act; count 2 alleged a violation of Section 22 of the Act; and count 3, a violation of Section 37 of the Penal Code relating to the Selective Services Act. The jury heard evidence from witnesses, including British Vice Consul C. White Mortimer and members of the American Protective League, before formally charging that Goldstein

> ... wilfully and unlawfully attempted to cause insubordina-
> tion, disloyalty, mutiny and refusal of duty on the part of the
> military and naval forces of the United States, in that he presented
> at Clune s Auditorium a certain moving-picture play entitled *The
> Spirit of '76,* designed and intended to arouse antagonism, hatred
> and enmity between the American people and the people of Great
> Britain, at a time when the defendant well knew the government
> of Great Britain, with its military and naval forces, was an ally
> of the United States in the prosecution of a war against the
> imperial government of Germany.

Unable to meet the $10,000 bond, Goldstein was held in the county jail until April 15, 1918, when he was convicted on two counts of violation of the Espionage Act. On April 29, Judge Benjamin F. Bledsoe sentenced him to ten years in the Federal Penitentiary at McNeil's Island and a fine of $5,000 on the first count and to two years imprisonment on the second count, both prison terms to run concurrently.

In August 1918, *Photoplay* published a blistering editorial that stated

> Goldstein is a bumptuous ignoramus more fool than villain,
> who mistook greedy aggressiveness for talent and business en-

ergy. His foot slipped when he tried to insult Uncle Sam as he had already insulted art. A theatrical costumier, he bought stock in *The Birth of a Nation,* made a bit of money, and decided to beat Griffith. He sold some of his stock, and produced *The Spirit,* a multi-reel whoop of bunk sentiment, fictitious history, coarse plot and insectivorous acting. Purporting to be a transcript of the war of American liberation, it was a fifty-fifty libel of the Colonies and Mother England. It was German propaganda, impure and simple. Goldstein knew very well the real source of his backing, and why he was backed.

In reality, Goldstein appears to have done little wrong. There is no evidence of German financing of his film. He just happened to have made the wrong film at the wrong time. The years of 1917 and 1918 were times of witch hunting in American history when it was a crime to criticize the Red Cross or the YMCA and when socialist leader Mrs. Rose Stokes received a ten-year prison sentence for writing a letter to a newspaper attacking the government.

The end of the war brought an end to the hatred and Goldstein was released after serving only one year of his sentence. In 1921, he re-issued *The Spirit of '76* with another opening in Chicago at the Town Hall. An enthusiastic audience cheered the American patriots and hissed the British. The only negative response came from critic Edward Weitzel, who suggested in *The Moving Picture World* (August 6, 1921) that Goldstein's prison sentence should have been "for an artistic crime and an offense against good taste and common sense."

Both Goldstein and the film disappeared.[15] Jane Novak recalled her last sighting of the man: "In '24, I was making a film in Berlin. One day I had a phone call from Mr. Goldstein. My companion and I had dinner with him that night. He was the same gentle, softspoken man I had known so many years before. I never saw him again."

When America eventually entered the war in 1917, it became a subject of prompt and easy exploitation. Mary Pickford's ship is torpedoed and she glimpses first-hand the brutality of the Germans in *The Little American* (1918). Walter Miller is a slacker whose Americanism is awakened after he witnesses the desecration of the flag in *The Slacker* (1917). Baby Marie Osborne not only persuades her father to enlist, but also captures a spy in *The Little Patriot*

(1917). Rita Jolivet relives her fateful voyage on the *Lusitania* in *Lest We Forget* (1918). In the fantasy storylines of *The Belgian* and *To Hell with the Kaiser* (both 1918), innocent peasants are ravished and killed; but, in the end, the Kaiser is captured. Enid Bennett vamps a German spy fomenting American labor disputes in *The Vamp* (1918).

Even after the war, it was still a topic for exploitation. Erich von Stroheim, as a German officer, viciously rapes Dorothy Phillips in *The Heart of Humanity* (1919). The Mack Sennett comedy feature *Yankee Doodle in Berlin* (1919) has a female impersonator (Bothwell Browne) vamping the Kaiser and finds humor in an American soldier dropping hand grenades down the front of the trousers of two German soldiers.

The most extraordinary of these postwar dramas is *Behind the Door*, directed by Irvin Willat in 1919. Jane Novak is the heroine, raped by a German U-Boat captain (Wallace Beery). After he and his crew are through with her, she is removed from the submarine via the torpedo shoot. Later, her husband (Hobart Bosworth) captures the German and takes him behind the door to skin him alive.[16]

To a lesser extent in 1917 and to a large extent in 1918, the American film industry was engrossed in propagandizing the allied war effort. Fifty-eight fictional features and 36 short subjects had the war as their primary subject matter in 1917, with an increase to 119 features and 28 shorts in 1918. Among the serials exploiting the war were *Patria* (1917), *The Fighting Trail* (1917), *The Red Ace* (1917), *The Eagle's Eye* (1918), *The House of Hate* (1918), *The Woman in the Web* (1918), and *Wolves of Kultur* (1918). Comedians starring in short subjects who lent their name to the war effort include Max Linder (in his first American film, *Max Comes Across*, 1917), Larry Semon, Mr. and Mrs. Sidney Drew, Harold Lloyd (who rescues Bebe Daniels from the Kaiser in *Knocking the Germ out of Germany*, 1918), and Charlie Chaplin (who captures both the Kaiser and the Crown Prince in *Shoulder Arms*, 1918).[17]

The last great exploitation effort by the American film industry in the teens was created as a result of the "Red Scare," which had Americans terrified by stories coming out of Russia of bloodthirsty revolutionaries and "the nationalization of women." The industry had, at first, been supportive of the Russian revolutionary movement and openly critical of the regime of Czar Nicholas II with films such as *The Nihilists* (American Biograph, 1905), *Russia, the Land of the Oppressed* (Defender, 1910), *The Russian Peasant* (Kalem, 1912), and *Beneath the Czar* (Solax, 1914). Many rising executives in the film industry were escapees from Czarist Russia and they found nothing to admire in the old regime. Unfortunately, the U. S. government quickly found nothing to admire in the new Soviet regime and filmmakers had little choice but to endorse the official U. S. government attitude. David K. Niles, chief of the Motion Picture Section of the U. S. Department of Labor, reminded the industry that "being American citizens," its members should be "unwilling to produce anything for the screen that violates the policies of the Government." [18]

During 1919 and 1920, some nine "Red Scare" films were released, the most important of which are *Bolshevism on Trial, The Red Viper, The Right to Happiness, Lifting Shadows,* and *Dangerous Hours.* Written by Thomas Dixon, *Bolshevism on Trial* (also known as *Shattered Dreams*) concerns the establishment of a socialist utopia on an island off the Florida coast. Religion and marriage laws are abolished, and the socialists are only saved from themselves by the arrival of the U. S. marines, who tear down the red flag and raise the Stars and Stripes. Based on the story "A Prodigal in Utopia," by Donn Byrne, *Dangerous Hours* shows a young college graduate duped into collaboration with Bolshevist labor leaders and includes a terrifying picture of life in contemporary Russia. So successful was *Dangerous Hours* in its depiction of the horrors of Communism that the general manager of the General Motors works in Saginaw, Michigan, purchased 5,000 theater tickets to enable his staff to witness first-hand the dangers of the "Red Menace."[19]

Arguably, the most exploitive of all American films from this period is *Auction of Souls,* also known as *Ravished Armenia.* It purports to depict, on a personal level, the massacre of some 2 million Armenians by the Turkish authorities between 1914 and 1918, with gory scenes showing newly severed heads sticking on the tops of poles and rows of naked, crucified Christian girls.

The film is the true story of Aurora Mardiganian, who arrived in the United States from Oslo on November 5, 1917, after escaping from Armenia through Russia. She witnessed cruelty on a scale that few can imagine:

> I didn't know my aunt was pregnant. The Turks took a knife
> and cut open her abdomen. They said, "This is how we are going

to end all you people." They pulled out a fetus from her, put it on a stone. They took the end of the gun which they had, which was heavy, and started to pound and pound and pound her baby. They killed my parents, and the blood was running red. No one was there to see. No Americans. Only God in his Heaven.[20]

Taken in by an Armenian family in New York City, Mardiganian was interviewed by Harvey Gates, a newspaperman with ties to the film industry. He turned her story into a book titled *Ravished Armenia,* sponsored by Near East Relief (now the Near East Foundation). The success of this book led to filming Mardiganian's story. Knowing little, if any, English, the young girl was persuaded by Gates and his wife, Eleanor Brown, to sign a contract to star in a film for the paltry sum of $15 a week. "I didn't understand English," recalls Mardiganian, "and they said $15 was a lot of money. I was naive. I didn't know nothing."

Filmed in Los Angeles late in 1918 under the direction of Oscar Apfel and produced by William N. Selig on behalf of the American Committee for Armenian and Syrian Relief, the production was a severe emotional experience for Mardiganian: "The first time I came out of my dressing room, I saw all the people with red fez and tassles on. I got a shock. I thought they fooled me—I thought they were going to give me to these Turks to finish my life. So I cry very bitterly."

As *Ravished Armenia,* the film was first seen at the Majestic Theater, Los Angeles, on January 19, 1919. A charity presentation took place at the Plaza Hotel in New York City on February 16, 1919, with the first public performance in New York at Loew's New York Theater on May 10, 1919, and the title now changed to *Auction of Souls.* Critical reaction was favorable. *Variety* (February 28, 1919) described the film as "superbly produced, in characters, settings and playing." Julian Johnson in *Photoplay* (May 1919) called it an "interesting, though sometimes horribly detailed pictorial recount of a little people's long struggle for liberty." Only one critic, Frederick James Smith in *Motion Picture Classic* (August 1919), pointed out the exploitive nature of the presentation: "The cheap sensationalism of its advertising panders to the worst in humanity. We are heartily sick of the screen's exploitation of atrocities under any guise."

Meanwhile, the exploitation of Aurora Mardiganian continued, as she appeared at each major presentation of the film. She was then safely removed to a convent school in New England while seven Aurora Mardiganian impersonators made personal appearances with the film around the country.

Certainly, *Auction of Souls* helped raise a large sum of money for a valid charitable cause. Certainly, the film helped legitimize the plight of the Armenian people. When Lord Bryce and Lord Gladstone attended a private screening in London in the fall of 1919, they noted, "all statements in the report were true, and, if anything, fell short of the facts." However, no more sorrowful exploitation by the film industry of a tragic event in world history exists than that of the filming of *Auction of Souls*.

Notes

1. Testimony of Siegmund Lubin, June 3, 1913, *Greater New York Film Rental Company vs. The Biograph Company and the General Film Company.*

2. Maurice Tourneur, "Meeting the Public Demands," *Shadowland,* Vol. II, No. 9 (May 1920), p. 46.

3. *The Vampire* is preserved in the International Museum of Photography at George Eastman House.

4. Kalem specialized in railroad dramas. As early as August 8, 1909, the *New York Herald* published a feature article on Kalem's hiring an entire railroad to stage a drama. Kalem was also the first studio to build sets in railroad yards, thus making it possible to show actual railroad scenes through the windows of the sets, rather than mere painted drops.

5. "Charming Dare-Devil," *Pictures and the Picturegoer* (March 13, 1915), p. 504.

6. *Who Pays?* is preserved at the UCLA Film and Television Archive.

7. The best general source of information on silent serials is Kalton C. Lahue, *Continued Next Week* (Norman, OK: University of Oklahoma Press, 1964). An annotated list of corrections to this volume, prepared by George Geltzer, is of tremendous value; copies are on deposit with various film libraries and archives.

8. For more information, see Mack Sennett, *King of Comedy* (Garden City, NY: Doubleday, 1954).

9. "Hal Roach on Comedy," *The Silent Picture,* No. 6 (Spring 1970), p. 2.

10. John B. Rathbun, *Motion Picture Making and Exhibiting* (Chicago: Charles C. Thompson Company, 1914), p. 53.

11. A good introduction to these types of exploitation films is provided by Kathleen Karr, "The Long Square-Up: Exploitation Trends in the Silent Film," *Journal of Popular Film,* Vol. III, No. 2 (Spring 1974), pp. 107-128.

12. For more information on the question of social issues in silent films, see Kay Sloan, *The Loud Silents: Origins of the Social Problem Film* (Urbana, IL: University of Illinois Press, 1988).

13. Wayne D. Shirley of the Music Division at the Library of Congress points out an amusing paradox in *The Fall of a Nation.* One of the subplots has an Italian-American family hoping that their son will grow up to be president. The son in question is played by M. Giraci, who is, in reality, a girl. Only the initial of the name was used because Dixon's film is, in part, about the danger of giving women the vote and the producer did not want to admit that his film portrays the first female candidate for president of the United States.

14. This and the other quote by Jane Novak are taken from an undated letter to Anthony Slide written in 1972.

15. For further information, see Anthony Slide, *Robert Goldstein and The Spirit of '76* (Metuchen, NJ: Scarecrow Press, 1993).

16. For more information on *Behind the Door,* see Anthony Slide and Edward Wagenknecht, *Fifty Great American Silent Films, 1912-1920* (New York: Dover, 1980).

17. The best survey of the American film industry's contribution to the war effort is Craig Campbell, *Reel America and World War I* (Jefferson, NC: McFarland, 1985).

18. *Variety* (November 29, 1918).

19. Russell Campbell, "Nihilists and Bolsheviks: Revolutionary Russia in American Silent Film," *The Silent Picture*, No. 19, pp. 4-36.

20. Interview with Anthony Slide, December 17, 1988.

12

The Language, Business, and Art of the Film

No one should doubt the importance of American cinema prior to 1920. So much was happening. The motion picture was constantly changing and developing. Somehow it seems so improbable, and yet many major actors and actresses flourished and died in those pioneering years. The ranks of the comedians diminished the most. The screen's first major comedy star, John Bunny, died of Bright's Disease on April 26, 1915. Eric Campbell, the brutish bully in early Chaplin two-reelers, died in an automobile accident on December 20, 1917. Sidney Drew, star of domesticated comedies for Vitagraph and Metro, died of uremia on April 9, 1919. Keystone comedian Fred Mace died on February 21, 1917. Matinée idol Arthur Johnson died on January 17, 1916. The beautiful and talented leading lady of the Thanhouser Company, Florence La Badie, was killed in an automobile accident on October 13, 1917. Young Robert Harron, who had been nurtured to stardom by D. W. Griffith, demonstrated that his vulnerability was not limited to the screen when he died by his own hand on September 5, 1920. Mary Maurice, a Vitagraph character actress renowned for her portrayal of mother roles, died on April 30, 1918. The 1918 Spanish influenza epidemic took the lives of both Myrtle Gonzales and Harold Lockwood on October 22, 1918.

Motion pictures also had an effect on other spheres of entertainment. Popular composers turned their attention to the new medium with songs such as "She's Only a Moving Picture" by C. E. Dittmann (1912), "Movie Rag" by J. S. Zamecnik (1912), "At the 10 Cent Movie Show" by Leo J. Curley and George Christie (1913), "Since Mother Goes to Movie Shows" by Charles Mc-Caron and Albert Von Tilzer (1916) "Since Sarah Saw Theda Bara" by Alex Gerber and Harry Jentes (1916), "Take Your Girlie to the Movies (If you Can't Make Love at Home)" by Edgar Leslie, Bert Kalmar, and Pete Wending (1919), and "At the Moving Picture Ball" by Joseph H. Santley (1920). Ironically, in 1914, Irving Berlin contributed "If That's Your Idea of a Wonderful Time—Take Me Home," in which Geraldine rejects Johnny's suggestion of an evening at the nickelodeon as a suitable date.

In the March 16, 1913, issue of *Life,* drama critic James Metcalfe wrote, "The moving pictures are said already to compete seriously with the theater in a financial way. That competition has only just begun."

As if to counter such competition, the legitimate stage began borrowing from the motion picture. On March 3, 1913, John Philip Sousa's opera *The American Maid* opened at New York City's Broadway Theater. Set in Cuba in 1898, it used film footage shot in Florida by the Kalem Company to depict American soldiers on the march. Two years later, Kalem turned to the world of opera, hiring the Metropolitan Opera's set designer, Arthur Seidle, to create a hotel lobby set for the company's *The Mysteries of the Grand Hotel.*

At that time, there were no agents to represent the actors and actresses to film producers. It was up to performers to approach prospective employers directly. Thus, Grace Cunard wrote to Selig on March 8, 1912, detailing her previous employment and adding that she could "Ride, row, paddle a canoe and drive."[1]

However, the promotion of films and their players became standardized fairly quickly. The use of still photographs was introduced as early as 1907 by the Vitagraph Company, and Terry Ramsaye, in *A Million and One Nights,* published a photograph from a 1901 Edison production that he dubbed "The First 'Still.'"[2] Film posters were first used in a major way by the Kalem Company in December 1909, and their size was determined by the standard dimensions for a theatrical poster. Lobby cards were in use as early as 1913 by Universal and their size of 11 x 14 inches was adopted because eight of them (seven scenes and a title card) took up the same space as a folded one-sheet poster and could easily be packaged with the poster.[3]

Contrary to popular belief, the concept of film preservation did not begin with the creation of the Department of Film at New York City's Museum of Modern Art in 1935. On December 1, 1906, *Views and Films Index,* with remarkable precognition, urged the use of film to document the past and the establishment of a National Archives and university film archives:

> We are making such rapid strides nowadays, the march of improvement is so great that we hardly keep in touch with what a few short years ago we thought wonderful. A large section of a city is torn down, another built in a few weeks' time, and the former state forgotten except to the film or photograph. Perhaps the day will come when motion pictures will be treasured by governments in their museums as vital documents in their historical archives. Our great universities should commence to gather in and save for future students films of national importance.[4]

On April 3, 1915, *Motography* pondered: "Can Films Be Preserved for Posterity?," noting that British scientists were studying the effects of aging on motion pictures and that "The British Museum officials decline to store film because of its inflammable nature and the consequent necessity for a special vault for its safe keeping."

Film preservation was also the subject of an April 1923 editorial in *Photoplay* in which Terry Ramsaye wrote of his efforts to track down documentation for what became *A Million and One Nights:*

> In the last year it has required two trips across the continent and one the length of the nation to find and see these things. How will the student of the motion picture find them ten years, or twenty years hence?
>
> It is still possible to see Edwin S. Porter's famous picture *The Great Train Robbery,* complete in its original form, just as it went on the screen to startle the world with the story telling powers of the motion picture two decades ago. There are perhaps a half a dozen copies of this classic in existence. Mr. Porter has in his experimental workshop the machine with which he pro-

jected the shows of the Eden Musée in the dim dark days of
ancient film history. In a basement bin and scattered about in old
desks at the Biograph laboratories in uptown New York are
mementoes and relics of early Biograph days that are worth their
weight in gold. There the curious searcher can find fascinating
fragments that tell of the early efforts of Mary Pickford, the little
girl star of *The Violin Maker of Cremona,* stills from the picture
when young David Griffith worked as an extra. And farther back
still, among the Mutoscope reels of Biograph's peep show days
are the little card wheel pictures of *Boxing Match at Canestota,*
the first product of the Biograph camera, the now famous *Empire
State Express,* motion picture of William McKinley and his
young friend Theodore Roosevelt, in his wasp waisted days in
the politician's frock coat of the nineties, Joe Jefferson in *Rip
Van Winkle,* and half the contemporary history of the world.

The legal files of the Motion Picture Patents Company and
the bookcases in the office of Henry Norton Marvin, where an
old brass plate still bears the once mighty legend of the company,
constitute a whole Alexandrian library of the screen.

A mutilated copy of the Gutenberg Bible, of the handiwork
of the accredited father of the modern art of printing, today costs
more money than would be required to bring all of the existing
relics of early motion picture history together and give them
adequate care while making them available to the public and
today's makers of screen history.

America sends expeditions of learned men to dig in the dust
of Egypt to seek out the gewgaws and bracelets where the
Shepherd Kings buried their harems. Meanwhile the beginnings
of the one great art that is more nearly America's alone than any
other are rapidly on their way to become at one with Nineveh
and Tyre.

The endowment of a museum of the motion picture presents
an opportunity for some of those so magically enriched by the
screen to make graceful acknowledgment of their debt to Yesterday. By this means the motion picture's beginnings may be
preserved to history and spared the sketchy inaccuracies of some
future archaeology. ˒

The only individual in early Hollywood who appears to have
had an interest in preserving the films of the past was George André

Beranger (1893-1973), an actor who worked with Griffith in the early teens. He collected 28mm prints, on noninflammable stock, of more than one hundred titles, including many of his mentor's films, as well as many French Pathé Frères subjects and interest shorts. Beranger took pleasure in screening films at the Hollywood Athletic Club for fellow members of the industry. Eventually, he grew tired of the collection and first tried to sell it, unsuccessfully, in 1927. He tried again in 1942, when he decided to leave the United States and return to his native Australia.[5]

To most Americans, the work "photoplay" is associated with a monthly fan magazine of that name that ceased publication in the summer of 1980 after making its initial appearance in August 1911. "Photoplay" was also once the preferred name for the motion picture and was coined in 1910. In July of that year, the Essanay Company announced a contest to discover a new, one-word name to substitute for "Moving Picture Show." In October, the judges—George Kleine, Fred C. Aiken, and Aaron Jones—awarded the $100 prize to a Sacramento, California, exhibitor named Edgar Strakosch who had come up with the name "photoplay."

It is, of course, "movies," rather than "photoplay," that has become the established term in the American language for what the British call the cinema. The word "movie" first gained prominence around 1906 or 1907, when it was in common use in New York City's Bowery District as a shortened version of "moving pictures." It was adopted by the Mutual Film Corporation, founded in 1912, as part of its advertising slogan, "Mutual Movies Make Time Fly." The word was not, however, without detractors. On September 7, 1912, *Motion Picture News* commented

> The season of housecleaning is invariably a moving occa-
> sion, but you wouldn't class the good housewife as a "movie."
> There are scenes in the picture theater that move you to laughter
> or tears, and there is the man who eats onions who moves you to
> another seat. You move, perhaps, but you and the theater should
> not be classed as "movies." "Movies" is a misnomer for the
> Moving Picture theater. Swat the term!

The Moving Picture World (November 29, 1913) joined the opposition when it editorialized

> Like most current slang, it [movies] has been widely ac-
> cepted but it is not in any sense a word that will advance the cause
> of photoplay. It is all right to argue that a nickname helps to
> popularize, but it should be the right sort of nickname and to take
> the coining of the streets and the children's playground is not
> going to give emphasis to the fact that the photoplay is not the
> cheap and nasty thing it was.
>   Educate your clients to use the more dignified "photoplay."
> Do a little missionary work on the screen with slides. The popular
> expression is a curse to the pictures and confirms the fanatic in
> his belief that the motion pictures are still the cheap rot that he
> saw back in '98.
>   Advertise that you do not show "Movies," but pictures in
> motion. Lay stress on the fact that your offerings are better than
> the word "Movies" would suggest. It will not hurt the attendance
> of those who employ the term. It will help to bring to your house
> many who do not know how good the photoplays are.

In September 1914, Los Angeles theater owners announced a
campaign to boycott the word "movie." "It is the opinion of the
theater men that a more dignified name should be used," reported
Motion Picture News (September 12, 1914). The Los Angeles
exhibitors also demanded that local newspapers should list their
advertising alongside legitimate theater advertising in order to
improve the public standing of the motion picture and put it on par
with the stage.

One cause for concern within the industry at the use of the word
"movies" was that it was frequently heard in placing blame for a
crime. Thus, when a Cleveland, Ohio, man set fire to a school
building in the summer of 1912, he blamed "the movie" (a version
of Dante's *Inferno* that he had just witnessed) for his act. The
industry opposition was, however, too late; by 1913, legitimate
publications such as *Literary Digest* had started using "movie" as
an acceptable term for the motion picture. Its use still tended to be
derogatory; for example, *Outlook* (April 5, 1913) wrote: "The
movie fan lays himself open to overtired eye nerves, with the
consequent headaches, indigestion, and general nervous com-
plaints."

Final approval of the word came in 1926, when film critic/his-
torian Iris Barry's classic British work, *Let's Go to the Pictures,*

was published in the United States. The American publisher, Payson and Clarke, Ltd., chose to retitle it *Let's Go to the Movies*.

The acceptance of the movies as an art form took considerably longer. Filmmakers themselves held no pretentious attitude towards their work. They called themselves "manufacturers," and as far as the early pioneers were concerned, they were manufacturing a product that the public wanted.

Despairingly, director Maurice Tourneur wrote

> Making pictures is a commercial business, the same as making soap, and, to be successful, one must make a commodity that will sell. We have the choice between making bad, silly, childish and useless pictures, which make a lot of money, and make everybody rich, or nice stories which are practically lost.[6]

On the whole, producers were not inclined to label their work "art." Admittedly, George K. Spoor told *The Moving Picture World* (June 12, 1908), "As an art the motion picture will take its place equally with the other arts," but such comments were generally the exception. The trade papers conceded that film was an art form prior to most producers and by its issue of September 27, 1913, *Exhibitor's Times* was writing of "the early days of the art."

After a brief acknowledgment of its beginnings in 1896, general periodicals paid scant attention to the motion picture. Film reviews were limited to those found in the trade papers, and were seldom negative, consisting of little more than plot synopses based on materials provided by producers. Fan magazines, with close ties to the industry, were loath to review films. Individual films were usually the subject of extremely lengthy synopses often taking much longer to read than the film would take to view and including nuances totally missing from the film's plot.

It was Julian Johnson who introduced reviewing to *Photoplay* in November 1915, with his "Department of Comment and Criticism of Current Photoplays." Johnson's comments were always scrupulously honest and often biting, as were those of his successor at *Photoplay,* the distinguished theater critic Burns Mantle, best remembered for his editorship of the annual "Best Plays" series of books. Once *Photoplay* had paved the way, other fan magazines began publishing criticism, notably *Motion Picture Classic* with Frederick James Smith, who joined the publication in January 1918.

Lillian Gish has repeatedly hailed D. W. Griffith as the first person to acknowledge silent film as the universal language, which he claimed was prophesied in the Bible. However, such recognition probably belongs to Julian Johnson, who wrote a blank verse poem on the subject, "I Am the Universal Language," in the April 1919, issue of *Photoplay*. Earlier, a similar comment on the cinema had been made by director George Loane Tucker in *Motion Picture News* (January 13, 1917) when he noted

> The motion picture is the only international language. It can be understood by the people of any land. At present America is pouring out its films to all parts of the world. These pictures in time will stimulate the more remote nations to produce film drama of their own. Americans should encourage them to do that.

Nonfilm publications were slow to consider the new medium worthy of review. It was not until April 22, 1913, that *The New York Times* began reviewing films with what was little more than a news item on the Astor Theater screening of the Italian epic *Quo Vadis*. "The production has many spectacular scenes and is full of pictorial effects that are striking," reported the *Times*' anonymous writer in a review that might just as well have been written by the film's publicist. So unimportant were films considered by *The New York Times* that its reviewers were not identified by name—except for the occasional major review essay by Alexander Woollcott until the mid-twenties, when Mordaunt Hall became the newspaper's official film critic.

James C. Metcalfe, the drama critic for the humor magazine *Life,* began occasionally reviewing a motion picture in the early teens, primarily because there were no new stage plays upon which to comment. His attitude towards the motion picture is typified by the following comment on *A Daughter of the Gods* from the issue of November 2, 1916: "With everything the moving-picture industry can provide and with the loveliest of natural settings, *A Daughter of the Gods* shows in emphatic form what a poverty of artistic brains is employed in the moving-picture business."

Drama critic and playwright Channing Pollock wrote

> Of the two hundred and sixty-four thousand, eight hundred and nine mistakes I have made in a brief but interesting career,

the two greatest have had to do with the motor car and the motion picture. When I saw my first "horseless carriage," I knew at once that the automobile was an utterly impracticable device. About the same time, a gentleman named Whiting Allen, newspaper man and circus press-agent, chaperoned a cinematograph into Willard Hall, in Washington. Mr. Allen's instrument showed horse races in which the grand stand jumped up and down more than the horses, and the only persons in the District of Columbia who thought well of the machine were the occultists. *The Post* went to press with my expert opinion that "moving pictures were a curiosity of no particular importance." [7]

Pollock changed his opinion in September 1914, when he began the regular review of films for the popular Hearst publication *The Green Book Magazine.* His first review was of *Neptune's Daughter* and he wrote of the star: "Miss [Annette] Kellermann undressed is a lovely creature, not so much because of her symmetry of body as because she seems vibrant with health, enraptured with life, drunk with draughts of the outdoors."

By 1916, the number of books and pamphlets on film was large enough that S. Gershanek, a cataloger with the New York State Public Library, was able to compile what is probably the first Motion Picture Bibliography—for the trade paper *Motography.*[8] (A second bibliography was published in 1919 by the St. Louis Public Library.) Many of the publications listed by Gershanek were in a foreign language and the majority dealt with technical aspects of filmmaking, notably the writing of screenplays. There is, however, one important literary text included: *The Art of the Moving Picture,* by poet Vachel Lindsay (1879-1931). Published by Macmillan and reissued in a revised edition in 1922, *The Art of the Moving Picture* contains Lindsay's often lofty views on the subject and shows his loving fascination for actress Mae Marsh, but it is a clear illustration of the intelligentsia's interest in the new medium and their gradual, but increasing, acceptance of it as an art form.

Lindsay's book was followed in 1916 by another important early text, *The Photoplay: A Psychological Study*, by Hugo Munsterberg. Published by Appleton, Munsterberg's book is divided into two parts: "The Psychology of the Photoplay" and "The Aesthetics of the Photoplay."

One of the proposals for which Munsterberg argued was the education of the motion picture audience so that it might demand standards in film equal to those in other art forms. In fact, film study at American universities dates from 1914, when a course in Photoplay Composition was first taught at Columbia University by Dr. Victor O. Freeburg, author of *The Art of Photoplay Making* (Macmillan, 1918). As a result of Freeburg's work, Vachel Lindsay urged in *The Moving Picture World* (September 9, 1916) that Columbia University become the home of the First Museum of Photoplay Writing and Production. This did not happen, but by 1920, Columbia did have a Department of Photoplay Composition with Frances Taylor Patterson as its head. In true academic tradition, she was a critic and had never actually sold any screenplays to the film industry.

In *Photoplay* (January 1920), she wrote

> Columbia has the distinction of being the first college or university to recognize the tremendous possibilities of the gentle art of story-telling by means of pictures, to realize that the photoplay in its highest form is essentially artistic, and that wielded by trained and skillful writers its power is illimitable.

Aside from Columbia, reference must also be made to the University of Chicago, where Professor Frederick K. Starr was possibly one of the first academics to acknowledge the motion picture, in an article titled "The World Before Your Eyes" in the February 7, 1909, edition of the Sunday *Chicago Tribune*. He called the moving picture

> not a makeshift, but the highest type of entertainment in the history of the world. It stands for better Americanism because it is attracting millions of the masses to an uplifting institution, drawing them to an improving as well as an amusing feature of city life. Its value cannot be measured now, but another generation will benefit more largely through its influence than we of today can possibly realize.

Edwin S. Porter was a technician. Thomas H. Ince was an entrepreneur. Jesse L. Lasky, Adolph Zukor, and Sam Goldwyn were businessmen. Mary Pickford was a personality. They all contributed much to early film history, but the man who almost single-handedly transformed film into an art form was D. W. Griffith. The stage could not make him immortal, so he turned to the motion picture; here he succeeded. When Griffith left Biograph in October 1913, he placed an advertisement in *The New York Dramatic Mirror* of November 26, 1913, proclaiming himself as "Producer of all great Biograph successes, revolutionizing Motion Picture drama and founding the modern technique of the *art*."

To D. W. Griffith, film was an art form and with the production of *The Birth of a Nation,* others—most importantly, the critics—agreed with his assessment. *The New York Dramatic Mirror* (March 10, 1915) hailed *The Birth of a Nation* with the heading "Summit of Picture Art." Not only had D. W. Griffith arrived, but so had the art of the film.

Notes

1. Letter in the Selig Collection at the Academy of Motion Picture Arts and Sciences.

2. Opposite page 410.

3. For more information on advertising matter and film memorabilia, see Anthony Slide, *A Collector's Guide to Movie Memorabilia* (Des Moines, IA: Wallace-Homestead, 1983).

4. "History and Motion Pictures," *Views and Films Index,* Vol. I, No. 32 (December 1, 1906), p. 1.

5. For more information on the subject, see Anthony Slide, *Nitrate Won't Wait: A History of Film Preservation in the United States* (Jefferson, NC: McFarland, 1992).

6. Maurice Tourneur, "Meeting the Public Demands," *Shadowland,* Vol. II, No. 9 (May 1920), p. 46.

7. Channing Pollock, "Even Channing Pollock Writes about the Movies," *The Green Book Magazine* (September 1914), p. 492.

8. *Motography,* Vol. XVI, No. 6 (August 5, 1916), pp. 339-342.

General Bibliography

Books and periodical articles dealing specifically with subjects covered in individual chapters are noted in the footnotes to the chapters. Because of their importance to the period and the wealth of published material about them, D. W. Griffith and Thomas H. Ince are the subjects of separate bibliographies.

Books

Agnew, Francis. *Motion Picture Acting.* New York: Reliance Newspaper Syndicate, 1913.

Balshoffer, Fred, and Arthur C. Miller. *One Reel a Week.* Berkeley, CA: University of California Press, 1967.

Bordwell, David, Janet Staiger, and Kristin Thompson. *The Classical Hollywood Cinema: Film Style and Mode of Production to 1960.* New York: Columbia University Press, 1985.

Bowers, Q. David. *Nickelodeon Theatres and Their Music.* Vestal, NY: Vestal Press, 1986.

___. *Muriel Ostriche: Princess of Silent Films.* Vestal, NY: Vestal Press, 1987.

Brownlow, Kevin. *Behind the Mask of Innocence.* New York: Alfred A. Knopf, 1990.

Burch, Noël. *Life to Those Shadows.* Berkeley, CA: University of California Press, 1991.

deCordova, Richard. *Picture Personalities: The Emergence of the Star System in America.* Champaign, IL: University of Illinois Press, 1990.

Donaldson, Leonard. *The Cinematograph and Natural Science*. London: Ganes, 1912.

Edwards, Richard Henry. *Popular Amusements*. New York: Association Press, 1915.

Fell, John L., ed. *Film Before Griffith*. Berkeley, CA: University of California Press, 1983.

Fielding, Raymond, ed. *A Technological History of Motion Pictures and Television: An Anthology from the Pages of the Journal of the Society of Motion Picture and Television Engineers*. Berkeley, CA: University of California Press, 1967.

Goldwyn, Samuel. *Behind the Screen*. New York: George H. Doran Company, 1923.

Goodman, Ezra. *The Fifty-Year Decline and Fall of Hollywood*. New York: Simon and Schuster, 1961.

Grau, Robert. *The Business Man in the Amusement World: A Volume of Progress in the Field of the Theatre*. New York: Broadway Publishing Company, 1910.

___. *The Theatre of Science: A Volume of Progress and Advancement in the Motion Picture Industry*. New York: Broadway Publishing Company, 1914.

Griffith, Mrs. D. W. *When the Movies Were Young*. New York: E. P. Dutton, 1925.

Hampton, Benjamin B. *A History of the Movies*. New York: Covici-Friede, 1931.

Hanson, Patricia King, ed. *The American Film Institute Catalog: Feature Films, 1911-1920*. Berkeley, CA: University of California Press, 1989.

Hartt, Rollin Lynde. *The People at Play: Excursions in the Humor and Philosophy of Popular Amusements*. Boston: Houghton Mifflin, 1909.

Hendricks, Gordon. *Origins of the American Film*. New York: Arno Press, 1972.

Hopwood, Henry V. *Living Pictures: Their History, Photo-Productions and Practical Working*. London: The Optician & Photographic Trades Review, 1899.

Hulfish, David S. *Cyclopedia of Motion Picture Work*. Chicago: American School of Correspondence, 1911.

Jacobs, Lewis. *The Rise of the American Film: A Critical History*. New York: Harcourt, Brace 1939.

Jobes, Gertrude. *Motion Picture Empire*. Hamden, CT: Archon, 1966.

Justice, Fred C., and Tom R. Smith, eds. *Who's Who in the Film World*. Los Angeles: Film World Publishing, 1914.

Kerrigan, Jack. *How I Became A Successful Moving Picture Star*. Los Angeles: The Author, 1914.

Koszarski, Richard. *The Rivals of D. W. Griffith: Alternate Auteurs, 1913-1918*. Minneapolis: Walker Art Center, 1976.

Lennig, Arthur. *The Silent Voice: A Text*. Albany, NY: The Author, 1969.

Lescarboura, Austin C. *The Cinema Handbook*. London: Sampson Low, Marston, circa 1921.

Lindsay, Vachel. *The Art of the Moving Picture*. New York: Macmillan, 1915.

Lyons, Timothy J. *The Silent Partner: The History of the American Film Manufacturing Company 1910-1921*. New York: Arno Press, 1974.

Macgowan, Kenneth. *Behind the Screen: The History and Techniques of the Motion Picture*. New York: Delacorte Press, 1965.

Milne, Peter. *Motion Picture Directing*. New York: Falk, 1922.

Motion Picture Studio Directory. New York: 1916-1921.

Moving Picture Annual and Yearbook for 1912. New York: The Moving Picture World, 1913.

Musser, Charles. *The Emergence of Cinema: The American Screen to 1907*. New York: Charles Scribner's Sons, 1990.

___. *Before the Nickelodeon: Edwin S. Porter and the Edison Manufacturing Company*. Berkeley, CA: University of California Press, 1991.

___. *High-Class Moving Pictures: Lyman H. Howe and the Forgotten Era of Traveling Exhibition, 1880-1920*. Princeton, NJ: Princeton University Press, 1991.

North, Joseph H. *The Early Development of the Motion Picture, 1887-1909*. New York: Arno Press, 1973.

Phelan, Rev. J. J. *Motion Pictures as a Phase of Commercialized Amusement in Toledo, Ohio*. Toledo: Little Book Press, 1919.

Pratt, George C., ed. *Spellbound in Darkness*. Greenwich, CT: New York Graphic Society, 1973.

Ramsaye, Terry. *A Million and One Nights: A History of the Motion Picture*. New York: Simon and Schuster, 1926.

Rathbun, John B. *Motion Picture Making and Exhibiting*. Chicago: Charles C. Thompson Company, 1914.

Reel, Oren Clayton. *The Life of Earle Williams*. New York: The Shakespeare Press, 1915.

Reid, Bertha Westbrook. *Wallace Reid: His Life Story*. New York: Sorg, 1923.

A Report on the Conditon of Moving Picture Shows in New York, March 22, 1911. New York: Office of Accounts, 1911.

Richardson, F. H. *Motion Picture Handbook*. New York: The Moving Picture World, 1910.

Royal, Lee. *The Romance of Motion Picture Production*. Los Angeles: Royal Publishing Company, 1920.

Slide, Anthony. *Aspects of American Film History prior to 1920*. Metuchen, NJ: Scarecrow Press, 1978.

___, ed. *International Film, Radio, and Television Journals*. Westport, CT: Greenwood Press, 1985.

___. *The American Film Industry: A Historical Dictionary*. Westport, CT: Greenwood Press, 1986.

___. *100 Rare Books from the Margaret Herrick Library*. Beverly Hills, CA: Academy of Motion Picture Arts and Sciences, 1987.

___. *Silent Portraits*. Vestal, NY: Vestal Press, 1989.

Slide, Anthony, and Edward Wagenknecht. *Fifty Great American Silent Films, 1912-1920*. New York: Dover, 1980.

Spears, Jack. *Hollywood: The Golden Era*. South Brunswick, NJ: A. S. Barnes, 1971.

Spehr, Paul. *The Movies Begin: Making Movies in New Jersey, 1887-1920*. Newark, NJ: The Newark Museum/Morgan and Morgan, 1977.

Talbot, Frederick A. *Moving Pictures: How They Are Made and Worked*. Philadelphia: J. B. Lippincott, 1914.

Tinee, Mae. *Life Stories of the Movie Stars*. Hamilton, OH: The Presto Publishing Co., 1916.

Vardac, A. Nicholas. *Stage to Screen: Theatrical Method from Garrick to Griffith*. Cambridge, MA: Harvard University Press, 1949.

Wagenknecht, Edward. *The Movies in the Age of Innocence*. Norman, OK: University of Oklahoma Press, 1962.

___. *Stars of the Silents*. Metuchen, NJ: Scarecrow Press, 1987.

Wagner, Rob. *Film Folks: Close-ups of the Men, Women and Children Who Make the Movies*. New York: The Century Company, 1918.

Welsh, Robert E. *A-B-C of Motion Pictures*. New York: Harper & Brothers, 1916.

Periodical Articles

Brown, Harry D. "The Evolution of Studio Lighting." *American Cinematographer*, Vol. VI, No. 10 (January 1926), pp. 8, 13.

Cator, Van Vorst. "The Growth of Motion Pictures." *Motion Picture Magazine* (May 1918), pp. 18-19.

Doublier, Francis. "Travels of a Cameraman in the 90's." *National Board of Review Magazine* (February 1940), pp. 10-12, 15.

Gershanek, S. "A Motion Picture Bibliography." *Motography*, Vol. XVI, No. 6 (August 5, 1916), pp. 339-342.

Grau, Robert. "Actors by Proxy." *The Independent* (July 17, 1913), unpaged.

Howard, Clifford. "The Cinema in Retrospect, Part I." *Close Up* (November 1928), pp. 16-25.

___. "The Cinema in Retrospect, Part II." *Close Up* (December 1928), pp. 31-41.

Johnston, William Allen. "The Moving-Picture Show, the New Form of Drama for the Millions." *Munsey's Magazine* (August 1909), pp. 633-640.

Karr, Kathleen. "The Long Square-up: Exploitation Trends in the Silent Film." *Journal of Popular Film,* Vol. II, No. 2 (Spring 1974), pp. 107-128.

Lang, Arthur J. "Cashing In on Europe's War." *Motion Picture News,* Vol. X, No. 21 (November 2, 1914), pp. 25-26.

Lusk, Norbert. "I Love Actresses!: The Last of Lubinville." *New Movies* (April 1946), pp. 26-30.

Meader, John R. "The Story of the Picture That Moves." *Bohemian Magazine* (September 1908), pp. 357-366.

Musser, Charles. "The Early Cinema of Edwin S. Porter." *Cinema Journal,* Vol. XIX, No. 1 (Fall 1979), pp. 1-38.

Pollock, Channing. "Even Channing Pollock Writes about 'The Movies.'" *The Green Book Magazine* (September 1914), pp. 492-497.

Smith, Frederick James. "Yesterday and Tomorrow in the Photoplay." *Shadowland,* Vol. II, No. 12 (August 1920), pp. 55, 80.

Staiger, Janet "Combination and Litigation: Structures of U. S. Film Distribution, 1896-1917." *Cinema Journal,* Vol. XXIII, No. 2 (Winter 1983), pp. 41-72.

Starr, Helen. "Putting It Together." *Photoplay* (July 1919), pp. 52-54.

Tourneur, Maurice. "Meeting the Public Demands." *Shadowland,* Vol. II, No. 9 (May 1920), pp. 46, 71.

Townsend, Edward W. "Picture Plays." *The Outlook* (November 27, 1909), pp. 703-710.

"Tricks in Motion-Pictures." *The Literary Digest* (March 21, 1914), pp. 615-616.

D. W. Griffith Bibliography

The primary source for research on D. W. Griffith is the Film Department of the Museum of Modern Art, which houses both the director's papers and films. Some American Biograph titles directed by Griffith and not at the Museum of Modern Art may be found at the Library of Congress, and the UCLA Film and Television Archive. The papers of D. W. Griffith have been published on microfilm by Microfilming Corporation of America.

The following bibliography is limited to major articles and books; articles and reviews dealing with specific films have been excluded.

"Actresses Must Be Young." *The Moving Picture World* (December 27, 1913), p. 1556.

Aitken, Roy E., as told to Al P. Nelson." *The Birth of a Nation Story.* Middleburg VA: Denlinger, 1965.

Barry, Iris, and Eileen Bowser. *D. W. Griffith: American Film Master.* New York: Museum of Modern Art, 1965.

Barry, Richard. "Five Dollar Movies Prophesied," *Editor* (April 24, 1915), pp. 407-410.

Bitzer, G. W. *Billy Bitzer: His Story.* New York: Farrar, Straus & Giroux, 1973.

Blaisdell, George. "At the Sign of the Flaming Arcs."*The Moving Picture World* , Vol. XIX, No. 1 (January 3, 1914), p. 52.

Bowser, Eileen, ed. *Biograph Bulletins, 1908-1912.* New York: Octagon Books, 1973.

Bravermann, Barnet G. "D. W. Griffith, America's Solely Great Contribution to Cinema." *Film Spectator* (July 13, 1929), pp. 7-9.

___. "Griffith . . . The Pioneer." *Theatre Guild Magazine* (February 1931), pp. 28-33.

___. "David Wark Griffith, Creator of Film Form." *Theatre Arts*, Vol. XXIX, No. 4 (April 1945), pp. 240-250.

Brown, Karl. *Adventures with D. W. Griffith*. New York: Farrar, Straus & Giroux, 1973.

___, "The Great D. W." *Sight and Sound*, Vol. XXXXII, No. 3 (Summer 1973), pp. 160-165.

Carr, Harry. "Griffith, Maker of Battle Scenes, Sees Real War." *Photoplay* (March 1918), pp. 23-28, 119.

___. "How Griffith Picks His Leading Ladies." *Photoplay* (December 1918), pp. 24-25.

___. "Life and the Photo-Drama: David Griffith Talks on the Film Play." *Motion Picture Classic* (December 1918), pp. 16-17, 70.

___. "Griffith: Maker of Pictures." *Motion Picture Magazine*, Vol. XXIV, No. 7 (August 1922), pp. 88-89.

Cook, Raymond Allen. *Fire from the Flint: The Amazing Careers of Thomas Dixon*. Winston-Salem, NC: John F. Blair, 1968.

Cooper, Miriam, with Bonnie Herndon. *Dark Lady of the Silents: My Life in Early Hollywood*. Indianapolis: Bobbs-Merrill, 1973.

Croy, Homer. *Starmaker: The Story of D. W. Griffith*. New York: Duell, Sloan & Pearce, 1959.

Cuniberti, John, ed. *The Birth of a Nation, by D. W. Griffith and Frank E. Woods: Shot-by-Shot Analysis*. Meriden, CT: Research Publishing, 1979.

Darnell, Jean. "The Personal Side of David W. Griffith." *Motion Picture Magazine*, Vol. VII, No. 12 (January 1917), pp. 95-97.

"David W. Griffith, Film Wizard." *Theatre* (May 1920), pp. 488-490.

"David W. Griffith, Motion Picture Director." *The Moving Picture World* (July 11, 1914), p. 184.

"David Wark Griffith: A Symposium by Lionel Barrymore, Cecil B. DeMille, Tony Gaudio, Lillian Gish, F. Hugh Herbert, Julian Johnson, Mae Marsh, Seena Owen, Mary Pickford, and Mack Sennett. "*The Screen Writer*, Vol. IV, No. 2 (August 1948), pp. 2-4, 18-20.

Dorr, John H. "Griffith in Hollywood." *Take One*, Vol. III, No. 7 (1972), pp. 8-11.

___. "Griffith's Talkies." *Take One*, Vol. III, No. 8 (1972), pp. 8-12.

___. "The Griffith Tradition." *Film Comment*, Vol. X, No. 2 (March-April 1974), pp. 48-54.

Everson, William K. "The Films of D. W. Griffith, 1907-1939." *Screen Facts*, No. 3 (May-June 1963), pp. 1-27.

Feldman, Joseph and Harry. "The D. W. Griffith Influence." *Films in Review*, Vol, I, No. 5 (July-August 1950), pp. 11-14, 45.

Films in Review. "The David Wark Griffith Centennial Issue." (October 1975).

Geduld, Harry M. *Focus on D. W. Griffith.* Englewood Cliffs, NJ: Prentice-Hall, 1971.

Gish, Lillian. "D. W. Griffith: A Great American." *Harper's Bazaar* (October 1940).

___ with Ann Pinchot. *The Movies, Mr. Griffith and Me.* Englewood Cliffs, NJ: Prentice-Hall, 1969.

Gordon, Henry Stephens. "The Story of David Wark Griffith." *Photoplay* (June 1916), pp. 28-37; (July 1916), pp. 122-132; (August 1916), pp. 78-88; (September 1916), pp. 79-86, 146-148; (October 1916), pp. 86-94; (November 1916), pp. 27-40.

Graham, Cooper C., Steven Higgins, Elaine Mancini, and João Luiz Vieira. *D. W. Griffith and the Biograph Company.* Metuchen, NJ: Scarecrow Press, 1985.

Griffith, D. W. "The Rise and Fall of Free Speech in America." Los Angeles: The Author, 1916.

___. "What I Demand of Movie Stars." *Motion Picture Classic* (February 1919), pp. 40-41, 68.

___. "Motion Pictures: The Miracle of Modern Photography." *The Mentor*, Vol. IX, No. 6 (July 1921), pp. 2-12.

___. "Youth, the Spirit of the Movies." *Illustrated World* (October 1921), pp. 194-196.

___. "The Movies 100 Years from Now." *Collier's* (May 3, 1924), pp. 7, 28.

___. "The Motion Picture Today and Tomorrow." *Theatre* (October 1927).

___. "An Old-Timer Advises Hollywood." *Liberty* (June 17, 1939).

___, with James Hart. *The Man Who Invented Hollywood: The Autobiography of D. W. Griffith.* Louisville KY: Touchstone Publishing, 1972.

Griffith, Mrs. D. W. *When the Movies Were Young.* New York: E. P. Dutton, 1925.

"Griffith Number." *The New York Dramatic Mirror* (May 20, 1919).

"Griffith Special Issue." *The Silent Picture*, No. 4 (Autumn 1969).

"The Griffith Way." *Photoplay* (April 1915), pp. 75 -77.

Gunning, Tom. *D. W. Griffith and the Origins of American Narrative Film.* Champaign, IL: University of Illinois Press, 1991.

Harrison, Louis Reeves. "David W. Griffith: The Art Director and His Work." *The Moving Picture World*, Vol. XVIII, No. 8 (November 22, 1913), pp. 847-848.

Hastings, Charles Edward. *A Biography of David Wark Griffith and A Brief History of the Motion Picture in America.* New York: D. W. Griffith Service, 1920.

Henderson, Robert M. *D. W. Griffith: The Years at Biograph.* New York: Farrar, Straus & Giroux, 1970.

___. *D. W. Griffith: His Life and Work.* New York: Oxford University Press, 1972.

Huff, Theodore. *A Shot Analysis of D. W. Griffith's The Birth of a Nation.* New York: Museum of Modern Art, 1961.

___. *Intolerance: The Film by D. W. Griffith: A Shot-by-Shot Analysis.* New York: Museum of Modern Art, 1966.

Leyda, Jay. "Film Chronicle: The Art and Death of D. W. Griffith." *Sewanee Review* (Fall 1948).

Merritt, Russell. "Dixon, Griffith and the Southern Legend." *Cinema Journal* (Fall 1972), pp. 26-45.

___. "Rescued from a Perilous Nest: D. W. Griffith's Escape from Theatre into Film." *Cinema Journal* (Fall 1981), pp. 2-30.

Mullett, Mary B. "The Greatest Moving Picture Producer in the World." *American Magazine* (April 1921), pp. 32-34, 144, 146, 148.

Nash, Alanna. "Remembering D. W. Griffith." *Take One,* Vol. IV, No. 7 (December 31, 1974), pp. 9-28.

Naylor, Hazel Simpson. "The Poet-Philosopher of the Photoplay." *Motion Picture Magazine,* Vol. XXVIII, No. 8 (September 1919), pp. 28-30, 102.

Niver, Kemp R. *D. W. Griffith's The Battle at Elderbush Gulch.* Los Angeles: Locare Research Group, 1972.

___. *D. W. Griffith: His Biograph Films in Perspective.* Los Angeles: Locare Research Group, 1974.

O'Dell, Paul. *Griffith and the Rise of Hollywood.* New York: A. S. Barnes, 1970.

Paine, Albert Bigelow. *Life and Lillian Gish.* New York: Macmillan, 1932.

Pearson, Roberta E. *Eloquent Gestures: The Transformation of Performance Style in the Griffith Biograph Films.* Berkeley, CA: University of California Press, 1992.

Petric, Vlada. *A Corner in Wheat: A Critical Analysis.* Cambridge, MA: University Film Study Center, 1975.

"A Poet Who Writes on Motion Picture Films." *Theatre* (June 1914), pp. 311-312, 314, 316.

Quirk, James R. "An Open Letter to D. W. Griffith." *Photoplay* (December 1924), p. 27.

Robinson, Selma. "Don t Blame the Movies, Blame Life!" *Motion Picture Magazine* (July 1926), pp. 33, 82.

"Romantic Estate Now Griffith's Studio." *Photoplay* (May 1920:), pp. 42-43.

Scheuer, Philip K. "D. W. Griffith, the Inventor of the Medium." *Los Angeles Times Calendar* (January 11, 1976), pp. 1, 34, 35, 39.

Silva, Fred, ed. *Focus on The Birth of a Nation.* Englewood Cliffs, NJ: Prentice-Hall, 1971.

Slide, Anthony. *The Griffith Actresses.* New York: A. S. Barnes, 1973.

___. *The Kindergarten of the Movies: A History of the Fine Arts Company.* Metuchen, NJ: Scarecrow Press, 1980.

Smith, Frederick James. "He Might Be the Richest Man in the World." *Photoplay* (December 1926).

Stanhope, Selwyn A. "The World's Master Picture Producer." *Photoplay* (January 1915), pp. 57-62.

Stern, Seymour. *An Index to the Creative Work of D. W. Griffith*. London: British Film Institute, 1944-1946.

___. "Griffith and Poe." *Films in Review,* Vol. II, No. 9 (November 1951), pp. 23-28.

___. "The Soviet Directors' Debt to D. W. Griffith." *Films in Review,* Vol. VII, No. 5 (May 1956), pp. 202-209.

___. "Griffith: The Birth of a Nation." *Film Culture,* No. 36 (Spring-Summer 1965).

Sterne, Herb. "Return of a Master." *The New York Times* (September 3, 1939), p. 4X.

___. "D. W. G.: A Poet Sings in Celluloid." *Rob Wagner's Script* (January 20, 1945), pp. 10-11.

Thompson, Paul. "David Wark Griffith: A Few Interesting Side Lights on the Movie's Belasco." *American Cinematographer* (October 1929), pp. 6, 38-39.

Tully, Jim. "David Wark Griffith." *Vanity Fair* (December 1926), pp. 80, 110.

Vardac, A. Nicholas. *Stage to Screen: Theatrical Method from Garrick to Griffith.* Cambridge, MA: Harvard University Press, 1949.

Wagenknecht, Edward, and Anthony Slide. *The Films of D. W. Griffith.* New York: Crown, 1975.

Watts, Richard, Jr. "D. W. Griffith." *New Theatre* (November 1936), pp. 6-8.

Welsh, Robert E. "David W. Griffith Speaks." *The New York Dramatic Mirror,* Vol. LXXI, No. 1830 (January 14, 1914), pp. 49, 54.

Williams, Martin. *Griffith: First Artist of the Movies.* New York: Oxford University Press, 1980.

Woolley, Edward Mott. "Story of D. W. Griffith: The $100,000 Salary Man of the Movies." *McClure's* (September 1914), pp. 109-116.

Thomas H. Ince Bibliography

The International Museum of Photography at George Eastman House has a considerable collection of early Ince productions while copies of later films (from the twenties) are available for study at the UCLA Film and Television Archive. A complete set of still books for Ince productions are housed in the Margaret Herrick Library of the Academy of Motion Picture Arts and Sciences. Papers relating to Ince can be found at both the Library of Congress and the Museum of Modern Art.

No claims are made that this bibliography is definitive, but it is the most detailed one yet available. In the case of certain entries, it was impossible to provide complete annotations; but rather than omit such listings, they have been included with as much information as possible.

It is fairly safe to assume that the articles attributed to Thomas H. Ince in the teens were written by Kenneth O'Hara, whom the producer hired as his publicist in August 1914. A brief biography of O'Hara appeared in *The Moving Picture World* (November 18, 1916, p. 990.) Articles attributed to Ince in the twenties were probably written by Hunt Stromberg.

"About Thomas H. Ince." *Paramount Progress* (July 12, 1917), p. 6.
Ariza, F. J. "Ince, el Innovador." *Cine-Mundial* (January 1925).
Beall, Harry Hammond. "Ince, Noted Producer, Dies." *Exhibitor's Herald* (December 6, 1924).
"A Bit of Spain in Hollywood." *Photoplay,* Vol. XXVI, No. 1 (June 1924), p. 63.

Bradford, Gardner. "Ince Was Never Satisfied with His Film Efforts."
    Filmograph (November 22, 1924).
Carr, Harry "Directors : The Men Who Make the Plays." *Photoplay*, Vol.
    VIII, No. 1 (June 1915), pp. 80-85.
___. "Ince: Rodin of Shadows." *Photoplay*, Vol. VIII, No. 2 (July 1915),
    pp. 81-84.
Condon, Mabel. "Thomas H. Ince's Rapid Rise to Fame." *The New York
    Dramatic Mirror*, Vol. LXXI, No. 1953 (May 27, 1916), p. 24.
"The Cross of Shame." *Motion Picture Magazine*, Vol. XVI, No. 8
    (September 1918), pp. 68-70.
Duncan, Robert C. "The Ince Studios." *Picture Play*, Vol. IV, No. 1 (March
    1, 1915), pp. 25-39.
Ellis, Frederick J. "The Passing of a Great Showman." *Story World*
    (January 1925), pp. 9-10.
"Emotional Ince." *The Moving Picture World*, Vol. XXIII, No. 7 (February
    13, 1915), p. 1000.
Everson, William K. "Thomas H. Ince." *Cinemages*, Vol. I, No. 5 (June
    1955), pp. 8 -10.
___. "D. W. Griffith and Thomas Ince, the American Civil War and the
    Early West." Theodore Huff Memorial Film Society Program Note
    (November 17, 1956).
"A Few More Inches about Ince." *Photo-Play Journal*, Vol. II, No. 1
    (January 1919), p. 44.
Grau, Robert. "Past and Present." *Picture Play*, Vol. IV, No. 3 (May 1916),
    pp. 211, 215-216.
Hewston, E. W. "Thomas H. Ince at Work." *Static Flashes*, Vol. I, No. 14
    (April 24, 1915), p. 8.
___. "Interviewing Ince." *Picture Play*, Vol. II, No. 2 (October 16, 1915),
    p. 25.
"Ideal Studio Location in Southern California." *The Morning Telegraph*
    (May 31, 1914).
Ince, Elinor. "Thomas H. Ince." *The Silent Picture*, No. 6 (Spring 1970),
    pp. 14-15.
Ince, Thomas H. "Present Needs of Photoplays." *The New York Dramatic
    Mirror*, Vol. LXXII, No. 1879 (December 23, 1914), pp. 23, 36.
___. "The Permanency of the Motion Picture." *Motion Picture News*, Vol.
    X, No. 26 (January 2, 1915), p. 29.
___. "Is the Motion Picture a Fad?" *Motography*, Vol. XIII, No. 2 (January
    9, 1915), p. 51.
___. "Getting Out a Feature." *The New York Dramatic Mirror*, Vol.
    LXXIII, No. 1891 (March 17, 1915), p. 27.
___. "Morality and Motion Pictures." *Reel Life*, Vol. VI, No. 1 (March 20,
    1915), p. 21.
___. "Troubles of a Motion Picture Producer." *Motion Picture Magazine*,
    Vol. IX, No. 4 (May 1915), pp. 113-115.

___. "The Western Drama." *The Moving Picture World* , Vol. XXI, No. 2 (July 10, 1915), pp. 225-226.

___. "New Technique of Photo Plays." *The Triangle,* Vol. I, No. 4 (November 13, 1915), p. 2.

___. "The Stage Star and the Screen." *Motography,* Vol. XV, No. 6 (February 5, 1916), pp. 299-300.

___. "What Constitutes Good Direction?" *Moving Picture Stories* (October 6, 1916).

___. " What Does the Public Want?" *Photoplay,* Vol. XI, No. 2 (January 1917), p. 66.

___. "The Art of Motion Picture Directing." *Pictures and the Picturegoer,* Vol. XI, No. 235 (August 10, 1918), p. 161.

___. "The Early Days of Kay Bee." *Photoplay,* Vol. XI, No. 4 (March 1919), pp. 42-46.

___. "Past Year Was One of Unexampled Prosperity for Picture Industry." *The Moving Picture World,* Vol. XXXXIII, No. 1 (January 3, 1920), p. 97.

___. *Your Opportunity in Motion Pictures.* Los Angeles: Photoplay Research Society, 1922.

___. "The Elements of Successful Production." *The Film Daily,* Vol. XXVIII, No. 70 (June 22, 1924), p. 47.

___. "Memoirs of Thomas H. Ince." *Exhibitor's Herald* (December 13, 1924-January 10, 1925).

"Ince a Pioneer." *The Film Daily* (November 20, 1924).

"Ince Camera Expert." *The New York Dramatic Mirror,* Vol. LXXI, No. 1953 (May 27, 1916), p. 25.

"Ince Community Dedicated with Reception and Ball." *Motion Picture News,* Vol. XIII, No. 4 (January 22, 1916), p. 346.

"Ince Completes a World Drama." *Photoplay,* Vol. IX, No. 6, (May 1916), p. 32.

"Ince Culver City Studios Now Open." *Motography,* Vol. XV, No. 6 (February 5, 1916), pp. 289-290.

"Ince Directing Out of Triangle." *The Moving Picture World,* Vol. XXXII, No. 13 (June 30, 1917), p. 2071.

"Ince Is in New York Arranging for Civilization Premiere." *Motion Picture News,* Vol. XIII, No. 22 (June 3, 1916), p. 3379.

"Ince Says Stage Stars Help Films." *The Triangle,* Vol. I, No. 13 (January 15, 1916), p. 2.

"Ince Studios," advertising matter. *Motion Picture News,* Vol. XIV, No. 26 (December 30, 1916), pp. 4243-4252.

"Ince Studios Are Models of Construction." *The Moving Picture World,* Vol. XXIX, No. 7 (August 12, 1916), p. 1087.

"Ince Talks of Culver City." *The Moving Picture World,* Vol. XXVIII, No. 10 (June 3, 1916), p. 1967.

"Ince To Make Three Mammoth Productions a Year." *Motion Picture News*, Vol. XI, No. 12 (March 27, 1915), p. 41.

"Inceville Busy Making 4-reelers for Mutual." *Motion Picture News*, Vol. XI, No. 10 (March 13, 1915), p. 46.

"Inceville Suffers from Fire." *Motography*, Vol. XV, No. 5 (January 29, 1916), pp. 227-228.

"Inceville Then and Now." *The New York Dramatic Mirror*, Vol. LXXII, No. 1879 (December 23, 1914), pp. 30-31.

"Inceville to Have Its Own Wild West." *Motion Picture News*, Vol. X, No. 18 (November 7, 1914), p. 34.

"Inceville Will Soon Become a City." *Motion Picture News*, Vol. X, No. 25 (December 26, 1914), p. 38.

"Industry Pays Its Tribute to Ince." *Motion Picture News*, Vol. XXX, No. 23 (December 6, 1924), pp. 2923-2924.

"Interesting Ince Figures." *The New York Dramatic Mirror*, Vol. LXXI, No. 1953 (May 27, 1916), p. 25.

Jessen, J. C. "In and Out of West Coast Studios." *Motion Picture News*, Vol. XIV, No. 16 (October 21, 1916), pp. 2523-2524.

Lahue, Kalton C. *Dreams for Sale: The Rise and Fall of the Triangle Film Corporation*. New York: A. S. Barnes, 1971.

Lusk, Norbert. "Pictures and Personality." *Moving Picture Stories* (July 30, 1920).

Melbourne, Dick. "Inceville." *Movie Pictorial*, Vol. II, No. 3 (September 1915), pp. 10-11.

Meyer, Art. "In Memoriam." *Motion Picture Bulletin* (December 3, 1924).

Milne, Peter. "Directors Schooled by Ince" and "The Method of Thomas H. Ince." *Motion Picture Directing*. New York: Falk Publishing, 1922.

Mitchell, George. "Thomas H. Ince." *Films in Review*, Vol. XI, No. 8 (October 1960), pp. 464-484.

Mitry, Jean. "Thomas H. Ince, premier dramaturge de l'ecran." *Cahiers du Cinéma*, Vol. III, No. 19, 20, and Vol. IV, No. 21 (January, February, and March 1953).

_____. *Thomas H. Ince: Maître du cinéma*. Paris: Cinémathèque Française, 1956.

_____. "Ince." *Anthologie du Cinéma*, No. 9. Paris: L'avant-Scéne du Cinéma, 1965.

_____. "Thomas Harper Ince." *Filmographie Universelle* VI (1966), pp. 169-290.

"Mr. Ince of Inceville." *The New York Dramatic Mirror*, Vol. LXXI, No. 1953 (May 27, 1916), p. 25.

Neil, Henry Judge. "Life Story of Thomas H. Ince." *Holly Leaves* (November 22, 1924).

"New Ince Studios at Culver City Finest in the World." *The Triangle*, Vol. II, No. 14 (July 22, 1916), p. 3.

"New Inceville Studios Represent Millions." *The Triangle,* Vol. II, No. 6 (May 27, 1916), p. 6.

O'Dell, Paul. *Griffith and the Rise of Hollywood.* New York: A. S. Barnes, 1970.

O'Hara, Kenneth. "The Voice of Genius." *Variety,* Vol. XXXIX, No. 6 (July 9, 1915), p. 15.

___. "Making an Eighth Wonder." *Picture Play,* Vol. IV, No. 6 (August 1916), pp. 25-31.

___. "The Life of Thomas H. Ince." *Picture Play* (January 1917), pp. 20-27; (February 1917), pp. 219-228; (March 1917), pp. 49-59; (April 1917), pp. 214-223; (May 1917), pp. 64-74; (June 1917), pp. 246-253.

"An Old Friend Goes Away." *Picture Play,* Vol. XXI, No. 6 (February 1925), p. 95.

"The Personal Side of Pictures." *Reel Life,* Vol. V, No. 12 (December 5, 1914), p. 18.

Pratt, George C. "See Mr. Ince. . . ." *Image,* Vol. V, No. 5 (May 1956), pp. 100-111.

___. *Spellbound in Darkness.* Greenwich, CT: New York Graphic Society, 1973.

"Produced by Thomas H. Ince." *Exceptional Photoplays,* Vol. V, Nos. 3 and 4 (December-January 1925), p. 6.

Quigley, Martin J. "Thomas H. Ince." *Exhibitor's Herald* (December 6, 1924).

Rall, Pearl. "Picture Industry Mourns Loss of a Genius." *Screen News* (November 29, 1924).

Shepard, David H. "Thomas Ince." *American Film Heritage.* Washington, DC: Acropolis Books, 1972.

"The Sign of the Rose. " *Photoplay,* Vol. VIII, No. 1 (June 1915), pp. 31-32.

The Silent Picture (Spring 1972). Special issue on Ince, including a chronology, interviews with Claire DuBrey, Jane Novak, and Blanche Sweet (on *Anna Christie*), and a study of *Hell's Hinges.*

The Silver Sheet. House organ published by Thomas H. Ince productions in the twenties to promote its product with each issue devoted to an individual feature.

Slide, Anthony. "A Research Guide to the Thomas H. Ince Collection at the Library of Congress." Washington, DC: privately circulated, 1971.

Spargo, John. "An Argonaut of the Screen." *Exhibitor's Herald* (December 6, 1924).

Stromberg, Hunt. "East Cannot Hope To Displace West as Picture Centre, Says T. H. Ince." *The Moving Picture World,* Vol. XXXXIII, No. 8 (February 21, 1920), p. 1205.

"Studio Improvements for Tom Ince." *The Moving Picture World,* Vol. XXXII, No. 1 (April 7, 1917), p. 102.

"Thomas H. Ince Dead." *Greater Amusements* (November 22, 1924).

"Thomas H. Ince To Produce for Paramount and Artcraft." *Moving Picture Stories* (July 27, 1917).

Usai, Paolo Cherchi, and Livio Jacob, eds. *Thomas H. Ince: il profeta del western.* Pordenone, Italy: Le Giornate del Cinema Muto, 1984.

Waller, Tom. "Death Claims Thomas H. Ince after Illness of a Day at Beverly Hills, Calif." *The Moving Picture World*, Vol. LXXI, No. 5 (November 29, 1924), p. 403.

Wing, W. E. "Tom Ince of Inceville." *The New York Dramatic Mirror,* Vol. LXX, No. 1827 (December 24, 1913), p. 34.

Index